WORLD DIRECTORS SERIES

Film retains its capacity to beguile, entertain and open up windows onto other cultures like no other medium. Nurtured by the growth of film festivals worldwide and by cinephiles from all continents, a new generation of directors has emerged in this environment over the last few decades.

This new series aims to present and discuss the work of the leading directors from across the world on whom little has been written and whose exciting work merits discussion in an increasingly globalised film culture. Many of these directors have proved to be ambassadors for their national film cultures as well as critics of the societies they represent, dramatising in their work the dilemmas of art that are both national and international, of local relevance and universal appeal.

Written by leading film critics and scholars, each book contains an analysis of the director's works, filmography, bibliography and illustrations. The series will feature film-makers from all continents (including North America), assessing their impact on the art form and their contribution to film culture.

Other Titles in the Series

Jane Campion

Forthcoming:
Lars von Trier
Yash Chopra
Emir Kusturica
Terrence Malick

YOUSSEF CHAHINE

Ibrahim Fawal

Publishing

First published in 2001 by the
BRITISH FILM INSTITUTE
21 Stephen Street, London W1T 1LN

The British Film Institute promotes greater understanding of,
and access to, film and moving image culture in the UK.

Cover design by Ketchup

Set by Alden Bookset
Printed in England by The Cromwell Press, Trowbridge, Wiltshire

British Library Cataloguing-in-Publication Data
A catalogue record for this book is available from the British Library

ISBN 0–85170–858–7 (pbk)
ISBN 0–85170–859–5 (hbk)

ACKNOWLEDGMENTS

It gives me pleasure to acknowledge the critical help and invaluable advice I have received from friends, colleagues and former supervisors in writing this book. In England, I would like to thank Robin Ostle, Ian Christie, my editor Andrew Lockett and Sophia Contento; in the United States, Michael Leslie and Gerald D. Johnson. In Egypt, I am indebted to many who shared with me either their fond experiences of working with Youssef Chahine or their intimate opinions of him as the thinker and poet of Arab cinema: movie stars Hind Rustum, Yousra, Magda, Mahmoud Hemeda and Seifeddin; film critics Ali Abu Shadi and Samir Farid; director/historian Muhammad K. al-Qalyoubi; film directors Radwan al-Kashef, Yousry Nasrallah, Khaled Youssef and Atef Hatata; and film producers Gabriel Khoury and Marianne Khoury. Also I would like to thank May Hossam at Misr International Films. Above all, I would like to register my great admiration and respect for Youssef Chahine himself who, with his thoughtful and compelling films, has brought honour to the Arab nation and enriched world cinema.

For Salem, Gina, Freeda and Rima

CONTENTS

INTRODUCTION

Mirroring Egypt's personality on the screen has been Youssef Chahine's lifetime obsession. For half a century, and in thirty-four features and six documentaries, he has created an astonishing body of work that alternates between ambiguity and brilliance. By shedding light on Egypt in all her moods and dimensions, Chahine reveals his own tormented self: an artist committed to define Egypt's identity as well his own, daring to tell the 'truth' as he sees it, and advocating humanistic values. As an influential voice of modern Egypt, the internationally acclaimed Chahine is to Arab cinema what the Nobel Laureate Naguib Mahfouz is to Arabic literature.

Throughout his long career, Chahine has doggedly pursued a complex cinema of ideas in a country prone to sentiment and escapism rather than sophistication and serious art. Son of a petit bourgeois family that aspired to high society, Chahine was born in Alexandria and educated at the prestigious Victoria College which was often compared to Eton, and whose alumni include King Hussein of Jordan, Edward Said and Michel Shalhoub (who became Omar Sharif). After studying theatre and television for two years at Pasadena Playhouse in California, Chahine returned to Egypt to launch his film career and, as it were, to deliver a jolt to the mainstream Egyptian cinema. Mixed blood runs in Chahine's veins: his mother was Greek, and his father Lebanese. His wife of fifty years is a French woman born in Egypt. He himself was born and bred in Egypt, and educated in a British-style school and in America. No wonder he is multi-lingual and cosmopolitan in mentality. His Christianity in a predominantly Muslim country has not been problematic for him, his clashes with the Muslim fundamentalists notwithstanding. Chahine prides himself on being, above all, an Egyptian.

Over the years, Chahine has developed his own film-making style, which is characteristically frenetic, non-linear, multi-layered, cerebral and demanding. Many of his films 'read' like modernist scripts: fragmented, convoluted, with a dash of the Theatre of the Absurd. Of particular interest to his admirers is his innovative use of time, space, *mise-en-*

scène, memory, and the blending of genres in a single film. Rare is the Chahine film in which history and politics do not resonate, or the film in which a part of his own life is not integrated in its fabric. His provocative cinema appeals mostly to thinking audiences, though mainstream audiences often respond to his unique films and stirring themes. Naguib Mahfouz worked on several of his scenarios, and one of Chahine's masterpieces, *The Earth* (1969), was based on an Arabic novel, considered by the literary critics as a modern classic.

Besides being a consummate director, Chahine has been blessed with multiple talents: writing, dancing, acting, in addition to a sharp intellect and moral rectitude. Early in his youth he fell under the spell of the American musicals, particularly those of Gene Kelly. Other influences are hard to discern, except for Julien Duvivier's *The Great Waltz* and the melodramas of Douglas Sirk. Some of Chahine's films invite comparison with Italian Neorealism or hint at the French New Wave. The shoestring budgets and inadequate apparatus of his early years are reminiscent of the hard times Orson Welles had to endure later in his career. Chahine's emphasis on the actor's performance, particularly the Stanislavsky style of acting, puts him in a league with Elia Kazan. On another level, Chahine's concern about postcolonial Egypt brings to mind the similar concerns of Satyajit Ray and Ousmane Sembene regarding postcolonial India and Africa respectively. Chahine is of the same ilk as two other mavericks: with John Cassavetes he shares the integrity and intensity but not the improvisation; with Robert Altman he shares the nonconformity and experimentation but not the lack of structure. But unlike these two independent Americans who operated on Hollywood's periphery, Chahine was and remains at the forefront and at the centre of the Egyptian cinema. In his confessional mode, however, Chahine is comparable to extrovert Fellini and introvert Bergman, both at once. Chahine's use of song and dance in the midst of high drama recalls Bertolt Brecht's *Mother Courage and Her Children* and Richard Attenborough's *Oh, What a Lovely War*, though there is no evidence that he has ever seen either of these two productions. In short, Chahine is hard to pigeonhole simply because he is an original.

* * *

Chahine became a film director in 1950, two years before the watershed
Revolution of 1952 which brought to power Gamal Abdel Nasser, the 'colos-
sus'[1] who has been described as the first native to rule Egypt in over two
millennia. But just before the monarchy was overthrown, Egypt was already
making more than fifty films a year, and had been involved in film production for at least thirty-five years. By the time Chahine arrived the cinema
industry in Egypt was already thriving. To understand the society in which
he lived and depicted on the screen, and to put the cinema within its political, social and cultural contexts, one should cast a panoramic look at the
way it all began. An infrastructure had to exist before such an industry could
take root, for it was the extended family of artists that staged plays and went
on to make movies, and it was novelists and playwrights who supplied both
stage and screen with scripts. When did all these art forms develop? And
who undertook the financing?

During the course of the nineteenth and early twentieth centuries, cer-
tain conditions were created which were ultimately favourable to the rise of
Egyptian cinema. The first crucial phase in this process was the reign of
Muhammad Ali (1811-49), who assumed power in the aftermath of
Napoleon's expedition (1798-1801). Though despotic and greedy,
Muhammad Ali was shrewd enough to realise that modernisation can be
used as an instrument of policy. Consequently he embarked upon a far-
ranging set of social reforms and extensive programmes to industrialise
Egypt and educate her vast populace. It was he who 'hired French officers
who had flocked to Egypt in search of employment once Napoleon's army
had been disbanded'.[2] Historians add that he 'who was illiterate until the
age of 47, had an enthusiasm for education that verged on being a fetish'. To
his credit, he did not limit this enthusiasm for education to his immediate
family. 'His modernisation of the army led to developing and expanding a
programme of education in terms of staff colleges, engineering corps,
medical surgeons and veterinary surgeons. Schools were opened in Egypt
and educational missions sent abroad to learn technology, not only in the
field of military science but in other fields as well'.[3]

It was Muhammad Ali's grandson Khedive Ismail, 'the impatient
Europeanizer',[4] who built the Cairo Opera House to celebrate the opening

of the Suez Canal in 1869, giving Egypt great prestige, especially after *Aida* was premiered in it two years later. The building was a magnificent structure which cost the national treasury a huge sum of money. And the premiere was a lavish affair, a grand spectacle in its own right, to which kings and queens and the rich and famous from around the world had been invited. Ismail's fascination with everything western led him to declare: 'My country is no longer in Africa, it is in Europe.'[5]

Birth of the theatre

It was during the reign of Khedive Ismail in particular that the conditions were created which favoured the rise of the theatre in Egypt. Though cinema is considered the liveliest art, its existence depends on literature, music, dance, photography, painting, sculpture, mime and acting. For the Egyptian cinema industry to emerge and thrive, a convergence of many of these elements had to occur first to make it possible. Cinema is not only the most expensive of all arts, it is also a business, requiring sophisticated means of production, distribution and exhibition. A form of capitalism, a fledgling industrialisation, relative political stability, a measure of independence, and the presence of a large community of cosmopolitan foreigners — all contrived to make cinema happen in Egypt. Cinema in the rest of the Arab world lagged far behind, precisely because those essential factors that were available in Egypt were lacking anywhere else. One of the most important of these factors was the rise and early development of the theatre in Egypt.

Long before Egypt's indigenous playwrights began to return from their studies in France, their artistic horizons enhanced — and in some cases before they had even been born — it was from Greater Syria (which then included Lebanon, Palestine and Jordan) that pioneers came to contribute to the establishment of journalism as a profession in Egypt and to stage theatrical productions, first in Alexandria and then in Cairo. The primary reason they came was Egypt's relative independence, where they could escape the oppressive Ottoman regimes in their countries. The first Arab to write a stage play was a Lebanese who came to Egypt in 1846, and who was followed by a succession of actors and theatre organisers from Greater Syria.

The first theatrical group 'consisted of 12 actors and 4 actresses',[6] preferring Alexandria to Cairo for its liberalism and tolerance. Though Egypt
could have developed theatre on her own eventually, the fact remains that
the Syrian and Lebanese contributions at this early stage were crucial. Thus,
due to a unique set of circumstances, the Egyptians found themselves
decades ahead of the rest of the Arab world that was just beginning to
emerge from the 400-year period of Ottoman rule. Consequently, Cairo
became the unchallenged cultural centre of the Arab world – its Hollywood
and Broadway.

Popular theatre

It is in the realm of the popular theatre that the relationship between stage
and screen is the most profound. Both are mediums for mass audiences
who find in them the least expensive and the most accessible entertainment. This was the case in America where performers in vaudeville found
their way to the nickelodeons. As Charlie Chaplin progressed from stage to
screen, so did two Egyptian comedians, Ali al-Kassar and Naguib al-Rihani.
Illiterate spectators who could not appreciate opera or drama found their
pleasures in music halls or the newly discovered language – cinema. For
actors, working in either medium seemed natural. With the arrival of
sound, the popular theatre became an essential training ground for playwrights who could write colloquial dialogue.

A founding father of both Egyptian theatre and cinema, Yusuf Wahbi, a
young aristocrat, became a living legend. It was he who produced *Zainab*
(1930), the first significant Egyptian silent film; and who wrote, produced
and starred in Egypt's first sound film *Children of the Aristocrats* (1932). He
is also credited for having established in 1930 'the first small studio in
Egypt'.[7] He called it Studio Ramses. Another founder of the Egyptian theatre was Fatma Rushdi, a remarkable young woman 'from traditional
Muslim background with no knowledge of a European language'.[8] From that
humble beginning, she rose to become the Sarah Bernhardt of Egypt. Her
Arabic plays were original historical dramas in classical verse. Adaptations
from the world's dramatic literature in which she starred included *Hamlet*,
Joan of Arc, *Camille* and *Anna Karenina*.[9] Like Yusuf Wahbi, Fatma Rushdi

was primarily a theatre person who made a successful transition to the screen and was able to make a considerable contribution. In 1939, she starred in *Determination*, which many consider the first important Egyptian sound film. She was also one of the first women in the world to become a film producer.

Rise of the novel

Without the novel, the Egyptian cinema would have been impoverished indeed, for some of the finest films were based on published narratives, or benefited from the contribution of a novelist who worked either on the scenario or the dialogue. It is said that the daughters of Naguib Mahfouz watch the films based on their father's novels but never read the novels themselves. It has also been suggested that the Nobel Laureate himself has written a number of his novels with the cinema in mind. And Tawfiq al-Hakim, one of Egypt's most prestigious novelists and playwrights, played himself as an old man in an adaptation of his first novel, *Bird from the East* (1986), which he had written in 1933 about his time as a student in France.

While the Arabic novel is now considered one of the highest forms of creative expression, in the late nineteenth century and in its present form, it was not a part of Arab writers and poets' heritage. It arose decades after the theatre had taken root in Egypt. But within the relatively short span of less than a century, it developed sufficiently enough to win Naguib Mahfouz, in 1988, the Nobel Prize for Literature. Only the cinema came to rival the novel in its capacity to explore complex issues in depth and at sustained length.

By mid-century, the Arab world was in turmoil. Colonialism, communism, Zionism and nationalism were explosive ideologies. *Coups d'états*, revolutions, wars of independence, assassinations and shifting alignments were as real as the refugee camps that were rapidly dotting the landscape. One of the best known novels in Egyptian literature was published one year after the Revolution of 1952: *al-Ard* (*Egyptian Earth*), by the Marxist Abdel-Rahman al-Sharqawi. It depicted the exploitation of the *fellahin* (peasants) by their feudal masters. Within the same year Yusuf Idris published his seminal collection of short stories, *Cheapest Nights*, which represented the lower strata of Egyptian society in a new way. Together, both books signified *iltizam*, a serious, committed approach to fiction. One of the most loyal adherents to the principle of *al-iltizam* is Youssef Chahine: a poet and thinker who happens to write his novels on the screen rather than the page.

The fine arts and music

The development of the fine arts and music in particular had salutary influence on the growth of Egyptian cinema. Film brings together hundreds of artists and craftsmen, but first the professions themselves have to exist. In most western countries such professions preceded the arrival of the cinema. In Egypt they almost emerged together as though in anticipation of providing a talent pool for the nascent cinema to draw upon. Towards that end, a few significant dates are worth noting. Three pioneers in the field of sculpture, music and painting were born within a few years of each other: the sculptor Mahmoud Mukhtar (1891), the musician Sayyid Darwish (1892) and the artist Raghib Ayyad (1893). The School of Fine Arts was founded in 1908.

If the song-and-dance genre is the most popular in Egyptian cinema, an individual or a group of people must have contributed to the rise of that tradition. And if Chahine mobilises the *ughniya* (song) for maximum dramatic effect, there must be songwriters and composers who provide the material with which to punctuate his films. The acknowledged pioneer here is Sayyid Darwish (1892-1923). His lyrics were full of pride and nationalistic fervour and his tunes were simple yet rousing. He was the unofficial voice and conscience of Egypt as it struggled under colonialism. All the musicians who followed him revered his name, as did the Egyptian populace.

Musicologists trace the beginning of Egyptian interest in symphonic music to the opening of the Opera House in Cairo on 17 November, 1869, not particularly on account of *Aida* which had its premiere in Cairo in 1871, but because of the Italian operas and other western music that continued to be performed in Egypt during every winter season thereafter. Such musical evenings had direct and positive influence on the Egyptian elite. Some of them even began to compose pieces for the piano.[10]

Serious study of music began with three young men who wished to become pioneers in this art form. Ironically the three had graduated from university in fields other than music: Yusuf Jiryes, in law; Hassan Rashed, in agriculture; Abu Bakr Khairat, in engineering. But their first love was classical music, to which they devoted their time and money. Some of their compositions are still remembered.[11] Subsequent generations of Egyptian film composers are indebted to these three pioneers for having instilled in them the love and appreciation of classical music and for having indirectly paved their way to careers in cinema.

Radio came to Egypt in 1926, the same year Youssef Chahine was born. One cannot overestimate the role it played in spreading Egyptian culture in general and in paving the way for the acceptance of the Egyptian film throughout the Arab world. Radio introduced singers, popularised songs, and made drama a precursor for touring theatrical troupes or cinema itself. Film audiences throughout the Middle East were always entertained by a medley of songs before the start of a film as well as during intermissions. In many ways, radio played a crucial role in familiarising Arab audiences with the Egyptian dialect and idiom, a fact of inestimable importance for having made the Egyptian film the film of choice, especially when the general film-going public had not yet acquired a foreign language or learned to read sub-titles. Consequently the Egyptian dialect and idiom are so dominant in the Arab world that they give the Egyptian film an advantage over films from other Arab countries.

With the infrastructure of the railway system, press, publishing, tele-graph, phonograph, theatre and radio all in place, Egypt's fledgling cine-ma was poised to become a regional power in its own right, supported by the other media. Colonialism was waning and the Egyptians were eager to rule themselves and to assume leadership over the Arab countries. The outpouring of books, magazines, records and films from Cairo went to all parts of the Arab world. The Egyptian dialect became familiar from Morocco to Kuwait. Cairo streets, Alexandria beaches and Egyptian *aryaf* (countryside) were as familiar to Arabs outside Egypt as their own neigh-bourhoods. It is difficult to overrate the extent to which the Egyptian media – and radio in particular – created the conditions, from 1950 onwards, for the increasing number of receptive audiences throughout the Arab world. Overlapping these cultural developments was the birth and growth of Egyptian cinema.

The advent of Egyptian cinema

Less than a year after the first film was shown to a paying audience any-where in the world, an Egyptian audience enjoyed a similar experience. The Lumière brothers' films were screened in the Salon Indien, a basement room of the Grand Café in Paris, on 28 December 1895; and on 5 November 1896, a Lumière representative screened a programme of their films in the back room of a café called Bourse Toussoun in Alexandria.[12]

'Bourse Toussoun' is a significant name not only because it marks the site of a historic cultural event in Egypt, but, more importantly, because it is not an Arabic name. Considering the number of foreigners who lived in Alexandria at the time, it is not surprising that they would play a major role in the development of the motion picture industry in Egypt. Even as late as 1927, when a Chamber of Cinema was established in Alexandria, the presi-dent, vice-president, secretary and treasurer were all Alexanderine of for-eign descent.[13] The history of Egyptian cinema is replete with names such as: de Langarne, Umberto Dores, Osato, Mario Volpi, Alvise Orfanelli, Togo Mizrahi, Rocca, Maurice and Alexander Aptekman, Carol Boba, Fritz Kramp, Willy Rosier, Rene Tabouret and Stelio Chiarni. These were not Egyptians. Why and how these outsiders came to play such a pivotal role in the develop-ment of Egyptian cinema reveal what a multi-layered and tolerant society Egypt was. At the turn of the twentieth century there were at least a quarter of a million foreigners living in Egypt. Without the Europeans' contribution, film would have arrived at the shores of the Nile much later.

The initial showing of the Lumière films in Alexandria in 1896 generat-ed great interest among the public. Before too long 'the public grew tired of always seeing these same imported films which presented foreign scenes without any connection between them and all unfamiliar to the Egyptian people'. So a certain de Langarne embarked on lavish productions revolv-ing around local scenes.[14] Until 1907 all filming in Egypt was by cameramen working for the Lumières, and all exhibition of film was carried out by foreigners living in Egypt. These early films whetted the public's appetite to the point that 'foreigners in Alexandria planned to produce dramatic films which they thought would earn substantial profits'. Again to satisfy demand another Italian 'set up the Italo-Egyptian Cinematographic Company with the Banco Di Roma as a silent partner. The company put up a number of buildings with glass ceilings and walls to provide the light needed for shooting.'[15] Unfortunately, Umberto Dores was no more successful than de Langarne had been before him. His dramatic films were so bad that 'These films (running time between 30 to 45 minutes) ... were not at all successful. The inconsistent subjects, the disconnected sequences, the French subtitles and non-Egyptian actors all contributed to the failure.'[16] Consequently, Banco Di Roma was forced to pull out, causing the company to collapse.

Muhammad Bayyumi

As in all colonised countries, one's ethnicity was a sensitive issue in Egypt where the wealth and power still belonged to foreigners, the royal house not excepted. Since the Revolution of 1919, Egyptians wanted to control every aspect of their life, including the cinema. Thus they dismissed the early film activities in Alexandria and Cairo as the work of foreigners, and relegated the maverick Muhammad Bayyumi as the pioneer of Egyptian cinema.[17]

After having studied cinema in Germany and been admitted to the Austrian Society of Cinematographers, Bayyumi returned to Egypt in the early 1920s and immediately established Amun Films, calling it the first Egyptian film studio. His breakthrough came in 1923, when Prime Minister Sa'd Zaghloul returned from exile in the Seychelles. Many film historians consider that short documentary about the national hero's return to be the cornerstone of the Egyptian film industry. According to his biographer, Bayyumi described his filming of the reception of Sa'd Zaghloul 'as the first film that was produced by *misri watani* – a native and nationalist Egyptian – thus emphasizing film production in Egypt as a patriotic and nationalistic act'. He dismisses all earlier efforts by Alexandrian film-makers as 'works by foreigners as compared to natives'. [18]

Bayyumi went on to write, produce, direct and edit *Barsum Looking for a*

Job (1925), which again he was quick to label 'the first Egyptian film come-dy'.[19] According to al-Qalyoubi, the twelve-minute theatrical was highly influenced by German Expressionism as well as Chaplin's *The Kid*. Though it is hard to imagine a film influenced by both Chaplin's film and Weine's *The Cabinet of Dr. Caligari*, he insists that this is not surprising considering that Bayyumi had studied in Germany. Probably the simple story was Chaplinesque while the photography 'looked' German.

A significant development in Bayyumi's career was his relationship with Tal'at Harb, the Egyptian industrialist and financial tycoon. After a conge-nial period during which Bayyumi headed a film subsidiary for him called Misr Film, the relationship between the giant and the novice floundered. In 1926, Bayyumi resigned, and for the rest of his life felt that he was cheated out of the industry he had founded. Though he made several silent films, he was a victim of his own failure to grasp that cinema may be an art and a tech-nology, but, above all, it is a sophisticated business. In 1963 he died in a charity ward.

Three silent films

The year 1922 witnessed a widespread interest among Egyptians in the use of the film medium for educational purposes.[20] Newspapers published many articles by prominent people advocating similar ideas. One such per-son was Victor Risotto, a lawyer, who was particularly interested in farming. He urged the government to license the establishment of a company to pro-duce instructional films dealing with new agricultural methods. His appeal was well received by the public. Ironically, many of the letters written to the newspapers called for a company to be controlled by natives and financed by local money.[21] Although he was of Italian descent, Risotto regarded him-self as a bona fide Egyptian and did not feel excluded. A year after he had published his letter to the government, Risotto took everyone by surprise. He released a fifty-minute theatrical film entitled *In the Land of Tut Ankh Amun*. He wrote, directed and produced it for £1,900, which he financed personally.

The plot revolves around an archaeologist, his kind daughter, his jealous and scheming adopted daughter, and the son of the Nile. The setting is the

Valley of the Kings in 1922, the year the tomb of Tut Ankh Amun was discovered. Described as 'Egyptian in meaning, foreign in structure', the film
offered much to fill Egyptians with pride. Although parts of it were deemed
by one magazine to be 'crude, disconnected and with scenes that were too
long',²² both reviewers and audiences loved it for being 'an Egyptian film'
and for its public relations value.

Much was written about *Laila* (1927) and its competition with *Qublah fil-
sahra (A Kiss in the Desert)* as to which one marked the 'real' beginning of
Egyptian cinema. *A Kiss in the Desert* was released five months earlier than
Laila, but it failed to qualify because it had been made by Ibrahim and Badr
Lama, two Palestinians who were born and raised in Chile. The issue
remained unresolved for almost half a century: recent discoveries by al-
Qalyoubi, however, give the distinction to *Laila*.

Laila is important for three other reasons. First, it was produced by a
woman in her early twenties. Aziza Amir was a popular stage actress who
had married well and had developed the project for herself. For a director
she chose Wadad Orfi, a Turkish writer of Jewish faith, who had recently
emigrated to Egypt. When difficulties arose between them, she replaced
him with Estephan Rosti, an Egyptian who had studied cinema in Paris, but
she retained the Italian cameraman, Stelio Chiarini. These are impressive
decisions for a very young woman to have made, especially then. Second,
Aziza Amir was among three women to enter Egyptian film production. As
she was making *Laila*, another woman, Assya, was producing *Remorse*,
directed by Ibrahim Lama. They, together with Fatma Rushdi, might have
been among the first women in the world to enter the field.²³ Third, *Laila*
touches on the problematic relationship between East and West, a subject
that preoccupies writers up till the present. The plot depicts a young
Egyptian woman whose misfortune is the result of an affair her betrothed
has with an American woman with whom he leaves to live in her country.
The lure of the West, as personified in that seductress, is what brings ruina-
tion to this innocent village girl.

The most important silent film was *Zainab*, directed by Muhammad
Karim who would be enshrined in an Egyptian film pantheon had there
been one. In the 1920s Karim travelled to Rome and then to Berlin for

training at UFA Studios. In his memoirs, he credits Fritz Lang, who at the time was directing *Metropolis*, for having given him an opportunity to watch the entire production and to 'look through the lens from every angle'. For this reason Karim called himself 'a graduate of *Metropolis*'.[24] Upon returning home in 1926, he was immediately employed by Tal'at Harb's film company, where he made a few shorts. He chose a distinctive novel, *Zainab*, for his theatrical film project. It was produced by Yusuf Wahbi, a famous stage actor and director.

Zainab premiered on 9 April 1930, and was an instant success. Dignitaries and high officials were in attendance. The 'Prince of Poets', Ahmad Shawqi, told the director in the presence of many journalists and literati: 'You have revealed poetry on the screen.' An important novelist wrote about the film in a weekly newspaper for three consecutive weeks. Every major magazine in Egypt covered its release. It was even covered in Turkish, French and German newspapers. The German magazine *Film Woche* told its readers: 'It is equal to the greatest of American films'.[25] The founder of Studio Misr wrote the director a letter congratulating him on his great success. However, the letter that touched the young director the most came from the author. He told Karim that the power and beauty of his images gave the subject 'greater clarity than any pen can dare show in a novel or a story'.[26]

Every film has its detractors, and *Zainab* was no exception. Some considered the story unworthy of all the effort that went into making the film.[27] Others objected to the husband kissing his wife immediately after saying his prayers,[28] something no devout Muslim would do. And in the view of another reviewer: 'The director gave us a picture of the Egyptian *fellah* wearing silk, sleeping in a bed, covering the floor with carpets and rugs, using mirrors, drawers, servants, cutlery, towels, eating meat, and giving up his plough to eat chicken. In other words, the *fellah* is a graduate of Oxford!'[29]

Sound comes to Egypt

Having led the Egyptian cinema towards realism, Muhammad Karim now turned his attention to the talking film. Here again he turned to Yusuf Wahbi, who was already having great success starring in *Children of the*

Aristocrats, a melodrama he himself had written. They decided to make it as their first vehicle into sound, with Wahbi himself repeating his stage per-formance on the screen. In preparation, Wahbi purchased additional film equipment and renovated his Ramses Studio. El-Charkawi says: 'The silent part of the film was shot in this studio with sets built by Muhammad Karim himself, while the sound part (40%) was shot in Paris. *Children of the Aristocrats* premiered at the Royal cinema on 14 March, 1932, and enjoyed a great success.'[30]

Again the plot deals with a theme that was already touched on in *Laila*: the relationship between East and West. It revolves around a married Egyptian man who has an affair with Julia, a French girl living in Egypt. When his wife discovers his affair, he and his mistress flee to France. But when he discovers Julia in the arms of a new lover, he kills her. The lurid story was hugely popular. The French and the European community in Egypt called the film racist,[31] because the French girl was blamed for the young man's misery, imprisonment and eventual death.

The significance of the controversy is that by 1932 the Egyptian film had already entered international discourse. Unwittingly, what the film-makers had produced was now being regarded as an expression of national character and personality, and not just an artefact intended to entertain. Egyptian cinema's merits as well as faults were now under scrutiny. It had assumed a new role: to reflect Egyptian values, attitudes, biases and beliefs – and through it the outside world was judging Egyptian society. That was a major leap into seriousness that neither Karim nor Wahbi had probably contemplated.

Singers as movie stars

Egypt did not have the same kind of problem with sound as Hollywood, but it was equally vexing. It concerned the nature of Arabic songs themselves, for in those days they did not lend themselves well to cinema. They were too long and repetitive. Although *Song of the Heart* (1932) was filmed at the Eclair studio in Paris, had two great singers and one of Egypt's best actors, it was a total disaster. That it was written by one of Egypt's leading authors, and directed by Mario Volpi, did not make it any more lively. The problem was that the Arabic songs did not consist of breezy lyrics and catchy tunes sung lightly. They were meant to be absorbed at leisure, and to intoxicate the aficionado. The average song lasted between fifteen and twenty minutes.

Once again Karim came to the rescue. For a new challenge, he looked towards the musical. He collaborated with Muhammad Abd al-Wahhab, the most famous singer and composer in the Arab world. Their first film together, *al-Warda al-Bayda* (*The White Rose*, 1933), became a major triumph for all concerned and led Abd al-Wahhab to trust the direction of his seven films only to Karim – the director never made any films of significance without his singing star.

Technically *The White Rose* broke some new artistic ground. The indoor scenes were again shot in Paris studios. In due course, Karim was able to set the standard (even the format) for the Egyptian musical for a long time. After shortening the song to six minutes, he would focus the camera on the singer while he or she was actually singing and then move the camera around while the orchestra was playing. During the musical bridge, he would 'cut away to two pigeons, or a scene of the Nile, or a sailing vessel with masts, or a garden, or a rural landscape – or whatever the song suggests'.[32] Now short and light, the songs 'developed to the point where, on occasion, they took the form of dialogue and constituted an integral part of the action'.[33] While popular, these musicals were melodramas with singing interludes – never 'musicals' in the Hollywood sense.

The role of capitalism

One of the most important figures in the history of the Egyptian cinema was the industrialist and banker Tal'at Harb, who was also a nationalist with a desire to see the arts flourish in Egypt. It was he who, in 1935, founded Studio Misr – a modern complex where artists and technicians could work. Modelling it after Hollywood studios, he went on to create all the departments from photography to carpentry, and to install in the sound stages all the latest equipment. In addition, he created a system that for the first time provided the film-makers with a sense of security, even putting employees, technicians and movie stars on contracts.

On 10 October 1935, Tal'at Harb officially opened Studio Misr 'with a lavish reception for over 500 guests, including outstanding figures in politics, finance, the arts, literature and journalism'.[34] Then he sent many promising young men to Paris to study all aspects of film production, and recruited those who were already studying in Germany. Shortly thereafter Egypt had several more film studios: Lama, Jalal, Lotus, Nassibyan and many more. Film production rose from three to five films a year during the silent period to about fifteen a year during the early sound period. Film societies had by now sprouted throughout the country.

A new landmark in the Egyptian cinema

Prior to Chahine's arrival as a director, the Egyptian cinema could boast of a few film-makers who were professional and serious enough to be considered his artistic predecessors. One was Muhammad Karim; another was Kamal Salim. Most film historians now agree that with *al-Azima* (translated either as *The Will* or *Determination*) Egyptian cinema reached a level of maturity. It was made in 1939, by a twenty-six-year-old whose death before the age of thirty-two was a major blow to Egyptian cinema. Unlike many contemporaries who had managed to study in Paris or Berlin, fate denied Salim the opportunity. He taught himself foreign languages so he could read cinema books, took private lessons in painting and piano, landed a job at Studio Misr, wrote scenarios and ended up directing.

The success of *Determination*, his second film, was unprecedented both commercially and critically. All the elements that are essential to making a good film are under control. Particularly commendable are the skilful use of camera movement and the handling of the *mise-en-scène*. For the first time Egyptian audiences were able to identify with the characters on the screen. The characters engaged the audience, spoke to them without reliance on song and dance, touched their souls, and they responded. In *Determination*, the protagonist, Muhammad, is one with his people. He is an ordinary fellow – just like them. He is *ibn al-balad*, a native from the lower classes, just like them. His aspiration matches theirs. Neighbours and strangers can relate to his troubles and to the obstacles in his path. And when he wins over the forces of evil, they are elated for him and themselves. Their values have been endorsed.

During the 1930s, Egyptian cinema reflected the gap between the rich and the poor, *ibn al-zawat* and *ibn al-balad*, educated and uneducated, tradition and modernity, native and foreigner. Egyptian society was an amalgam of competing strands. The gulf between classes was obvious, but they did not know how to bridge it. Like all art, cinema began to play a role in making the Egyptians examine and assess themselves and their society. The enigma of their identity began to materialise on the silver screen.

What may be considered Egyptian cinema's booming age began after World War II. One historian cum film director describes those years of expansion and prosperity. 'By 1944,' he writes, 'the Egyptian cinema faced a serious problem in the form of shortage of actors. Directors made do with singers and dancers and no longer bothered to train or discover new talents [*sic*]. The problem stood out particularly in this period when the total number of films screened rose from 106 during the War, to 364. The production companies likewise increased from 24 to 120',[35] for commercial cinema was robust and a potent Egyptian export. Actors were transformed into stars. Distribution reached out to audiences across the Arab world and as far as South America where there are large Arab communities. Large crowds queued up to greet the release of every Egyptian film in order to see their movie idols. If the success of an industry is measured by its audience's response, the Egyptian cinema can claim that it had succeeded in creating generations of film addicts. That many of these Egyptian films were imitative of Hollywood films was unnoticed by the general public. What mattered was that the stars and characters spoke and sang in Arabic, appeared in Arabic settings and wore Arabic clothing. Huge, glossy photographs of these stars adorned magazine covers and the walls of the cinema lobbies next to Hollywood stars. Tal'at Harb's wish for Studio Misr to make 'Egyptian films for Egyptian people' was more than fulfilled.

While it obviously fulfilled a national need and satisfied cultural appetite, Egyptian cinema up to the Revolution of 1952 was undermined by greed. The profit motive, however, was not unique to Egypt, for it was also the driving force elsewhere, albeit with local variations. In Egypt, between 1945 and 1951, 'film mongers'[36] began to multiply. This was the condition of Egyptian cinema when Youssef Chahine inaugurated his film career with

Daddy Amin in 1950. Creative and obsessed, he never ceased to make films that are a far cry from the legacy he had inherited. Yet it is possible that he might not have been the artist he has become without the traditions established in Egyptian cinema, even though he has often seemed to struggle against them.

Over fifty years, Chahine has directed thirty-four features and six documentaries. He is renowned for using *al-ughniya* (song) in most of his films – several of his features starred famous singers: Farid al-Atrash, Shadia, Laila Murad, Majda al-Rumi, Daleeda, Latifa; and a number featured Muhammad Munir. His only operetta was with the inimitable Fairuz. The classification of a film as a musical is problematic because Egypt has no celluloid equivalent of *Singing in the Rain*, *All That Jazz* and *A Hard Day's Night*. Except for a relatively few films that successfully balanced narrative and singing – such as the irresistibly charming *Khalli balak min Zuzu* (*Beware of Zuzu*, 1972) – the Egyptian musical genre remains a hybrid rather than a pure form.

Like all industries, Egyptian cinema was directly affected by the political tides that swept Egypt during Chahine's years of productivity. Revolution, nationalisation, de-nationalisation, wars, plus the normal vicissitudes of commerce, have all helped shape his career. Little is printed on the economics of Egyptian cinema, yet Chahine's financing can be charted in two phases: reliance on small independent producers; establishment of his own production company, Misr International Films, and co-production arrangements with other Arab countries, such as Algeria and Lebanon. Since 1985, his financing problems have stabilised, mainly through mutually satisfying co-productions with France.

Stars forgo their salaries just to be in a Chahine film. It is true that many stars do the same in the United States or United Kingdom, in order to be in low-budget and art movies. But in Egypt, where stars' salaries are infinitesimal by Hollywood standards, the sacrifices are much greater. Producer Marianne Khoury says, 'Stars don't get paid much when they work in a Chahine film. They work for him for very little because what they seek most is the prestige of having appeared in any of his films and for the opportunity to observe and learn. They value the experience, exposure and prestige far more than money.'[37]

Mahmoud Hemeda who starred in three Chahine films – *The Emigrant* (1994), *Destiny* (1997) and *The Other* (1999) – concurs. For *The Emigrant*, he only took token payment. Hemeda's case, however, may be special. A founder of a new film company, he had his own reasons for forgoing his salary. He explains:

> Chahine's films are costly, and he doesn't have money to pay his actors. His distribution is limited and he's not making the millions people assume he's making. Nothing of the sort. He's on the run. He's basically a semi-institution. He has a few services that he offers to foreign producers making films in Egypt. He now has a few movie theatres. But he doesn't have any laboratories or such. He rents Studio Galal from the government. So when I decided to work with him, it was because I wanted to learn. For me to shave my head and sit around seven months working for him for nothing, that's something else. But I learned from him administration and how this semi-institution is run.[38]

On the other hand the employees of his company are well paid. Chahine is considered the best paying producer in Egypt: his generous nature also makes good business sense. According to Gabriel Khoury, Chahine's nephew and partner,

> Chahine takes pride in knowing that he's providing employment to so many people: eighty working at the office and at the cinemas, and an additional hundred-and-twenty whenever we're in production. Two hundred families depend on the checks they receive from Misr International Films, and this to Chahine is reason enough to keep the company running.[39]

The mutual loyalty between Chahine and his cast and crew is unparalleled in Egyptian cinema. After calling Chahine enigmatic and rebellious, and after comparing him to soft moving sands that hide a volcano, Hind Rustum, star of *Cairo Station* (1958), waxes elegant when she talks about him. Yousra, who starred in several of his films, considers him her friend and mentor. She dismisses the twenty-five films she made before appearing in his *An Egyptian Story* (1982), adding, 'I began making quality films with him.'

And yet, the winner of film awards around the globe, who is also the premiere director in the Arab world, Chahine is not free of worries. 'My tor-
ment is sometimes physical, not just spiritual or internal,' he admits.
'Sometimes I hit my head against the wall.' As to being called rebellious, he
adds: 'I agree, although we must watch out for the different meanings the
word carries to different regimes. It has become a slogan. It's normal for
me that when I see cowardice or treachery to try to do something about it.'[40]

What is significant about Chahine is that despite (or perhaps because of)
being tormented, and despite operating under difficult circumstances –
financing obviously being only one of them – he has carved for himself and
for Egypt a respectable niche in the pantheon of world cinema.

*   *   *

Because Chahine's corpus is relatively large, I had to settle on a manageable
number of films for analysis. Thus the problems of selection and arrangement arose. The chosen fourteen films are those I believe to be his best and
which are the most illustrative of the diversity of his style. Chahine himself
concurs. There are three films I would also like to have included. *Al-Yawm
al-Sadis* (*The Sixth Day*, 1986), and *Bayya' al-Khawatim* (*The Ring Seller*,
1965), 'which the critic Jean-Marie Sabatier called the finest musical comedy of the Arab cinema'[41] were both excluded because of lack of space. *Al-
nas wa al-Nil* (*People and the Nile*, 1968), a controversial Egyptian-Soviet
co-production depicting the building of the economically vital Aswan Dam,
was another film I was eager to find, but the only print Chahine recom-
mended for me to see proved inaccessible. Further confirmation of my
choices came in September 1998, when the Film Society of the Lincoln
Center, in New York, held a retrospective on Chahine. Their selection of
fifteen films coincided precisely with my fourteen (plus one extra). Then
came the question of arrangement. A chronological approach promised to
be the easiest but it proved to be the least satisfactory. Within a short time
span Chahine made films in different genres, going on to repeat the cycle.
To move rapidly from social drama to a war film to a historical film and then
flip back and forth would have been too confusing. Instead, I have chosen

to group them thematically, and to arrange the genres so that there is a broadly chronological projection. The clustering around themes is more logical and illuminating than following a linear succession, even though there is an element of overlapping in the arrangement.

One
The Formative Years

Though they belonged to two different generations, Youssef Chahine and Gibran Kahlil Gibran – the celebrated author of *The Prophet* – share much in common. Their ancestral roots are in Greater Syria (which included Lebanon until 1920); their families emigrated towards the end of the nineteenth century, and largely for the same reasons – escape from Ottoman oppression, and economic hardship exacerbated by the abandonment of mother or grandmother by their husbands. Both were outsiders in their own countries. Both were born Christian in a predominantly Muslim world: Gibran focused on spirituality, Chahine on humanism – but neither was religious in the institutional sense. Both were loved by the public and attacked by the clerics for their 'radical' ideas. Gibran's books were rumoured to have been burned in one of Beirut's public squares and he himself was vilified from the pulpit;[1] one of Chahine's films was banned by Muslim fundamentalists and he himself was put on trial in a court of law.[2] Both had a connection with France: Gibran went to Paris and studied sculpture under Rodin but never became a Francophone; Chahine married a French girl born and raised in Egypt, and he himself is as French as a foreigner could be, but never at the expense of his Egyptianness. Both achieved international acclaim: one in literature, the other in cinema.

Where Gibran and Chahine part company is in their yearning for home. To Gibran, home was Lebanon; to Chahine, home is Egypt. In his youth Gibran returned from New York to Beirut to further his schooling;[3] in his youth Chahine went to America instead. Gibran specified in his will a wish to be buried in Lebanon's mountains; Chahine would not consider such an option. When Chahine went to Lebanon it was to make a film with Fairúz, the Arab world's singing idol. Although he had his chances to live and work abroad, Chahine chose to remain in Egypt in body and soul. When he dies he will be interred not in the shadows of the cedars, but on the shores of the Nile.

Having been abandoned by her husband, in 1898 or thereabouts, Chahine's paternal grandmother journeyed from Mount Lebanon to Egypt, carrying with her two babies – the cause of the abandonment was never known. Chahine himself had no idea; nor did he recall any contact between his grandfather and the family since his disappearance. The only things he remembers of the whole affair are that he once saw a piece of paper indicating that his grandfather had finally settled somewhere in the United States and become an American citizen, and also that his family was from Zahleh, Lebanon, with the Chahine family emerging out of a marriage between the Mir'i and Sawaya families. As to the origin of the name Chahine, he speculates that it is probably his grandfather's middle name.[4] His mother was the daughter of a Greek who had married a girl from Aleppo, Syria. Chahine describes his mother, Marie Kharrisis, as extremely beautiful. He then adds, 'I must've come out looking like my father.'

The dauntless grandmother settled with her children in cosmopolitan Alexandria which was then a haven for multiple ethnic minorities. Residents of the Levant were known then as Syrians, and the abandoned Chahines joined the Syrian community. Chahine remembers his grandmother making marmalades for family use but not for sale. How the poor woman managed to raise her family and educate her son, Chahine's father, to become a lawyer remains a mystery to him. But it is a mystery couched in respect and admiration for her instinct for survival and appreciation of education.

Childhood and family

Chahine was born in Alexandria on 25 January 1926, and apparently had a happy childhood. His parents were affectionate and he adored both of them. Even as a child he never doubted what he wanted to become. When he was young his grandmother took him to see a shadow play, which consisted of a screen of cloth onto which shadows were cast by moving objects in front of a lamp (behind the cloth). It must have been an important moment for him, for he went home and duplicated it and continued to do so throughout his childhood. He spent hours under the bed, imagining himself in a big cinema hall, in a production room, in a projection room, in front of a big screen, etc. He recalled:

> I used to attend American films then gather a few friends and bring them
> home where we would re-enact what we had seen. As I grew older, at the age
> of eight, I discovered that 9.5mm films and a small projector were being sold
> in the stores. The projector didn't cost more than 30 piasters, and each film
> cost three and a half piasters. I saved from allowances enough to buy the pro-
> jector and then became a regular customer for the *Rabbani Bibi* (*Bibi Raised
> Me*) short films. I used to gather the children of the neighborhood to show
> them these films. Some of them didn't care for cinema and would come up
> with all kinds of excuses not to attend. So I had no choice but to form a gang
> to beat up those who were late coming to the show.[5]

His mischief was not limited to boys and girls of the neighbourhood. If his
parents did not bother to watch his master-work, he would fuse the lights.
At the age of nine he received a Baby-Pathé, the kind that showed five-
minute reels. He told the same journalist:

> One of the longest Baby-Pathé films I can remember was *Destiné*, a film on
> Bonaparte. Perhaps it was a film by Abel Gance, I do not remember. In those
> days my mother used to take me to the local cinemas where French films
> would always be shown, with Henri Garat and Annabella or Jean Murat. I also
> remember films with Fernandel. In fact, I would mostly see films from
> Marseilles. Of course, once Egypt started importing Parisian films I would
> find the Parisian accent quite funny. The accent from Marseilles was closer
> to our own and I expect I understood it better.[6]

In his formative years Chahine was torn between two attractions: indulgence in sexual fantasies and cinema. Part of the struggle was due to his
youth and to not having settled yet on a career path. The conflict between
the two urges – cinema and 'the dark side' of sexual fantasies – raged in him
constantly 'because both were attractive to me'.

But tragedy crept into their modest home and young Chahine was
introduced to mortality. The worst shock of his childhood was the death of
his brother, Alfred, who was only two years older. When Alfred was eleven,
after playing a football game, he caught pneumonia, which then was almost

incurable. But being young, Chahine thought it was partly his fault. The reason for this was that two Christmas seasons earlier, when he was seven and Albert nine, he had tried to light a candle and instead burned the paper in the crèche, causing a fire. When they asked him who did it, he said Alfred did. It was a small fire and they were able to extinguish it quickly. It definitely did not cause Alfred's death. But when Alfred died, Chahine's grandmother went around the house lamenting, 'Why did he have to die? Why didn't the young one die instead?' That remark must have stung Chahine, for it resurfaced in one of the most touching scenes in *Alexandria ... Why?* (1978).

What Chahine recalls most about Alfred was that he was a dark boy with big eyes. Since then most of his male actors have eyes that resemble Alfred's. They do not necessarily have to be beautiful eyes, but they must be interesting just like his brother's were. 'In 90% of my films,' he explains, 'you'll find eyes communicating with eyes because the eyes are very important for me. The French have a word for it. You don't just look at somebody, you *see* him. You see profoundly. You see inside that person.' All great directors regard eyes as important, but Chahine attaches extra

Like the young Chahine: a child fearful of fire in the creche (*Alexandria ... Why?*, 1978)

significance to them on account of his brother's beautiful eyes.

Chahine characterises his father as 'a block of honesty'. In the ways of the world, he must have been artless. His lack of cunning helped Chahine develop his own will-power to remain honest. So when Chahine hears of people on the street saying that they may not understand his films but they respect him because he's *sadiq* (honest), he feels flattered even though he does not like flattery. For his honesty to be recognised gives him satisfaction, not only for himself but as a tribute to his father. 'Unfortunately', Chahine says, 'he was in the worst profession for him.' Roy Armes describes the father as a 'scrupulous but financially unsuccessful lawyer'.[7]

Besides probity, his father instilled in him the love of books. 'When I grew up I found a library at home, philosophy and the like,' Chahine recalls. He became a book addict. In preparing for *Adieu Bonaparte* (1985), he did intensive research. He is fluent in Arabic, French and English, and proficient in two or three other languages. Another influence the father left on his son was exuberance. 'First of all, he loved life,' Chahine remembers. 'On that score, he was very Egyptian. I said a lot about him in *Alexandria ... Why?*' Chahine speaks warmly of his father's sacrifice for him in order that

Paternal influence: father and son in *Alexandria ... Why?*

he should become educated. He closed his law office and took a job 'as a sub-head in the legal department of Alexandria's municipality' to be able to pay the tuition fees. 'How can I forget this?' Chahine asks. 'It's what I remember most. We had a hard time during the war [World War II], yet he enrolled me in the prestigious and expensive Victoria College.' Hardship and sacrifice, however, did not deter the father from pursuing happiness. He particularly liked fishing, which Chahine shows in some of his films.

From the many days of bird hunting with his father, Chahine learned to appreciate the topography of a place. He credits his father for having taught him how to look at the desert. Because there are very few roads in the desert, the father would tell his son how to look for landmarks such as a piece of twisted iron or a pile of bricks to remember which way to turn. Scouting locations for a film now reminds Chahine of those days. Early on he learned to pay attention to where the sun rises, and where the shadows fall on a dune. He explains:

> Sometimes when you go to the desert around eleven o'clock, you see nothing. Everything is white. I have a way of doing things: if the location doesn't give itself to you and tell you look at me, I want to be photographed, I'm pretty and so on ... then how can you film? You and the location must connect. So I sit in the desert and wait for the sun to move. Suddenly a dune tells me look how pretty I am, and I start filming.

Chahine and his mother were also very close. He remembers her as 'a beautiful woman who was often quoted'. Though at times in his youth she and other family members were not sufficiently sensitive to his interests, he still holds her in deep affection. He calls her 'absolutely brilliant'. She was sociable and articulate. She was also well read, although her formal education was rather superficial. Her marriage to a much older man created some very tangible problems. Chahine now admits that it took much courage on his part to address the issue in the second part of his autobiographical film *An Egyptian Story*, because it cast a shadow on a person whom he loved dearly and who was still living. She liked the film, then made a tiny remark that he finds interesting. Referring to the actress who portrayed her, she said, 'But I was prettier, wasn't I?' She did not get upset, for the film was preserving her for posterity. Everyone wants to be remembered, he explains, and he uses the word 'posterity' in a number of his films. In Arabic it means *al-khuloud*, which he employs in *Destiny* in reference to those who seek to usurp power with an eye on history.

Comparing his parents to each other, Chahine considers his mother far more intelligent than his father. He was humble; she was proud. Though they were *petits bourgeois*, their manners were always the manners of the upper class. Children were forbidden from using the wrong word at the dinner table or eating the wrong way. Both parents were sticklers for proper manners. If Chahine or his sister made a mistake they were punished for a whole week and had to eat in the kitchen. The family were acting like aristocrats at home, yet his father would not feel shame carrying a watermelon on the bus. Nor did he aspire to owning a car. It was his mother who wanted respectability and upward mobility. She was not a spendthrift, but rather careful with her money. 'As I remember,' he says, 'sometimes money was so tight we couldn't breathe.' Still his parents were very generous and lived beyond their means. They did not pay attention to bank statements. Aristocracy to them meant that they always had guests for dinner. When Chahine was already directing in Cairo, his mother invited Jeanne Moreau and Tony Richardson (who were filming in Egypt) to their home in Alexandria. He does not know how the invitation came about. Her cabin on the beach was open for all their friends. To compliment her about her food meant repeated invitations. One popular comic actor used to tell her (and here Chahine mimics him perfectly), '*ya salaam*, your food is absolutely delicious', and she would tell him to come the next night for dinner, which meant every night. One of the qualities she passed on to her son is caring for the poor. 'The whole neighbourhood must love her,' Chahine says. 'She needed love very badly.'

Three facts have emerged so far in this sketch of Chahine's upbringing that were to colour and condition some Egyptians' perception of him: that he is of 'foreign' descent rather than an indigenous Egyptian; that he is a Christian (albeit a lapsed one) rather than a Muslim; and that he was born and raised in Alexandria of the Mediterranean culture rather than in Cairo of the Muslim culture – all these factors were to prove problematic for him later in his career, especially after having made some controversial films. You would expect Chahine to ridicule such attitudes as nonsense; he might dismiss the image of the insider / outsider they try to attach to him as narrow-minded, but we his readers would be remiss not to pay attention to that image.

The American experience

The journey of a child interested in shadow plays to becoming one of the masters of world cinema took decades to achieve. Financially vulnerable yet determined to give him a good education, his parents enrolled him at Victoria College in Alexandria. Little is known about Chahine in those years or about the nature of the school itself. But in his memoir, *Out of Place*, Edward Said paints it as an inhospitable, racist and colonial institution where students were caned by a 'Europeanized Eastern Jew' who is not above declaring *'Ne manage pas comme les Arabes'*.[8]

Chahine graduated from Victoria College in 1944 and his immediate wish was to study dramatic arts abroad. But money was a major hurdle to overcome. His family could not afford the expense and his father was opposed to the idea of theatre as a profession, preferring something more secure. His father himself had wanted to be an engineer, to create something new, but had failed and therefore wanted his son to fulfill his dream. But the son balked, wanting to be an actor. At the age of seven-

A blow-up from an 8mm film showing Chahine in his school days at Victoria College

teen, and prior to taking the matriculation examination at Victoria
College, Chahine saw a film on Ziegfield, the famous Broadway producer
of lavish musicals, and was convinced that he could produce similar
shows.[9] After persuading a princess to sponsor a stage production for the
benefit of her charities, he rented the Alhambra cinema in Alexandria.
But the cinema owner would only allow him two hours for rehearsals. The
result was a fiasco. Spectators left in droves, noisily demanding their
money back.[10] To his family, this was proof positive that he should not
pursue a theatrical career. To him, it only proved that all he needed was
experience. He suggested that they let him study in France. 'When they
said no,' he recalled, 'I nearly had to blackmail them. I wanted to throw
myself through the window.'[11]

Still trying to dissuade him from pursuing a theatrical career, his parents enrolled him in the college of engineering at Alexandria University.
While there Chahine staged another musical in the style of the American
musicals. The show was a huge personal triumph for him. He used it to
demonstrate to his father that he would not succeed as an engineer. 'Even if
I could succeed, I wouldn't let myself succeed.'[12] With great sacrifice on his
family's part he eventually set out for California.

Eventually most of Chahine's experiences surface in his films. Such
an experience took place as he sailed from Alexandria on his way to
America. That moment taught him something about courage, the quality
he admires most. 'When you go to the cinema,' he says, 'the scenes during which you can't hold the tears back are scenes that usually depict
courage. Courage is one of the most important values in a human's life. I
admire it deeply.' Referring to his own mother and himself, he provides
an example:

> The mother who lost a son and is worried about the only son left to her tries
> to persuade him not to travel to a distant land. She reminds him that his
> stage production was a disaster, hoping he'd change his mind. The boy is
> crying desperately about leaving his family. They are so poor that he wor-
> ries that they might not have enough money to bring him back. Then, as the
> ship moves into the sea, the boy is instantly captivated by the lovely colour

of the waters below him. It is bluer than anything he had seen before. Suddenly he stops crying.

Remembering the purpose of his journey, the boy channels his love of his parents to the new love of the sea, the love of a new adventure. He summons up the courage to face the new challenge before him. He knows that he can never forget his family, but he puts them aside for the time being to concentrate on the new world he was about to enter. There is much that he wants to learn before returning to carry on the task he has prescribed for himself.

The transformation of the boy's love from his parents to the blue sea constitutes for Chahine an act of courage. 'Love changed him,' he says. 'Love can give you a qualitative charge. There's nothing but love, although the word is hard to define and is often trivialised. It's wonderful to love, but love is something you have to teach yourself.' In keeping with his method of weaving part of himself into every film he made, Chahine included the boy's transformation at the sea in part one of his autobiographical trilogy, *Alexandria ... Why?*.

At Pasadena Playhouse he finished a three-year course in twenty-seven months, studying theatre. Stanislavsky's method acting was then the rage in American drama schools and Chahine was influenced by it. He also took courses in television production, but not film. Film had not yet gained a foothold in American academies. He recalls an argument with a member of the camera crew, and asserting his authority as director on the set. He was later to test and hone all that varied experience. He also remembers learning that every movement on stage had to be inherent in the scene. It had to be justified, a principle he was to adapt to the screen. 'The spectator must not be conscious of the camera,' he explains. 'Something is wrong if he is. As a director, or spectator, you should follow the action. The camera movement constitutes for me the visual syntax, which is very important.'

Little is known of his years at Pasadena, except that he studied under Leonore Shanwise, was friends with Victor Jory and Robert Preston, and was impressed by Richard O'Connor, who had lectured on direction. While

Chahine studying acting at the
Pasadena Playhouse in California

still a student, Chahine abandoned his pursuit of acting. He had aspired to
be as great a Hamlet as John Gielgud had been, from the age of fourteen, but
he decided that his acting ambition had to wait. However, he had to perform
to gain admission. He explains:

> The way I interpreted it gave meaning to every word. Something was com-
> ing out of it, a bit like suffering. The other 'comedians' would sing the role
> in the usual way. Yet, each time that Hamlet or a similar role was offered, I
> wouldn't get it. The little African with a big nose and big ears that I was did-
> n't fit. They preferred to give the role to a blond guy, even if he was an
> absolute idiot. I could've waited for years. Already by then the star system
> was more important than talent.[13]

But he must have been excellent in the rest of his studies, for of the 200 students attending, only thirteen sat for the final examinations and of those
only four passed. He ranked first, and upon graduation he was offered a
teaching position.[14]

Two incidents from those days illustrate Chahine's determination and
irrepressible youth. The first concerns a visit to a Hollywood studio. Told to
remain quiet while filming was in progress, the impetuous Chahine could
not keep quiet. Consequently, he was literally thrown out of the sound stage.

The second involved finding his way to an acting class. Unable to get in through the front door, he descended through the chimney. When the instructor saw the trouble he had gone through to be there, she told him, 'If you get in this way all the time I'm not going to stop you.'[15] Characteristically, Chahine used the latter incident in his film *The Emigrant*.

Homecoming

Strangely, upon returning from Pasadena in 1948 with a Pasadena Playhouse diploma, Chahine did not work in the Egyptian theatre. It is uncharacteristic, and rather anticlimactic, for him not to have done so. Considering the agony he and his family had gone through before he could travel abroad to study theatre, it is difficult to understand why he did not seek employment on the stages of Cairo. Convinced that his looks were a hindrance to his being cast in leading roles, he must have made a mental adjustment to shift his interest from actor to director and from the declining theatre to the booming cinema. Of the latter this is what he had to say:

> I had never met a director in Egypt. I didn't know anything about cinema. I could only guess. For example, to choose the rhythm between two scenes, I would place my hand on my heart and I would count the number of beats between a change of scenes. I don't know if it taught me anything but it already demonstrated my interest in the problem. And why would they change?[16]

Instead of working either in the theatre or in film production, Chahine worked in the publicity department of Twentieth-Century Fox in Cairo, where his brother-in-law, John Khoury, was manager. From then on, Chahine was on his way. From the fragments of biographical sketches available, we learn that 'he spent the next year acting and working with the Egyptian-born documentarist Gianni Vernuccio and the distinguished cameraman Alvise Orfanelli'.[17] When an Egyptian film director quarrelled with his producer and walked off the set, the producer turned to Chahine to complete the film for him. Instead of welcoming the chance to prove himself, Chahine had the boldness to refuse. Should the producer, however, need him in the future to start a film, he would be glad to oblige. Though the words sound haughty from someone at his age who should have welcomed the opportunity, Chahine was astute in observing an unwritten ethical code which forbade one director from taking over a production in the case of a dispute between another director and the producer, unless the aggrieved director designated him as his replacement. The combination of determination, self-confidence and professionalism obviously served him well. Surprisingly, though, when he was offered a job as an assistant director, he had the temerity to turn it down, too, claiming that it was beneath someone like him who had 'participated in directing films in Hollywood'.[18] It is said that it takes more than talent to succeed in 'showbiz', and Chahine had both talent and that mysterious quality that propels those who have it into fame.

Besides the lack of experience, Chahine had another problem which is not normally mentioned as a prerequisite for film direction. Now internationally acclaimed, he laughs about it. He admits that at twenty-one he looked ungainly. 'I had a six-meter-long nose and ears like ship sails. One of the producers told me I couldn't be taken seriously. He told me to put on some weight and to change my appearance. Perhaps I would be noticed that way. Even as a film director my appearance counted.'[19]

Chahine does not remember any Egyptian film that might have had an

The greatest influence on Chahine:
Julien Duvivier's *The Great Waltz*
(1938)

impression on him. He does remember, though, that the first film that had a strong influence on his technique was Julien Duvivier's *The Great Waltz*, which he claims to have watched forty times. That was during the difficult years, he now recalls, when he was about fifteen or sixteen years old. Almost fifty years later, he used a segment of it in his film *The Other*. But the films he 'was crazy about' were the American musicals. He liked them because he loved to dance, and considered Busby Berkeley a phenomenon. Above all, Chahine wanted to dance like Gene Kelly to whom, years later, he dedicated *The Sixth Day*.

In 1951, Chahine fell in love. The way it happened reveals him as a man who does not need much time to know what he wants. One day he was sitting around in Alexandria telling stories about his school days and regaling his friends with memories of the musical fiasco he had staged at the age of seventeen. Among those who were enjoying his company was a young French girl, Colette Favaudon, who, like him, was born and raised in Alexandria. Some of his friends claim that her ancestors were friends of Napoleon's. At the end of the day, Chahine had to return to Cairo but was already smitten with Colette (Coco). After a sleepless night, he rang her up in the morning and blurted out that he simply had to marry her. Startled, Coco could not believe that he would propose to her on the phone. He told her to say yes and he would rush back to Alexandria and marry her. She consented and they were married immediately. The morning after their wedding night he had to report to work, starting *Nile Boy* (1951).

Chahine's lifestyle is unpretentious. His film company is located in the congested heart of Cairo, and his offices are so crammed that the small production room doubles as a projection room. The room where the film cans, new film stock, videotapes, television set and VCR unit are stored is tiny. One would expect a well-established enterprise that many consider an Egyptian 'institution' to be on a grand scale. What matters to Chahine most is putting every pound where it counts – on the screen, and not on fancy offices. One is inclined to believe him when he says, 'Every penny I make goes back into cinema'.[20] Similarly his car is sixteen years old, for to him a car is a means of transportation and not a luxury or a status symbol. He and his wife Coco live in Zamalek, a smart suburb by Egyptian standards. The high-rise apartment building is close to a major boulevard, but its entrance faces a side street that is narrow and dark. His study is cosy and its walls are lined with bookshelves and CDs, not unlike the inner sanctum of a professor, content to be alone with his thoughts or one of his friends. White German liqueur, however, is his passion.

Having no children of his own, Chahine looks upon his films, his students at the High Cinema Institute and his protégés as his legacy. Profit for its own sake is secondary. In contrast a Hollywood studio mogul reputedly admonished his subordinates by reminding them that they were not in the business of making movies: they were in the business of making money. Though the producer to whom this remark is attributed is anonymous, he undoubtedly spoke for the majority of producers.

Two
Chronicle of Chahine's Career and its Context

It is instructive to situate Chahine's bio-filmography within the context of Egyptian cinema and the overall political and cultural scene, for the seeds of many of his films were sown in historical events which he witnessed. It is significant, for example, that the year he made his debut as a film director (1950) happened to fall in between two major historical turning points. In 1948, the Arabs lost Palestine and Israel was born; in 1952, Colonel Gamal Abdel Nasser led the bloodless Revolution which ended a corrupt monarchy. The significance of these two watershed events, artistically speaking, is that they shaped the society which Chahine chose to portray on the screen for the next fifty years. It is useful, then, to divide his career into three phases, each of which contributed to shaping him as a director and allowed him to tackle national themes that became the hallmark of his cinema.

In his early period (1952-70), Chahine was preoccupied with the large issues of his time: the liberation movements that were sweeping the Arab world, be it colonialism or monarchy; the Egyptian *fellah*, whose welfare was central to the Revolution; the rise of a new kind of leadership, as exemplified by the charismatic Nasser; and by Arab socialism and the betrayal of it by those who put self-interest above national interest. The seismic Revolution of 1952 which ended the 141-year-old dynasty that Muhammad Ali had started in 1811, made the Free Officers who engineered it instant heroes, and inaugurated the new era of pan-Arab Nationalism. Serious Egyptian film-makers were also encouraged by what they were hearing in regard to their own medium. The first president of the new Republic, General Muhammad Naguib, delivered a major speech which resonated throughout the Egyptian film industry. After criticising the '[e]ffimency and moral depravity' that had reflected the old regime, he added, 'Today we cannot accept from Art or from those in charge of it any-

thing like what used to happen in the past.'¹ The industry was now in con-
cert with the policies advocated by the new regime. While some directors
were in favour of the government becoming involved in the film industry,
Youssef Chahine 'was satisfied to listen and not comment'. ²

* * *

Two years before the Free Officers' Revolution, Chahine had his own ideas
on film-making. With his first film, *Baba Amin* (*Daddy Amin*), which he
made at the age of twenty-four, he conceived an agenda for himself: while
accommodating genuine requirements of local tradition, he would deal
with more urgent themes. This introduced a new departure from contemporary Egyptian cinema in seriousness and originality. From the very
beginning Chahine began to lay bare parts of his autobiography, for the
father in the film is modelled on his own father. Even though *Daddy Amin*

A new kind of cinema: entertaining but not frivolous (*Daddy Amin*, 1950)

Nile Boy (1951): the first Chahine feature to be submitted to an international film festival

contains three songs, imposed on him by the producer, the film is fundamentally serious and deals with family values and fiscal responsibility. More important, with *Daddy Amin*, Chahine was heralding a new kind of cinema: entertaining but not frivolous. The young Chahine might have *looked* ungainly, but his debut as a director was extraordinarily promising.

The day after his wedding in 1951, Chahine started his second film, *Nile Boy*, which was 'an adaptation of the stage play *Nature Boy* by the American Grant Marshall'.[3] The film is important for two reasons. One, it deals with the Egyptian *fellah* a subject to which Chahine would return several times. The plot revolves around a young Egyptian *fellah* who is lured into and corrupted by the city, but finds his redemption upon returning to his village and family. Two, the film marks Chahine's entrée into international film festivals. The way he went about it is also illustrative of his resolve to broaden his horizon and to bring attention to Egyptian cinema in general. Still in his twenties and unaware of procedures, Chahine carried his film cans

under his arm and headed for Venice, only to be told that his film could not
be scheduled. Because he had neither submitted an application nor been
invited to enter his film, it would not be shown. But Chahine stood his
ground. He argued and sought assistance from another Egyptian director,
Niazi Mustapha, who happened to be there, until *Nile Boy* was given a slot
out of competition at ten o'clock in the morning.

In one of his early films, *The Blazing Sun* (1954), Chahine introduced
Omar Sharif to the screen. Omar Sharif was at that time still known by his
real name, Michel Shalhoub. He was a fellow Alexanderine and a graduate
of Victoria College, which Chahine had attended six years earlier. In this
film, Chahine again dramatised the exploitation of the Egyptian *fellah*. And
for the first time in Egyptian cinema, Chahine shocked audiences by showing the hanging of an innocent man, and by suggesting that the taboo of a
marriage between a boy and a girl from two different classes could be broken. Visually, *Blazing* represented something new in Egyptian cinema. The

Omar Sharif's introduction to the screen – courtesy of Chahine. (*The Blazing
Sun*, 1954)

chase and the extremely long shots and high angles in the exotic setting of the monumental columns at Luxor reminded viewers of the director's affinity with Hollywood. This last characteristic became particularly apparent in some of the musicals he directed at this time, such as *My One and Only Love* (1957), which contains one of the loveliest and most inventive duets in the history of Egyptian cinema. Here we find two singers enacting the love / hate relationship of young lovers, with charm and liveliness that was often missing in Egyptian musicals. During his first seven years, however, Chahine also became known as the 'wrecker of producers'.[4] He earned the epithet after *Devil in the Desert* (1954), also starring Omar Sharif. While the film was Chahine's first major box-office failure, the label itself was really placed on its young director too early in his career.

A series of political upheavals intervened before the next phase of Chahine's career. Their relevance to Chahine was more indirect than direct, but nevertheless they help reveal his political growth and the psychological condition of his potential audiences. On the positive side, Nasser was able to negotiate a peaceful evacuation of the British troops from Egypt, but after the United States reneged on its promise to finance the Aswan Dam, Nasser retaliated by nationalising the Suez Canal. The crisis escalated into the British-French-Israeli invasion of the Suez Canal zone in 1956. After the shooting had stopped, the Canal remained in Egyptian hands and Nasser was hailed as a hero in much of the Arab world. Syria invited Egypt to form a union with her. Though reluctant, Nasser agreed to form a republic with him as its president, and many thought of the newly formed United Arab Republic as a harbinger to the Arab unity they desired.

During the late 1950s, Chahine's own star was also in the ascendant. He made the significant *Cairo Station*, which depicted the tormented life of a marginalised segment of the Egyptian society. The early screenings pleased the critics but incensed general audiences. Chahine says that he 'was literally spat on by one of the viewers'[5] for having given Egypt a bleak image. The experience was so traumatic that Chahine felt he had no right to gamble with other people's money. Then he was asked to make a film on the subject of the Algerian Revolution. Consequently, *Jamila* (1958), marked a turning point in his career, for it was his first overtly political film to date. Co-scripted by Naguib Mahfouz and some of Egypt's best writers, and filmed on a lot near the Pyramids, *Jamila* proved to be a powerful film and an instant triumph throughout the Arab world. In this film, Chahine began to experiment with mixing genres, one of his signature traits. A year later, in 1959, the Higher Cinema Institute was established in Cairo for the training of a new generation of Egyptians in the arts and sciences of cinema. Chahine was one of its founders and a regular member of its faculty. The Institute proved to be a vital source of new talent on which the cinema counted.

These two successes by Chahine were followed by a string of failures, primarily because they were commercial vehicles rather than artistic expressions. The years 1959-61 marked his lowest period as a director. Four commercial and artistic flops – *Forever Yours* (1959); *Only You* (1960); *Lovers' Complaint* (1961); and *A Man in My Life* (1961) – filled him with self-doubt to the point that, at the age of thirty-five, he dusted off the books on the shelf in hopes of re-learning dramaturgy. It was one of his gloomiest periods. On the national level, too, the motion picture industry was experiencing a major crisis. Nasser's sweeping nationalisation of all industries did not spare it. The agrarian reforms might have been badly needed, but the cinema industry was a casualty. In 1961, a law was passed to nationalise Misr Bank, with all its motion picture subsidiaries. Besides Studio Misr, other studios were also nationalised. The end result was devastating. Military men, ignorant of cinema practices, were now running the studios. They offered contracts, paid out huge sums of money, but most of the films were never made. It was a period of unparalleled chaos. Outside interference took its toll and did incalculable damage. The cinema industry as a whole has yet to recover from that debacle.

Despite these dire conditions, Chahine found himself inheriting a colleague's pet project. Director Izzidin Zulfiqar had written a script he was about to start filming when he discovered that he was terminally ill. Although he had a brother, also a film director, the dying man chose Chahine to realise his dream. *Saladin* (1963) was an epic composed for the greater glory of Gamal Abdel Nasser, equating him with the legendary liberator of Jerusalem during the Crusades. The 195-minute epic was the biggest production in Arab cinema up till then. During filming (1961), the union between Egypt and Syria collapsed. Chahine himself regarded *Saladin* as the awakening of his consciousness regarding the realities of international power politics. It was also his first use of colour and widescreen. Suddenly things went askew. Despite the enormous logistical support Chahine had received from Nasser's regime in the production of *Saladin*, he was denied seventeen awards. The problem had arisen because of an acrimonious confrontation with the Deputy Minister of Culture over a script Chahine was preparing on the building of the Aswan Dam, to be called *Tomorrow Life Begins*.[6] The only award *Saladin* received was for a minor technical achievement, which was correctly perceived by Chahine and his allies as a public rebuff of the film's creator. The award deliberately highlighted the fact that *Saladin* was indeed in competition but lost. That year's top award went to an inconsequential film called *Soft Hands*, based on Tawfiq al-Hakim's stage play. *Saladin*, however, did garner an award from the Egyptian Catholic Centre for Cinema.[7]

With his eighteenth film, *Dawn of a New Day* (1964), Chahine addressed the subject of socialism which Nasser's regime had adopted for Egypt. Like many intellectuals, Chahine embraced socialism as a means to salvation. Poverty and illiteracy in Egypt were endemic, further exacerbated by a population that was exploding. The social problems were so immense and serious that although socialism might not have been a panacea, it was a badly needed remedy. He aimed his salvo at the greedy bourgeoisie who betrayed socialism. Contrary to some accounts[8], it is one of the few Chahine films which featured a woman in the central role.

While attending *Dawn of a New Day*'s premiere in Lebanon, Chahine was approached by the Rahbani brothers, famous musicians throughout the Arab world, to make a film starring Fairuz. Chahine welcomed the opportunity, thus abandoning *Tomorrow Life Begins*, the film about the Aswan Dam, which was already in bureaucratic trouble. Chahine was among thirty-five Egyptian directors to flee 'to Lebanon looking for opportunities to make their films'.[9] The film Chahine made in Lebanon was *The Ring Seller*. He loved listening to Fairuz's singing and to the music of the celebrated Rahbani brothers, but the Lebanese technicians were too inexperienced to suit him. Then he went to Spain, where he made *Golden Sands* (1966), an unabashed adaptation of *Blood and Sand* (1941), starring Tyrone Power. Although his film in Lebanon was evocative, with images worthy of Fairuz's voice, his effort in Spain was one of his poorest even though it starred Fatin Hamama, the first lady of the Egyptian screen.

Out of Egypt Chahine felt homesick and at a loss. Worried about the state of the cinema industry in general and his recent failures in particular, he regarded himself as in a self-imposed exile and out of place. Then a message reached him that President Nasser had hinted that *al-magnoon* (the madman) Chahine could return. Chahine was overjoyed. He was apprehensive, too, for he did not know whether the red carpet or the red cap (symbol of a death sentence) would be awaiting him. Neither was in sight.[10] Instead, he was asked to direct the first Egyptian-Soviet co-production. Immediately he started planning what would become *People and the Nile*. In the meantime, he made *Eid al-Mairoun (Sacred Oil*, 1967) a thirteen-minute documentary on the origin, preparation and significance of holy oil in the Coptic church. It is a beautifully haunting film which, in its chiaroscuro photography and striking compositions, recalls Andrey Tarkovsky's *Andrey Rublyov*. Its slow tempo represents a departure from Chahine's usually frenetic style, and reveals a spiritual side to him that is rarely seen. And it marks the first time he alluded to his Christian roots. Born a Melkite Catholic, he is not an observant of any organised religion.

The region was soon engulfed in a new war. Within only six days in 1967, Israel decimated the Arab armies and occupied Sinai, the West Bank and the Golan Heights. The *blitzkrieg* and the depth of defeat forced Nasser to offer his resignation, but he stayed in power by popular demand. A few years later, Chahine would return to analyse the roots of that catastrophe in *The Sparrow* (1973), one of his most poignant and intelligent films.

In 1968 Chahine commenced filming the much-publicised *People and the Nile*. It was a huge production which he shot on location in Aswan, Moscow and Leningrad. Egyptian and Soviet technicians collaborated on it, but the result was a major disappointment. Chahine managed to displease both sponsors, for each demanded certain changes. Some of the objections seemed petty. The Egyptians objected to a Soviet engineer walking ahead of his Egyptian counterpart. The Soviets objected because they had telephone booths on the streets of Leningrad, which Chahine did not show. Adamant that the film was less than they had expected, both sponsors, for disparate reasons, insisted on major alterations. Chahine re-shot many scenes with a new cast, disgusted with what he considered a 'made-to-order' film.[11] The version he himself preferred was stored at the *Cinématheque française*, which, according to him, 'contains some of the best footage in my career'.[12] The experience taught him never to get involved in a project sponsored by governments. His private version of the film was not exhibited until 1999 — and in France before Egypt. As late as 1999, the film was still not acknowledged in the records of the Egyptian Chamber of Cinema.[13]

But Chahine forged ahead, not waiting for the controversy to subside or for *People and the Nile* to be released. For his twenty-second film, which he made in 1969, he turned to a subject he cherished, the exploitation of the Egyptian *fellah*. *The Earth* was based on a modern Egyptian classic, written in 1953 by his Marxist friend, Abdel-Rahman al-Sharqawi. It was a big project which had taken Chahine ten years to realise. This time the public's verdict was quick and heartwarming: *The Earth* was hailed an instant triumph and the word masterpiece has been attached to it ever since. It was screened in competition at the Cannes Film Festival, and its distribution throughout France was the first international recognition of Chahine as an artist. The last shot in the film remains one of the most memorable in Egyptian cinema, for it shows the protagonist clawing at the land as he is being dragged away.

As he had vilified the bourgeoisie and the betrayers of socialism in *Dawn of a New Day*, in 1970 Chahine vilified the Egyptian intellectuals, including himself, for not having done their share in building the new society the 1952 Revolution had promised. This indictment was the subject of *The Choice* (1970), of which he says: '*The Earth* was about a man who said "NO", and *The Choice* is about a man who said "YES". By compromising and betraying himself, he lived a schizophrenic life'.[14] *The Choice* was screened at the Carthage Film Festival, which honoured Chahine with a lifetime achievement award. It was in the course of the festival that he was approached by Algerian film-makers to co-produce films with them. The co-operation that ensued between Misr International Films and the Algerian film industry is significant for it allowed Chahine to make three of his important films: *The Sparrow*, *Return of the Prodigal Son* (1976), and *Alexandria ... Why?*, in collaboration with Algerian television.

Chahine's first twenty years as a director reveal that he was a man of great energy working in great haste. The energy is commendable, the haste less so. High-powered productivity does not allow time for meditation and reflection. This trend continued: some of his films could have been more cogent or sharp, and some of his pitfalls could have been avoided, had he been less obsessed with being in constant motion.

Chahine's middle period spanned 1970-81. In 1970, Nasser suddenly died of a heart attack and was mourned by millions. No sooner had Anwar Sadat succeeded him and settled in office than he embarked on abolishing most of his predecessor's policies. In the main, Sadat's 'corrective revolution' replaced socialism with capitalism, wrested Egypt out of the Soviet bloc and aligned it with the United States. After crossing the Suez Canal and achieving a partial military victory over Israel in the October War of 1973, Sadat felt emboldened enough to launch his policy of *al-infitah*, 'an opening to increased economic relations with the west and especially to western investment'.[15] Sadat's economic liberalisation led to 'the growth of a new-rich class of entrepreneurial middlemen and demi-monde of wealth allied with graft that impedes efficiency and alienates ordinary people'.[16] A class of millionaires soon arose and the gap between the rich and poor again widened. In one of his darkest films, *Return of the Prodigal Son*, Chahine was to address the economic imbalance that resulted from such policies.

While Sadat was instituting those 'corrective' measures, the cinema's fortunes continued to languish. Unable to get financing from the public sector (before the cinema was denationalised in 1972), Chahine established Misr International Films. Reflecting on those days, Marianne Khoury says: 'When he first started his company he had one of the richest men in the Arab world as a partner, and then another. Both times the relationship failed. Chahine cannot work with partners.'[17] During that period, Chahine began to respond to the sea change that was reshaping Egyptian society. He refused to compromise his art by pandering to public taste, and his suspicion of officialdom persisted.

In fulfilment of his agreement with Algeria, Chahine, in 1973, directed his twenty-fourth film, *The Sparrow*, which is a brutal dissection of the Six Day War catastrophe. Upon watching it, the Minister of Culture was furious. Believing that the villain on the screen was modelled after his own brother, he wanted to burn the negative.[18] Luckily, the negative had been stored in a Paris vault. Arab intellectuals meeting in Beirut reacted more positively. They issued a strong statement defending the film and exhorting Arab governments to release it. An example of the way some of Chahine's films evolve out of each other can be found in the case of *The Sparrow*. During its filming Chahine had a heart attack, and was rushed to hospital for open heart surgery. The imminence of death became the genesis of the second part of his autobiographical trilogy – *An Egyptian Story*.

In 1973, Sadat abruptly launched a massive military campaign to liberate Sinai from Israeli occupation. With one act of courage, Sadat restored pride to a nation yearning for a modicum of victory. Even Israel's quick recovery on the battlefield – mainly due to Washington's limitless support – did not diminish the Arabs' feeling of satisfaction. Chahine produced a ten-minute film for the Egyptian Army, *Forward We Go* (1973), celebrating what became known as the October War. Shortly thereafter, the ban on *The Sparrow* was lifted. His abiding concern with the economic deterioration and the spread of corruption all around him, inspired Chahine to direct *Return of the Prodigal Son*, a film which he termed a 'musical tragedy'. It was his twenty-fifth film. Acting as a self-styled barometer of the Arab world, not just Egypt, he foresaw the inevitability of an internecine tragedy, thus predicting the civil war in Lebanon. The film was produced by Chahine's newly formed company and the Algerian cinema. It was the second such collaboration between the two countries. During the same year (1975), Chahine invited Salah Abu Seif to direct a film for his company. The result was *Death of the Water-bearer*, considered by many to be one of Abu Seif's finest films.

Empowered by his success during the October War, and perhaps succumbing to American pressure, or both, Anwar Sadat once again jolted the region when, in 1978 he committed the unforgivable in the eyes of fellow Arabs by unilaterally signing a peace treaty with Israel. The Camp David Accords shattered the fragile solidarity among the Arabs, leaving each state from then on to fend for herself. Demonstrations erupted throughout the

Arab world, with many groups and individuals publicly vowing to kill 'the traitor'. Egypt was now isolated, and the Arab League's headquarters were moved from Cairo to Tunis.

Chahine was caught in the crossfire. When he released his latest film, *Alexandria ... Why?* in 1978, the controversy over the Camp David Accords was raging. Arab intellectuals, who were eager for a film which would give vent to their frustration and would fuel their anger at Sadat's defection, were stunned. What they saw, instead, was a film depicting the Egypt of the 1940s, and speaking of forgiveness at a time when the Arabs felt surround-ed by enemies. Some went so far as to accuse Chahine of complicity with Sadat in promoting normalisation of relations with the Jewish state. *Alexandria ... Why?* constituted the first part of his autobiographical trilogy. It won the Silver Bear at the Berlin Film Festival, and its star won an acting award. Furthermore, the German television channel ZDF supported Chahine's company with a grant of approximately 400,000 Egyptian pounds.[19]

During this second period, Chahine was at the pinnacle of his creative power. It is likely that the slower pace of his productions contributed posi-tively to their artistic impact. Instead of making a film a year, here he only made six films in eleven years. Four out of these six are among his most challenging and demanding. It was at this time, too, that his films began to generate controversy. The rumbling that surfaced after *People and the Nile* took root with the release of *Alexandria ... Why?* ten years later. From then on, bitter controversy accompanied each of his films.

Chahine's latter period (1981-2001), was imbued with conflict and con-troversy. The overwhelming characteristic of this period, which began with the assassination of Anwar Sadat, is Chahine's clash with the rise of extremism. Chahine viewed the Muslim fundamentalists as intolerant, and they viewed him as subversive. The controversy that surrounded his films in the 1990s seemed to be in direct proportion to the acclaim the outside world bestowed upon him, which in turn made him more suspect.

The issues that preoccupied Chahine in this period were personal and national identity. By completing his autobiographical trilogy, he sought to come to terms with himself, and to aspire for Egypt to rise as a nation with boundaries that are broad and inclusive, not narrow and exclusive. And by mediating between the past and the present, as in *The Emigrant* and *Destiny*, he hoped that Egypt would avoid repeating past mistakes. The freedom of the individual and that of Egypt herself were at stake, and Chahine sounded the alarm.

Nearly a decade after his open heart surgery, Chahine wanted to take stock of his life. The result was his twenty-seventh film, *An Egyptian Story*, in which he played himself as a successful film director tormented by memories. It was based on an article by a famous writer and novelist, Yusuf Idris, who himself had had open heart surgery in London. Chahine's filmic adaptation – which he calls 'cinematic vision' – became the second film in which he appeared as an actor.

In 1985 Chahine's financial situation seemed to stabilise. In that year he met the French producer Humbert Balsan who provided him with new opportunities. The co-production of *Adieu Bonaparte* with France became possible because the president of the main French television channel (at the time a public service broadcaster, TFI), Hervé Bourges, was interested in the Middle East and the Arab world.[20] Since then, a co-production arrangement has been maintained between Chahine and France. Film production money is packaged from different sources: from his own company, Misr International Films; from French cultural organisations, television stations in France and other European countries; and in the form of advances from theatre chains and video distributors. The relationship has been both satisfactory and problematical for Chahine. It has sustained his ability to make films, but created some political difficulties for him among detractors who view his professional dealings with France as a sort of 'collaboration' at Egypt's expense. The accusation does not come only from Muslim fundamentalists, for Chahine's friend and fellow film director, Tawfiq -Saleh, echoed comparable sentiments.[21]

The controversy which engulfed *Adieu Bonaparte* raged to the extent that when the film was about to be shown at the Cannes Film Festival, the Egyptian government sent a committee to Cannes to watch and listen. Eventually *Adieu* was allowed to be screened, but the controversy has yet to subside. Continuing his relationship with France, Chahine made *The Sixth*

Day, a novel by Andrée Chedid, an Egyptian writer living and writing in France. It dealt with the cholera epidemic that had swept Egypt years earlier. It starred Daleeda, an Egyptian of Italian descent who had migrated to France and become a famous singer, in her first and only role as an actress. Chahine himself turned the poetic novel into a blend of drama and complex musical numbers, and paid homage to Gene Kelly by dedicating the film to him. Chahine appeared in a minor role, playing a Palestinian villager living in Egypt who returns home to do his share of the fighting to regain his occupied homeland.

During the same year, and for the first time in the history of Egyptian cinema, the Actors' Union held a general strike. For several weeks, actors – and sympathetic directors – barricaded themselves inside the Actors' Union building, in protest against the government's arbitrary revamping of the laws governing their industry. Chahine took a leading role in the whole affair. Three years later, he utilised the episode in *Alexandria Again and Forever* (1989), which concluded his autobiographical trilogy.

Paradoxically, during the 1990s Chahine was both the recipient of a high honour and the target of fierce condemnation. Immediately following the Gulf War in 1991, upon seeing young people demonstrating in the streets, he focused his camera on them and made a twenty-two minute documentary, which was to cause him problems. Instead of producing a sort of public relations film, which the average Egyptian had expected, he delivered *Cairo … as Told by Chahine* (1992), a powerful indictment of the authorities and society at large for having neglected the younger generation. From then on, Chahine's detractors kept a watchful eye on him. But his film activity was interrupted when, in 1992, he was invited by the *Comedie française* to direct a stage play of his choosing. He directed *Caligula*, by Albert Camus. The choice is significant, for exposing tyranny is one of Chahine's favourite themes. The play opened on 15 February, 1992, with a French cast. In 1993, the civilised world was stunned at the stabbing of Naguib Mahfouz, the feeble eighty-four-year-old Nobel Laureate, at the hands of Muslim fundamentalists. His 'punishment' was for having written a book decades earlier which the Islamists still resented.

It was in 1994, and in this climate of cultural conflict, that Chahine released *The Emigrant*, which caused an immediate and protracted squabble. This time the fundamentalists accused him of committing sacrilege by portraying the prophet Joseph on the screen. Chahine's protestations went unheeded. Relying on the fact that the Qur'an proscribes representations of prophets, the fundamentalists sued him in a court of law. The film, which was drawing crowds at the cinemas, was suddenly banned. Soon things got more precarious for Chahine. Having uncovered a plot to harm him physically, the Ministry of Interior assigned him round-the-clock protection, which he at first accepted and then declined after three days.[22] Chahine went so far as to visit al-Azhar and to submit his case to the clerics. After explaining his position, he declared that he would rather be killed than allow security police to trail him day and night.[23] The trial was held in the glare of the press and television cameras. A few weeks later Chahine was acquitted, but he has yet to silence his critics. Throughout this ordeal, the Board of Censors was a witness on his behalf.

* * *

Honours and rejections came to Chahine concomitantly. The first two accolades of the 1990s that came his way were the Locarno Film Festival's thirteen-day retrospective of all his films (1996), and *Cahiers du cinéma*'s special October issue on his career. Then in May 1997, the Cannes Film Festival screened his latest film, *Destiny*, in competition. The film was shot in Syria, Lebanon and France. Its general release in the Arab world again exposed Chahine to the wrath of the fundamentalists. The film depicted the twelfth-century philosopher Ibn Rushd (Averroës), who, Chahine's critics claimed, was not treated with suitable dignity. The Islamists also took issue with Chahine because he, they claimed, depicted many of them as fanatics. But Chahine had as many admirers as detractors. Though he did not win the Palme d'Or he had hoped for, he did receive the Cannes Film Festival's 50th Anniversary Prize for Lifetime Achievement. A year later (1998), the Lincoln Film Center in New York held a retrospective of fifteen of his films. The programme was so successful that it toured many American cities and also went to Vancouver, Canada. While in New York attending the retrospective, Chahine filmed a cameo with Edward Said to include in his next film, *The Other*, which was screened at the film festivals in Cannes, New York and London.

Also in 1999, Chahine's favourite version of *People and the Nile* was released in France under a new title: *The Nile and Life*. This was the Egyptian-Soviet production about the building of the Aswan Dam (1968), which displeased both the Egyptian and Soviet authorities. France's continual interest in Chahine's cinema is evident in the fact that during summer of 1999 two of his films (*The Other* and *The Nile and Life*) were simultaneously shown throughout the country.

During the 1980s and 1990s, Egyptian cinema was in steady decline. Production fell from over fifty films a year to around fifteen, and the number of cinema salons shrank from 200 to 120.[24] It is true that local and national cinemas everywhere have declined, unless financed by television (which is what is missing in Egypt), but the decline in Egyptian cinema cannot simply be attributed to a worldwide trend. There seems to be a tacit apprehension of the inherent power of the film medium itself to sway the masses. Enough concrete examples exist to prove that the decline is deliberate and not generic. The taxes levied on Egyptian producers and exhibitors are exorbitant; the restrictions posed at every turn, frustrating. The government does not seem to value the cinema as an industry. Nor does it seem interested in exporting and promoting the Egyptian film, even when the fruits of such endeavours are obvious. Government-controlled television itself is a culprit, not only in keeping audiences at home, but also in denying production companies adequate residuals for screening their films. Recent attempts to rectify the situation do not impress Chahine. New legislation stipulates that no film production company can be formed without a capitalisation of a minimum of 200 million Egyptian pounds (approximately U.S. $40 million). Film-makers worry that such an exalted level of financing will destroy independent companies and stifle creativity. Nor is Chahine excited about the proliferation of the new multiplex cinemas, for he and other like-minded artists view them as showcases for the Hollywood blockbuster – not the Egyptian film.

Chahine voiced reservations about these matters in October 1999, when the Goethe Institute in Cairo honoured him by showing eleven of his films. On that occasion he reminisced about having won the Silver Bear for *Alexandria ... Why?* at the Berlin Film Festival in 1979, and about the financial support that the German television channel, ZDF, had given his company. Then he accused successive Egyptian governments of choking the film industry. As to the 200 million pounds required for starting a new company, he exclaimed sarcastically: 'I don't even know how many zeroes there are in a million. I even get confused when I count ten pounds.'[25]

Chahine's two latest films recapitulate themes and motifs of his earlier films. Half a century of celebrity and a canon of films to his credit do not seem to have diluted his concern for the common people. In *Al-Akhar* (*The Other*, 1999), he exposes globalisation as a charade played out by the industrial nations for their own benefit. The poor and developing countries should expect nothing from it except false hopes and broken promises. The reviews were mixed, mainly on account of over-simplification. *Skout... Hansawar* (*Silence...We Are Shooting*, 2001), depicts a female singer who allows love affairs to distract her from her duty to herself and her audiences. To Chahine, Art is a sacred mission, and the Artist's commitment should be tantamount to taking a 'vow'.

Even in this light piece of entertainment, Chahine reiterates his concern for the Egyptian *fellah*, his pride of being an Egyptian, his love for the musical genre, and his derision of inane comedies. Since it is a film within a film, the title may be construed as the usual command on the set just before filming. But nothing in a Chahine film is that obvious or simple. The title is a barb aimed at his critics and detractors. 'Stop bothering me,' he is admonishing them, 'and let me do my work.'

Three
Social Dramas and Melodramas

It is often suggested that Chahine's political awakening was gradual, and did not manifest itself until 1958 when he made *Jamila*, presumably because it was the first overtly political film he had made up to that point in his short career. This is surprising, though, bearing in mind the political fervour in Egypt during the 1950s, with the Revolution of 1952 and the arrival of the charismatic Nasser who was destined to reshape history. No Arab could have remained passive to the sea change the whole region was undergoing. No intellectual like Chahine would have remained immune to any of this. The quibbling may be over semantics as to the definition of political 'awakening' or 'consciousness'. What is indisputable is that Chahine's concern for social justice was embedded in him from the beginning of his film-making career. Despite the Revolution's considerable achievements, millions of Egyptians were still neglected as they had been for centuries. It was natural then for a committed artist to address their problems, be he 'politicised' or not.

Filming in earnest

One can trace his social concern in his first two films, which, in fact, preceded the Revolution. In his first film, *Daddy Amin*, Chahine departed completely from the Egyptian norm of the day. Instead of relying on one of the three formulaic topics popular then (the girl who is blind or has a heart condition, the girl who can sing, or the girl who can dance)[1], Chahine chose to make a film about a father who has ambitions to get rich. But to do so he needs to invest all his savings in a business venture that was more likely to fail than not. When he unfolds his plans to his wife and children, they refuse to risk everything in such an uncertain scheme. Being a good father (Amin means trustworthy, faithful), he ponders their response. Then, in the tradition of Capra's *It's a Wonderful Life* (1946), he fantasises about what his family's life would be like should he lose all that money. Their future looks so grim that when he wakes up he rejoices that it was only a bad dream and abandons his plans. It bears a resemblance to Capra's film, with an affectionate allusion to Chahine's own father who was so inept as a businessman that he jeopardised his family's security. The film demonstrates Chahine's new brand of serious cinema where the welfare of families and ordinary people is centre stage. His second film, *Nile Boy* pits the innocent village against the corrupt city. A young man who is dissatisfied with rural life and is fascinated by the train that cuts through the countryside, hops on it one day and heads for the glittering metropolis where he is ensnared in the 'exciting' life of women, gambling and drugs. After rotting in prison for several years, he returns to his senses and to his village and to save a child drowning in the big river. Though melodramatic and predictable, it points to the kind of social themes in which Chahine was interested (the subject of the *fellah* in particular).

Concern for the Egyptian *fellah*: Chahine's early feature (*The Blazing Sun*, 1954)

In 1954, and perhaps in harmony with the aims of the Revolution, Chahine again turned his camera on the Egyptian *fellah*, whose primitive life had hardly improved since he had toiled building the pyramids. To the average Egyptian viewer, *Sira' fi-l-Wadi* (*The Blazing Sun*) is important because it introduced Omar Sharif to the screen. Its true significance, however, lies in the evolution of Chahine as an artist. Here, too, he depicts the exploitation of the *fellahin* by the rich and powerful. Ahmad is the son of the overseer of the pasha's country estate. Returning home after graduating as an agricultural engineer, he is (unconvincingly) bubbling with hopes and plans to increase the sugarcane output and to bring prosperity to his village. His dedication to his task pays off when the purchasing company determines that his village's crop that year is the best and that it will buy it at a higher price than that of the pasha's. This triggers a conflict between the village and the pasha, who is enraged by the sugar company's decision. The

Would pre-Revolution Egypt have allowed a Pasha's daughter to marry a *fellah*'s son? (*The Blazing Sun*, 1954)

pasha has a wicked nephew and the two conspire to flood the villagers'
fields and spoil their crop. They do so, but the villagers sense the conspiracy and threaten retaliation. The conflict escalates and the pasha's nephew
arranges to have the blind old man who had confronted the pasha killed,
and to falsely accuse the overseer of murder. The overseer is jailed,
tried and convicted. The hanging itself is the first in the history of Egyptian
cinema, and the fact that the victim was innocent makes it doubly emotional.
Ahmad vows revenge, even though he is in love with the pasha's only daughter.

* * *

Bab al-Hadid (*Cairo Station*, 1958)

With his eleventh film, Chahine was able to chart new territory for himself
and for Egyptian cinema. At the age of thirty-two he was already established
as a director of formidable talent and skill. His reputation was further
enhanced with a film that many still consider his masterpiece. It is one of
those rare instances in film history when forces converge to produce a work
of art that is of lasting value.

As a cripple, Chahine gives an astonishingly gripping performance

The main action revolves around a cripple named Kinawi, who is a newspaper vendor working at Cairo's railway station. Everything about him – his limp, stutter, scrawny physique, tattered clothes, demeanour – depict him as a wretch. But he is witty, and a sharp observer of the world around him. Despite his handicap he can even dance, practising his steps along the pavement. Above all, he has an eye for beautiful women, particularly their legs. Deprived of female companionship, he plasters the walls of his hovel with posters of semi-nude models. Beneath the rough surface, there is an imagination and a talent, for we see him retouching the photographs with his own sense of humour. In real life, he is drawn to Hannouma, a voluptuous young woman selling lemonade at the same station. But Hannouma is almost engaged to Abu Srei' (meaning Speedy), a tall, strong porter who is trying to organise a labour union. This does not deter Kinawi from proposing marriage to Hannouma. In a moving scene played against the statue of Ramses II, who dwarfs them with his gigantic size, he tries to woo her with a necklace. She humours him and listens to his expressions of desire to live with her on a farm, but she rejects him out of hand and laughs at his daydreaming. He continues to spy on her and her fiancé, and takes out his frustration on the posters, cutting them up with scissors. When he hears Hannouma and her fiancé giggling during a tryst in the warehouse, he becomes convinced that their wedding is imminent and decides to kill her. That morning the newspaper kiosk owner reads him a news item about a man who butchered his woman with a knife and stuffed her in a trunk, giving Kinawi an idea. Instead of killing Hannouma, however, he mistakenly kills her friend. When the mistake is discovered, he chases Hannouma with a knife in his hand. The police are alerted and they discover him on the railway track on the verge of stabbing her to death. The kiosk owner recognises his madness and the police let him cajole Kinawi into thinking that all is well and that that day is going to be his wedding day. Kinawi softens, they apprehend him and confine him in a straitjacket.

The theme of social awakening permeates the film. Most prominent among the subplots is that of Abu Srie' trying to organise a labour union. The workers at the station are controlled by a primitive 'mafioso', who exercises favouritism with their schedule and pay. He threatens Abu Srei' and his followers with dire consequences. Undaunted, Abu Srei' explains that without a union to look after the needs of all those workers, a man, such as the one who was almost crushed by the train that morning, would have no way of earning a living. He makes an appeal to all those attending and he eventually has sway over many of them. A government official appears and ratifies the formation of the union. Then there is the feminist leader who is campaigning to raise consciousness among Egyptian women. We see her delivering a speech from the window of a stationary train and we hear her a couple of more times calling women to a general awakening.

The most touching subplot concerns a teenage girl who is at the station to say goodbye to her boyfriend who is travelling to Europe with his family. The big divide between their social backgrounds, in addition to the mores of the time, prevents them from openly spending the last hour together. They rely on signals, and steal their way for a few minutes of privacy. Kinawi is watching this love play, and the viewer does not know with whom to sympathise more: the frustrated young girl who cannot say goodbye to the one she loves, or with deformed Kinawi who has no one to love him at all. The last shot of the film is of the young girl standing on the railway track after her boyfriend had departed with his family to Europe, and after Kinawi had been hauled away to a lunatic asylum. Kinawi's fate had been sealed; hers is uncertain.

The railway station provides a setting for Chahine to examine a diversity of issues. The police, who should have better things to do, are forever chasing the group of women who, like Hannouma, slave in the heat to sell a bottle of Pepsi to a thirsty customer. It would seem more decent to leave these young women alone to eke out a living than to chase them around like criminals. And how quickly characters in the film slap one another; on five or six occasions an argument is settled with a slap in the face. Even Abu Srei' who is normally polite and considerate, and who is an advocate for social justice, is not above slapping Hannouma when he hears of her dancing on the train to entertain her customers. As a group of young men rock and roll down the pavement, a couple of Muslim clerics invoke God's name to protect them from the devil.

Film style

Hind Rustum, the star of the film, considers Chahine 'a mad man when he's filming', and most demanding of his actors. She still shivers recalling her experience with him in *Cairo Station*. But then she adds, 'Listen, I love Youssef Chahine. Every time I worked with him I felt that I had really given of myself.'

The structure of the film is classic in that it observes the three unities of time, place and action. It never wavers from its main theme, which is embedded in the tragic fate of its protagonist. Heavily relying on visuals rather than dialogue, and revealing as much as concealing, Chahine paints a bleak picture of the underprivileged in Egyptian society. What lifts the film above provinciality is the fact that it isolates a situation and then extrapolates it so that it can yield meaning to viewers anywhere and any-time. As a character in Chahine's trilogy comments on this film, 'Everyone of us, in one way or another, is a cripple. We all need sympathy.'

Much has been written about the influence of Italian neorealism on *Cairo Station*. Roy Armes maintains that 'Chahine admits a debt to the Italians', though only obliquely. No one was unaware of that special kind of cinema that emerged in Italy after World War II, when Rome was reduced to rubble and the rate of unemployment was over 60 per cent. The depiction of ordinary people living uneventful, even sordid, lives became a suitable mode of film-making. True, *Cairo Station* is about ordinary people. But whereas neorealism emphasised the de-dramatisation of events,[2] *Cairo Station* heightened the tension. It almost became a melodrama, were it not for the honesty with which the characters are created. And whereas the situation in a neo-realistic film can happen to anyone,[3] Kinawi's situation is an extreme. Like De Sica's bicycle thief, many people find themselves unemployed and some might be tempted to commit petty crime. And like De Sica's *Umberto D* some might find themselves destitute in retirement, and end up selling their books or going to charity halls for a meal. Fortunately, most people neither crack up nor are hauled away to lunatic asylums as Kinawi is. The universal identification with him is only metaphorical, for most people do not fall off the precipice as he does. In De Sica's two films, the unemployed worker whose bicycle gets stolen is final-

Chahine and Hind Rustum: one of the most famous scenes in Egyptian cinema (*Cairo Station*, 1958)

ly reunited with his young boy whom he had alienated; similarly, the civil servant with no place to stay is reunited with his only friend – his dog. Kinawi's fate is bleaker and more tragic.

Appearing for the first time as a film actor, Chahine played the central role. But he does not seem to be acting; rather, he latches onto the character until they become one. The fusion is so convincing that, according to Egyptian film lore, the jury at the Berlin Film Festival denied him the best actor award, assuming he was a cripple playing himself. True or not, Chahine himself treated this rumour as a fact in the second part of his autobiographical trilogy, *An Egyptian Story*. Equally memorable in *Cairo Station* is Hind Rustum as Hannouma. She exploded onto the screen with such charm and vivacity that no one can blame Kinawi for wanting to win her affection. Farid Shawqi, the union organiser and Kinawi's rival in his love with Hannouma, delivers another sterling performance. Ensemble acting is one of the hallmarks of Chahine's cinema. A practitioner of

Stanislavsky's Method, Chahine chooses his actors with an uncanny eye and instills in them the sense of belonging to one family. The coming together of all this talent to bring alive a poignant script is the dream of every director. Such was the rarity of *Cairo Station*.

The start of controversies

Egyptian cinema depends mostly on dialogue. Actors and audiences alike derive much pleasure in verbal exchanges. But from the outset Chahine was a visual artist, and in *Cairo Station* he tells a story and reveals emotions mostly with images. This must have baffled his actors; it certainly displeased his audiences. The style, as much as the bleakness of the content, confounded the public, but not the professional critics. The violent reaction devastated him and drove him to blame himself. He had no right to talk above the audience's head or to risk other people's money. In time, though, especially after the film had been well received abroad, the audience's reaction shifted. It swung around and people learned to appreciate the film's value. This reversal of attitude taught Chahine a crucial lesson: trust your own creative instincts, for in time what now seems obscure will become apparent.

Besides being a landmark, *Cairo Station* charts the course Chahine's cinema would take. Sympathy for ordinary people and understanding of the plight of the individual are leitmotifs that can be traced back to this film. That Chahine was able to define and encapsulate his agenda at such an early age is remarkable. That he adhered to it for half a century attests to the clarity of his vision and the resoluteness of his purpose.

Though for entirely different aesthetic and social reasons, some foreign critics share with the Egyptian masses some reservations about *Cairo Station*. After calling Chahine's performance marvellous, one of them adds:

> This film from Egypt's most distinguished director is bursting with ideas and themes – worker exploitation, the corrupting influence of the Coca-Cola culture, the dangers of sexual repression. And that's the trouble. A Neo-Realist approach encloses what is essentially a melodrama, leaving no room to explore these themes and presenting characters drawn in broad simplistic strokes.[4]

One must agree with the praise, but take issue with its being 'essentially a melodrama'. Many national cinemas were using the genre of melodrama to deal with social issues, and *Cairo Station* is Egypt's superb contribution to that tradition. Chahine succeeds in providing a microcosm of his times, and in giving us a picture of Egypt with its longings and some of its warts. Yet one of Chahine's admirers finds *Cairo Station* lacking in depth: 'The crucial limitation of both the De Sica-Zavattini team and Chahine at this period is the inability to go beyond mere description of individuals and offer an analysis of society as a whole.'[5] A film artist is neither a social worker, nor a psychiatrist, nor a politician. It is not his job to put the world in order. It is enough for him to state the case and provoke a general debate.

Though *Cairo Station* is noted for its grim reality, Erika Richter situates the film within the context of the nationalisation of the Suez Canal, and 'senses a strengthening of self-confidence. The people we encounter dur-

Kinawi's fate is far bleaker than that of De Sica's characters (*Cairo Station*, 1958)

ing the course of a day ... porters, beverage vendors are full of demand for
better life.' [6] Despite such optimism, *Cairo Station* remains a protest against
stifling conditions. That the Revolution gave hope is granted, but that
seems hardly enough to save Egypt's misfits.

* * *

*Fajr Yawm Jadid (Dawn of a New Day,*1964)

Genesis of the film
By 1964, the Revolution's Free Officers had already been twelve years in
power, and had transformed Egyptian life altogether. The cornerstones of
the new era were a new constitution, political reorganisation, agrarian
reforms, nationalisation of industries and the introduction of socialism.
Some of these concepts were either embraced or rejected at the outset; others were first embraced and then rejected. The nation-building turned out
to be a slow process, full of agony and pitfalls. The burning question was
whether or not the ordinary Egyptian would benefit from all this upheaval.
An early admirer of Nasser's and an enthusiast about the revolution,
Chahine, like many intellectuals of his generation, soon became disillusioned. What had mattered to him most was socialism. It was, in his eyes,
Egypt's new dawn.

Plot and characters
The film centres on Na'ila, a middle-aged woman, married to Hamouda, a
drunkard who rejects the new social order. Both are from bourgeois families: her father had been a rich man who lost his fortune in the stock market;
his father was a war profiteer who had made his in scrap metals. The couple's
reduced status does not seem to be a direct result of nationalisation, but perhaps of bad business judgment or unfavourable circumstances. The script is
not clear on this. The couple have an unhappy marriage for other reasons as
well: she wants children and he does not. Once he even forced her to have an
abortion. The situation is exacerbated by his heavy drinking and constant
flirtations with other women. Thus, at the outset, Na'ila emerges as a sympa-

thetic woman trapped in unholy matrimony. To escape loneliness and depression, she joins a ladies' charity group that looks after orphans. At one of the balls, she works behind the counter selling drinks and sandwiches. There she meets Tariq, a handsome university student who eventually becomes her lover. As her relationship with her dissolute husband worsens, she entertains the idea of leaving with Tariq for Europe where he plans to pursue higher education. At the railway station, she has second thoughts. Realising the age difference between them, she changes her mind. 'I'm the past, you're the future,' she says as the train pulls away.

Soon after she meets Tariq, Na'ila gives him a lift to town. Frightened by the way she drives, he asks her why is she speeding. 'Because I want to settle the score,' she answers. A few mornings later she has a confrontation with Hamouda. She reminds him of who she is, boasting that she is the daughter of Ratib Pasha. Hamouda sneers at her and her family. If it were not for him and his father's money they would all be starving. 'The rich only loan to the rich,' he lectures her, 'and when your father lost his money no one would give him a millieme. You have all been living on our money.' Deriding his fondness for dancing, she says it was a mistake to have married the son of a war profiteer, one who holds a degree in ChaChaCha. After an altercation over the cook, Ossta Hassan, who wants his back wages to buy medicine for his dying son, Hamouda heaps insults on the stupid poor who have no sense but to breed like rabbits. He runs out of the house screaming and she leaves the house to roam the streets aimlessly.

When he returns from a month-long trip, she finds him ensconced in a big armchair waiting for her. 'It's two o'clock in the morning,' he says. 'Where have you been?' She tells him that she did not expect him to come home a day early. Still keeping his cool, he tells her that he has been hearing rumours about her. His friends have been making innuendoes which he pretended not to notice. Is she seeing someone else? She admits that she is. 'How can you jeopardise my name?' he explodes. 'What will people say?' He will not permit her to see her lover any more, but she defies him saying that she will. 'All you care about is money and your name,' she tells him. He coaxes her into revealing that Tariq lives in an attic, then sneers at his poverty. Learning that he is only twenty-two years old, he blurts, 'You've always wanted to be a mother. Now you are.'

Hamouda is libertine, self-indulgent and despicable. There is nothing redeeming about him. He holds no job, and perhaps he never did. Addicted to dancing, drinking, partying, and to wearing tuxedos when he is destitute, he is unlikely to work from nine to five or to sit behind a desk. His treatment of the poor cook and his icy reaction to his son's death are inhuman. His philandering in public and his hypocrisy at learning of his wife's affair are typical of his decadent class. The new social order cannot penetrate his foggy mind.

On the opposite side of the spectrum is Husayn, Na'ila's brother. A serious journalist, he is never impressed by the rich ladies, even when they throw a charity ball to help the orphans. An idealist, he prefers to resign than to have his articles rejected by the conservative editor. It is most significant that the last article he writes, which the editor summarily dismisses, is about *al-mithaq*, the National Charter, which was passed in 1961, and which laid down the socialist laws for the new Egypt. Though a secondary character, Husayn, is Chahine's alter ego. Husayn is wistful about the good old days when he was taking care of his young sister, Na'ila, when she was sick. Recalling their youth, he reminds her of the days when she used to give her food away to the poor. Both had shared a happy childhood, and both grew up to be upright citizens. Aware of Hamouda's bad influence on her, Husayn tries to awaken her innate gentleness. To revive her interest in the poor, he tells her, 'My greatest wish is for you to discover the goodness under their shabby clothes.' Though young and immature, Tariq provides her with solace. Through his eyes and in his company she revisits Cairo, the city she had almost forgotten. Above all, Tariq helps her rediscover herself. He swears eternal love to her while in bed, yet he is not above having a girlfriend of his own age on the side. He means well by Na'ila, enjoys her company, wants to do right by her and helps her survive a difficult period in her life. She, too, will always have a soft spot for him.

Another man who affects Na'ila profoundly, and who is central to the theme, is the cook, Ossta Hassan. Once, during a raucous party at her house, she participates in the drinking and dancing, until Ossta Hassan gets a telephone call. After he answers it and returns to the living room, the noise and music suddenly stop. Then he informs her that his only son has died. She is stunned but Hamouda is unmoved. A few days later she refuses to join Hamouda on a month-long trip to Alexandria. Still feeling guilty toward Ossta Hassan, she visits him at his house to apologise to him for what had happened. She comes out a changed woman. When she meets Tariq in his room she is overcome with Ossta Hassan's goodness. He was not angry with her, she says, only appreciative of her visit. She floats around the room, unbelieving that such a kind human has worked for them all those years without her realising his dignity and moral worth. 'Not once did he complain, not once was he impertinent,' she tells Tariq, adding, 'He taught me everything about love.' In a flourish, she shouts 'Curtains' and pulls a long red-and-white piece of cloth and swirls it around the room. The red colour dominates. Except for the white lower half, it seems conspicuously like waving the communist red flag.

The resignation of a frustrated wife (*Dawn of a New Day*, 1964)

As the central character, Na'ila wavers between her degenerate husband and idealist brother. At the outset she is, more or less, in Hamouda's camp. She recognises his shortcomings and knows that he is unfaithful to her. But she lacks the courage, as one of her friends tells her, to leave him. Eventually she does, but along the way she wavers in her attachment to the lifestyle of the rich and the need to relocate the missing pieces in her life. She savours reminding Hamouda of her respectable heritage, loves luxuriating in her plush bedroom and enjoys pushing the button to have breakfast served to her in bed. During her brief employment at the magazine, she expends no effort to befriend the other employees. Instead, she hides away from them in her brother's office. Her quitting the job is ostensibly motivated by her dislike for being in close proximity with her female rival – Tariq's secret girlfriend – but this is not the only factor. She, the daughter of a wealthy man, feels humiliated to be working for a living. In one respect, she differs from her idealist brother, Husayn, who defends his secretary and refuses to let his own sister attack her character. He even resigns over ideology. Husayn is committed; Na'ila, up till the very end, seems irresponsible. How else can we explain her leaving the orphan child on top of the Tower of Cairo, where she and Tariq had taken him, so she can journey abroad? At forty, she still needs to mature; but she does, when she realises the futility of running away with a student half her age.

Assessment

On the surface, the title promises more than the film delivers. If *Dawn of a New Day* is meant to celebrate the Revolution and its achievements, it is a decade too late. Had it been made in 1955, three years after the end of monarchy and a year after the British evacuation, it would have reflected the euphoria that was sweeping the Arab world. Had it been made in 1957, one year after the nationalisation of the Suez Canal and the repelling of the tripartite aggression, the title would have been more appropriate. But by 1965, the lustre of the Revolution had already been tarnished: the union between Egypt and Syria collapsed; Egypt's involvement in the war in Yemen cost Egypt thousands of lives and the internecine fighting dismayed the Arab people; the confiscation of lands and the nationalisation of industries forced many aggrieved Egyptians to leave the country. Above all, Egypt had become a police state. In his book, *In Search of Identity*, Anwar Sadat writes, '... as the Revolution of July 23 was gigantic in its accomplishments during the Fifties, it was gigantic in its mistakes during the Sixties'.[7] Upon what horizon, then, was the new dawn shining?

With this film Chahine is both celebrating the advent of socialism and lamenting its uncertain future. To him, the suffering of the Egyptian masses could only be alleviated by humane social reform. Socialism was the salvation. Concomitantly, he is attacking all of its opponents. He says, 'I wanted with *Dawn of a New Day* to give an expression to the birth of new Egypt under socialism. I was completely aware of this. I also wanted to show the old Egypt which tried to abort that experiment and destroy all those socialist decisions.'[8] Critics were not as enthusiastic as Chahine, and were divided in their opinion of the film. One referred to it as *'Dawn of a New Day – According to a Tourist'*.[9] Another called it 'relatively important' and then dismissed it altogether as an 'ordinary' film.[10]

The misreading is not wholly unwarranted. Part of the problem is the discrepancy between Chahine's intention and execution. The issue of socialism is never contextualised, although the intelligent dialogue is written by Abdel-Rahman al-Sharqawi, the renowned socialist and author of *The Egyptian Earth*. We know that Na'ila and her husband came from the privileged class that had lost its fortune, and are now coping with little or no money. We can also see the gap between the idle rich who get drunk and dance on furniture and the poor cook who begs for and still cannot get his back wages to buy medicine for his dying son. Chahine's preoccupation with socialism led him to wrong assumptions about what the viewer knows or does not know about the couple's loss of fortune. With a few judicious changes the script could have clarified the issue and given socialism more centrality. Subtlety here is perceived as vagueness, and the film ends up being less than it could have been. Individuals at different levels of political awareness can be interesting, but first one needs to know more about what divides them.

Personal cinema

Regarding Chahine's blending of genres, David Kehr says:

> Chahine possesses the technical skill to evoke the styles he is seeking with
> accuracy and respect, and because (in the manner of Scorsese), he actively
> reimagines his sources, using their spirit and sense to solve problems, rather
> than purloining their substance.[11]

Dawn of a New Day provides an excellent example of how mixing different
genres works in one film. Reflecting on them one wonders how the content
would have been affected had they all been shot in the same style instead.
Three scenes illustrate the significance of the approach: a bedroom, a party
at home, and a walk in the city. In the bedroom scene we find Na'ila lying in
bed, the morning after her second encounter with Tariq. She picks up the
hand-mirror and scrutinises her face as though to determine whether or
not it reflects the change within her. She blows on the mirror letting her
breath cover its surface, then draws a smile. She holds the mirror up and
lets the light reflection travel across the walls of the room until it falls on a
chaise longue. On it we see her red gloves, her peignoir and the white envelope Tariq had given her the day before. It contains the money for the sand-
wich and beer she had given him at the charity ball. She languidly rises out
of bed, walks to the chair, picks up the envelope, returns to bed, lies down
and caresses her face with it. Contented, she rings the servants for breakfast. This is the scene that reminds Kehr of Douglas Sirk – a favourite of
Chahine's. But the scene also brings to mind the exquisite opening shot in
Max Ophuls' *The Earrings of Madam De*. In both cases, inanimate objects
define the character. In both cases, the message is conveyed visually rather
than verbally. A married woman is contemplating an illicit affair and we, as
incorrigible voyeurs, savour the moment with her.

The party at home, following a rendezvous with Tariq, displays the idle
rich Egyptians. Even Na'ila is intoxicated and dances around as if in a
trance. The music is loud, the songs are in English, the dancing is Latin
American. In the heart of Cairo, the centre of Arab culture, there is nothing
Arabic, nothing Egyptian – except, perhaps, the opium or hashish. These
people are as alien to their country as the staffs in the foreign embassies.

The scene ripples with depravity and politics. The rich are a breed apart. They know nothing about the suffering around them; more important, they cannot care less. Again, the scene is reminiscent of Federico Fellini's *La Dolce Vita*, when the rich spend their afternoons lazing about and Nadia Grey dances over strewn bodies. Fellini, however, never resorts to external devices to convey his meaning. The interiority of the characters and the interplay among each other are bizarre enough. His camera sits and observes the *mise-en-scène* as the human menagerie expose themselves. Chahine, on the other hand, relies on lens distortions, image rotations and colour blending to render visually the mental chaos and spiritual emptiness of his characters. In the 1960s, film technique was celebrated by the new film school graduates who, unlike the masters of old who deliberately subdued technique, relished reinventing and manipulating the medium. Dissolves, super-impositions, out-of-focus, slow and fast motions, split-screens and a number of special effects were the vogue, and Chahine could

Rife with decadence: Fellini's *La Dolce Vita* (1960)

not resist the temptation. Yet the scene has power, for it underscores the superficiality and artificiality of those in it. Hamouda and his chic friends, even Na'ila, are caught in delirious poses.

Film noir is never mentioned in regard to Chahine's fusion of genres. *Dawn of a New Day* provides a rare example. After the confrontation with Na'ila, Hamouda storms out of the house screaming and showering abuse on the poor and their 'rabbits'; she too leaves the house. She drifts into dreary, dark, inhospitable streets. It is a descent in search of her own identity. Noisy Cairo is eerily quiet. She walks all night: passing half-lit bridges, steel columns, parked trucks and a movie marquee with an undecipherable title. The wetness of the streets belies the dryness of her feelings. Shadows fill the screen, bringing to mind the cinema of Fritz Lang in his Hollywood period. She drags her feet without purpose, without direction. The unhurried camera, often from high angles, stays with her: at once minimising her and keeping her wandering under surveillance. Dawn breaks. Drained and exhausted, she finds herself disoriented, talking to strangers, and asking about Tariq. Finally she is led to his attic. She knocks and waits. He opens the door, drops his school books and she falls into his arms and bed.

The fusion of these three genres enhances the film rather than detracts from its effectiveness. Techniques are there for a reason: to be used. The only restriction is whether or not they are used properly. If they illuminate meaning then it would seem foolish not to take advantage of them. Aesthetics either work or do not work. Or as Pauline Kael says, 'Surely there are no hard and fast rules: It all depends on how it's done.'[12] More important is the realisation of the director's intentions. What does not work in *Dawn of a New Day* is having Tariq's secret girlfriend working as Na'ila's brother's secretary. It is too convenient a ploy, for Cairo at the time was a city of nearly ten million people. Here Chahine is using the convention of melodrama, and it does not ring true.

al-Ard (*The Earth*,1969)
The novel on which the film is based is about the Egyptian *fellah* and his land; the film itself is about the same subject and much more. In 1969, with all of Palestine, the Golan Heights, southern Lebanon and Sinai occu-

pied by Israel, it was inevitable for Chahine to resume his effort to trans-late into film the best Arabic novel addressing the attachment of people to the land. Abdel-Rahman al-Sharqawi's novel, *The Egyptian Earth*, is a sombre, mournful testimony to the *fellah*'s feeling of loss without his farm. Published in 1953, but depicting rural Egypt in the 1930s, it tells of the corruption of the ruling class and the exploitation of the peasant. Reading it one wonders at the depth of depravity that drives human beings to be so heartless. That such cruelty is inflicted by Egyptians against Egyptians makes it doubly tragic. Chahine improves on the novel, enlarges its scope and amplifies its implications, creating in the process one of the glories of Arab cinema.

Like John Steinbeck's *The Grapes of Wrath*, *The Egyptian Earth* itself is a sprawling narrative that needed compression. But its evocation of time and place is so powerful that one feels engulfed in the harsh reality of that

As the quintessential Egyptian *fellah*, Mahmoud el-Milligi gives a memorable performance in *The Earth*

remote Egyptian village. What gives it weight is the author's depth of compassion and the honesty in his telling. It moves our sensibilities as a cry for justice. A Marxist, Sharqawi questions and we question with him the system that treats the *fellah* as sub-human. And Chahine etches the *fellah*'s drama with the same care, the same tenderness and the same revulsion.

Basically, the novel is the story of a village standing up against the authorities. An unscrupulous Pasha wants to build a palace, and to do so he inflicts pain on the villagers nearby. First he cuts their irrigation days from ten to five, and then confiscates their land to build a road that leads to his mansion. That they will suffer and might go hungry does not deter him. That they are so poor that women fight over camel dung and a girl exchanges sex for a cucumber does not matter. The corruption has its own hierarchy: from the Pasha all the way down to the *umda* (village headman) they all prey on the decent and utterly destitute people of the village. They jail innocent people to organise a welcoming parade for the visiting dignitaries, they rig elections and punish those who boycott them, take bribes and never honour a promise. A colonial power is compassionate in comparison.

Adaptation

Chahine tightens and improves on the novel, which is told from the perspective of a twelve-year-old boy who has been away studying in Cairo for the last five years. He opens and closes the novel, and the events unfold during his summer vacation. Sharqawi encounters major problems with the narrative viewpoint; even the more compact English translation does not solve the structural flaw. Except for the parts narrated by the boy, the novel assumes an omniscient viewpoint. But when we return to the boy in the last chapter the viewpoint shifts around as though it is still told from the boy's perspective. We see incidents and hear conversations that are beyond his purview.

The adaptation reduces the number of characters, hones the plot and focuses the conflict. While the film remains the story of a village standing against authority, it offers a more sharply delineated protagonist. Abu Swaylim owns less than an acre of land from which he scrapes a living for his family. He fought in the snows of Palestine during World War I, participated

A good girl never dishonours her father (*The Earth*, 1969)

in the Revolution of 1919, and was a Chief Guard in his village until the corrupt government of Isma'il Sidqi came to power in 1930, heralding a notori-
ously oppressive decade. Sidqi had been installed as prime minister to serve
two masters: the British and their stooge, the King, both of whom worked in
tandem to crush any spirit of nationalism. When Sidqi's party was up for
election, Abu Swaylim and his fellow patriots recognised it as a sham and
boycotted it. Consequently, he was dismissed and reduced to tilling the
patch of land to make a living. But his dignity remained intact.

Despite their poverty, the villagers exude warmth and gentleness. They
fight, but they embrace and forgive quickly. They own little, but a guest is
always welcome. Tea, coffee, cigarettes and watermelons are shared.
Towards the end of the film, a captain of the Camel Corps comes to suppress
the village and ends up sitting on Abu Swaylim's threshold. They talk about
serving and when Abu Swaylim disparages the captain's mission, the captain takes offence and tells him he should not talk like this to a guest. Abu

Swaylim retorts, 'If you were a guest I'd welcome you with open arms. You came to beat us.' Shortly, even this rift is remedied. Before leaving town, the peasant captain makes peace with his 'offender'.

A telling scene occurs early in the film. The farmers are fighting over the irrigation of their pieces of land. Each is trying to be first and to divert the water to his lot. A serious fight ensues and they trade blows without mercy. Then a woman wails: her cow has fallen in the well and she, the owner, is going to be financially ruined. Suddenly they forget all about their quarrel and work together to pull the cow out of the water. The contrast between these decent people and the ruthless regime is one of the hallmarks of both novel and film. The metaphor of solidarity is in the novel, but Chahine makes it more powerful. And here we have a motif that is dear to his heart. Ever since *Saladin*, unity, cooperation and collective effort have been a touchstone in his cinema. Unity is essential in this remote Egyptian village as it is on the pan-Arab scale.

The perennial exploitation of the Egyptian *fellah* (*The Earth*, 1969)

But all villagers are not the same. Careful not to lose his job, the *umda* fulfills his superiors' orders faithfully. Not once does he try to help his people, or tell Mahmoud Bey that five days are insufficient to irrigate the land. Not once does he try to intercede on behalf of all those farmers who are about to lose their land. A self-seeker, he is not above suppressing the news about the death of a woman to use the incident to blackmail others. Then there is Shaykh Yusuf who owns the only shop in the village. He and the teacher (who makes four pounds a month) are the only ones who have any money. But when the government labourers arrive to build the road, he withholds the goods from the villagers to sell them to strangers at higher profit. Even the respected Shaykh Hassouna, the headmaster, who comes to town to help the villagers in their hour of need, eventually turns out to be a disappointment. When he tries to protect Abu Swaylim's farm, he is silenced by the Bey with a bribe: be quiet and your and your nephew's land will be spared. He betrays the village, betrays his old friend Abu Swaylim, and slips out of town like the traitor he is.

Shaykh Hassouna's treason is the more poignant because of his background. He and Abu Swaylim and the shopkeeper, Shaykh Yusuf, were friends from the days of their youth. Together they fought in World War I and participated in the Revolution of 1919. In one of the best scenes in Mahmoud el-Milligi's distinguished career, Abu Swaylim reminds him and others of those days and draws a contrast between then and now. In the old days, he bemoans, 'we were men and stood up like men'. And now, each one is out for himself. That spirit of patriotism and duty has dissipated. Nothing is left of it but the memory. It is a powerful speech and delivered with restrained hurt, so much so that Shaykh Hassouna rises to embrace him and to renew his friendship and his solidarity with him and the village. In the very next scene – he betrays them.

Visual richness

Three scenes will suffice to show the kind of visual beauty Chahine uses to illuminate his drama. One scene involves Shaykh Hassouna leaving town. The scene is shrouded with smoke. On the side of the frame is his cousin, Muhammad Effendi's mother. Shaykh Hassouna emerges on top of the steps, enveloped with smoke as though he were emerging from a furnace. His descent down the staircase is a descent into hell. He stops by his cousin, who, in her innocence, asks God to protect him. The irony renders him speechless and he leaves wrapped in disgrace. The second scene involves Abu Swaylim, in prison on some trumped up charge. In a stark close-up, one soldier holds his head and another shaves his moustache. To an Arab, this is the ultimate act of humiliation. In Arab culture a moustache is a man's symbol of manliness. To have it forcibly shaved is to dishonour him. For a long time after he is freed, Abu Swaylim walks around with his head-piece covering his mouth and upper lip. How could he face the public, knowing that they might suspect his shame? The novel speaks of a beating, but the film develops this much further, giving it a devastating visual con-creteness. Chahine's cinema is rich with imagery, but there are two scenes that are indelible on the viewer's mind. One comes at the end of *The Sparrow*, when Bahiyya runs down the street screaming 'NO!' to Nasser's resignation and 'NO!' to the end of fighting. The other is here in *The Earth*. When, at the end of the film, soldiers arrest Abu Swaylim because he had the audacity to have his own cotton picked before they confiscated his land, they smite him until his face and body are covered with blood. Then they tie him up and drag him behind a galloping horse. Again, in a tight shot, we see his strong hands exerting a tremendous willpower to cling to the land, as though he were leaving his soul behind. The grooves his fingers make on his precious land remain imprinted on the mind.

Madonna and whore

The women in the family are marginal, except for Wassifa and Khadra. The comparison and contrast between them register on different levels. Wassifa is Abu Swaylim's beautiful daughter with whom every bachelor is in love. She provides relief from the gloom that permeates the novel, and acquaints us with the mores and values of the village. She exudes beauty and sexuality, but she knows her limits. She desires romance, but she is the daughter of proud Abu Swaylim and would do nothing to tarnish his good name. On the other hand, there is Khadra, the village whore who is used, abused and discarded. Her death at the hand of a phony holy man is an

Hope comes with solidarity (*The Earth*, 1969)

indictment of religion and a metaphor of what would happen to those without land. In both novel and film much is made of the fact that she is
doomed: not because she is poor or without family, but because she owns no
land. She provides Chahine with another opportunity to sound the alarm
bell: woe betide those who sacrifice an inch of their land. Cling to it, he
warns. The transfer of the warning from the personal to the national is
obvious: Arab land must be reclaimed. Arab land belongs to the Arabs and
no one else. Without it we are doomed, just as Khadra is doomed. Palestine,
the Golan Heights, south Lebanon and Sinai must all be liberated – by
force, if necessary. Thus, Sharqawi's theme of cruelty and exploitation
becomes in Chahine's film a foundation for another theme: the land. The
totality of these themes is his message, and that is how Arab viewers read it.

Popular as it is in the Arab world, *The Earth* has many admirers abroad
as well. Roy Armes calls it 'a masterly rural epic'.[13] David Kehr deems the
water in it an 'image of political change, as in the irrigation project that

rejuvenates the parched fields of the peasant farmers'.[14] Jean-Louis Bory
first considers it a masterpiece comparable to Tarkovsky's *Andrey Rublyov*
(1966), then lavishes on it the highest praise: 'Youssef Chahine finds the
accents that recall the great era of Russian cinema. *The Earth* by Youssef
Chahine, United Arab Republic, 1969: a date not only in the Arab cinema
but also in international cinema.'[15]

Four
Wartime and Postwar Films

The residue of wars is often as debilitating as the carnage of war itself. In this section, Chahine tackles colonialism and subsequent wars and their aftermath. Cataclysmic defeat, the melting of a national dream, the death of the hero and the corrupt economy disturb his psyche. In response to these historic events, Chahine puts on display the full range of his themes: identity, justice, integrity, self-expression and censorship. Their interaction attests to the richness of his cinema. As he mixes genres to tell his stories, he also combines elements of ideology, history and entertainment, in varying balance, to communicate his message.

Like all Arabs of his generation, Chahine is burdened with history. This is not surprising, considering that the twentieth century alone has seen the Arab world embroiled in nearly thirty wars and revolutions. Such horrendous waste of life and resources is difficult to duplicate in any region, at any time. One war might have been self-inflicted and avoided: the Gulf War in 1991. The rest — including the internecine fighting — are instigated by outsiders coveting their land or wealth. Therefore the Arabs feel not only wronged but victimised by the imperialists. Even independence, which followed centuries of occupation, yielded nothing but disillusionment.

Jamila al-Jaza' iriyya (Jamila, the Algerian, 1958)

Occupation in perpetuity

The French occupation of Algeria began in 1830 and lasted till 5 July 1962, when the country was declared independent. By all accounts the 132-year rule was brutal in the extreme. Treating the Mediterranean sea as a mere creek running through the French countryside, the colonists had the conceit to declare Algeria 'l'Algérie française'. Before the country was finally liberated, 'Over a million Algerians had been killed out of a population of 9 million, 800 villages were destroyed, and over three million peasants were dislocated.'[1] Apparently the lofty ideals of the French Revolution did not apply to the oriental 'Other'.

Rebellion against the imperialist began in 1920 and developed into a full-scale resistance movement after World War II. The heavy sacrifices the Algerians were paying for their freedom was an outrage and an inspiration. From those freedom fighters, who faced the tremendously superior French forces with valour, emerged the Arab world's new heroine: Jamila. Egypt's powerful radio station, Voice of the Arabs, broadcast the triumphs and defeats in every battle and skirmish. It turned Jamila's heroism into the stuff of legends. A simple young girl who had been tortured at the hands of the colonists, Jamila transcended her oppressors and wrenched the hearts of an entire nation. She became the Arabs' Joan of Arc. Chahine could not resist the opportunity to tell her story on film.

Synopsis

The appealing true story depicts the heroism of an innocent young girl who is meant to fall in love, get married and have children. Jamila is portrayed as kind and peaceful, giving a gift to a child (unwittingly a toy gun) and settling disputes among classmates. Instead of living a normal life, she chooses to follow a different path. One day she is shocked to see one of her girlfriends arrested by the French military. Since her own uncle and his friends are active in the underground movement, she volunteers to join the struggle for national liberation. She begins work as a messenger and quickly rises to an organiser because of her intelligence. Her anger mounts after watching her uncle being shot in the street by the French, who had just released him from prison. Eventually she is wounded and arrested, while helping the freedom fighters negotiate their way to carry out some military operation. In prison, she proves to be indomitable. Cutting her long hair, applying electric shocks to her nipples, forcing her to watch her brother being drowned in a tub full of water, all fail to turn her into an informer. While she braves her imprisonment, her comrades release her story to the foreign press. Details of her torture arouse sympathy for her around the world. Confounded, her captors decide not to eliminate her lest she become a martyr to her people. Instead, they put her on trial in a military court, hoping to deflect world attention. But the trial is a travesty. Soon a defence lawyer arrives from Paris. The military try to have him 'accidentally' killed (as they disposed of many witnesses). Surviving, he fights valiantly on Jamila's behalf. Still, the court condemns her to death. The resistance movement retaliates by waging a major attack on a military camp and inflicting heavy losses on the occupiers. Thus, Jamila becomes a symbol of defiance and inspiration to the whole Arab world.

Direction with vengeance

Chahine's style is unrelenting. The film's opening bristles with documentary footage of fighting during World War II. The impassioned narrator informs us of the sacrifices the Algerians had suffered on behalf of their French occupiers, with the promise that after the war they would be

Magda's Jamila has a striking resemblance to Falconetti's *Joan of Arc* (1928)

rewarded with independence. The promise was a sham. 'France betrayed us,' the narrator declares. 'We paid the price for her victory. We lost 45,000 people to liberate her ... to keep her head high. We restored life to them ... we restored their freedom. We were betrayed. Yes, we were betrayed. But will we be betrayed again?'

Scripted by some of Egypt's finest writers, including Naguib Mahfouz, the story can be described as a *bildungsroman* of Jamila, who achieves maturity as she defends her country against the foreign aggressor. With almost shaven head, bent neck and twisted hands, she looks like the character played by Falconetti in Dreyer's *The Passion of Joan of Arc*. Jamila's determination is reminiscent of Rossellini's *Rome Open City*. What these two films share is the indomitability of the human spirit. Paradoxically, these three films are painful yet heartwarming to watch. Agony is unbearable; victory, uplifting. Gillo Pontecorvo reprised in *The Battle of Algiers* (1965) what Chahine had done seven years earlier. Both films are distinctive, but the conditions under which they were made are different: Chahine made his film on a shoestring and in the thick of the battle for liberation (albeit shot in Egypt); Pontecorvo made his on a much bigger budget and after the French had evacuated. It is safe to assume that *The Battle of Algiers* became more popular on account of superior worldwide distribution.

Critical appraisal

Jamila is framed between two sequences taken from newsreel footage. By summarising and legitimising the conflict, they plunge the viewer into the drama and send him away with heightened emotion. Thus, quickly, the viewer gains considerable understanding of the brutality of foreign occupation and of a people's desire for freedom. That Chahine is able to do this so economically is due to his mastery of the film medium which allows him to employ 'highly Vertovian tones — rapid montage, stirring music, grand visual abstractions'.[2]

Comparison between *Jamila* and *Open City* is inevitable. As a result of the conditions under which the two films were produced, *Jamila* lacks the immediacy one finds in *Open City*. Chahine shot his film on a set built on a three-acre lot in Cairo; Rossellini shot most of his exteriors from Rome's rooftops while the German tanks were rolling out in retreat. Also, one misses the comic relief which ameliorates the agony in Rossellini's film. Chahine sustains his advocacy at a high pitch, even though one of the characters makes attempts at humour. The warmth and charm of a priest-turned-revolutionary is one of the aspects that makes *Open City* so appealing. There is no equivalent for him in *Jamila*. Portraying a real-life hero, Magda gives a credible performance. Her Jamila comes off as decent, intelligent and patriotic, albeit precious. Though moving, Magda has none of the spontaneity and fire of Anna Magnani who flings herself into the middle of the street, wailing from the depth of her soul while her skirt rides up her thigh.

One particular sequence is incredibly intricate, both in the scripting and the execution. Planning an attack in the heart of the casbah, the freedom fighters escape detection, and design a series of signals that permit no mis-

Jamila became a symbol of the Algerian Revolution

take. Although it looks slightly exaggerated, it is probably a duplication of battlefield tactics. David Kehr finds the scene dependant 'literally on the precise calibrations of camera angles and points of view – the conspirators communicate with each other by passing light and hand signals from window to window and street to street'. [3]

Chahine's penchant for the use of songs in his films is evident here too. The nightclub scenes are among the best in a film full of admirable scenes. The atmosphere foreshadows many such scenes in later works. But the naturalness is compromised towards the end, when a young boy and an old man embrace physically and emotionally. The boy is Jamila's

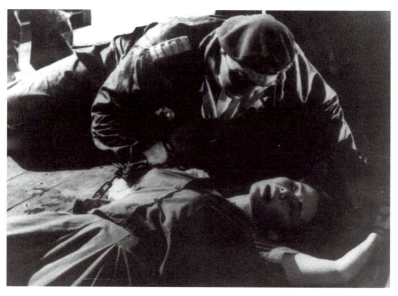

Jamila's torture and death pricked the conscience of the world

brother who we were led to believe had died when the soldiers drowned him in a tub full of water. Our concentration is broken when the old man opens his mouth to sing and nothing comes out. Instead of hearing his voice, we are treated to a professional singer's voice, leading the collective singing of the multitudes. The martial song is a fitting ending, but that split-second lapse between expectation and performance is jarring. A smoother and more honest rendition would have been to let the man start the singing and then segue to the robust choral chanting. Another minor point leaves us wondering how Jamila escaped the death sentence. Presumably, outraged world opinion saved her. But superimposing Jamila's face in a circle over the montage of the masses is glossing over the French change of heart. Such blemishes – which seem perfectly normal and acceptable in Soviet-style techniques – do not minimise the film's overall effectiveness. *Jamila* remains a landmark in Chahine's career, not simply because it glorifies a real-life heroine: Chahine's strengths as a film artist are evident here, though he would hone them further over the years.

Though hailed throughout the Arab world and the Eastern bloc countries, the film was banned in Algeria. This is understandable, for at the time Algeria was still under French rule. But it was also banned by the Algerians after their independence, because after the trial Jamila fell in love with and married the French attorney who had defended her – an act which amounted to treason in the eyes of the Algerians. They could not forgive her marrying one of 'them'. Then there was the question of glorifying one person. To the Algerians the real hero of the film should have been the masses – not an individual. It was the large-scale resistance at all levels of society that had forced the colonisers to pack up and leave. Similarly, Chahine himself later became 'suspect' in the eyes of some Egyptians. He, the militant against the French occupation in Algeria, was himself attacked for being 'soft' on the French in *Adieu Bonaparte*. That the two films were made twenty-five years apart, and under different circumstances, was immaterial.

The producer remembers

Magda, the producer and star of *Jamila*, makes the incredible claim to have been seventeen at the time. It was she who offered Chahine the opportunity to make one of his most powerful films. She is quick to assert that it is the only Chahine film that is also associated with her name and not only his. It is a testament to Chahine's stature that everyone who ever worked with him, in whatever capacity, desires to have his or her name linked to his. Magda is proud of the fact that *Jamila* opened up new markets for Egyptian cinema, for it was shown in countries as distant as Czechoslovakia, Hungary, Germany, Pakistan, Soviet Union, Afghanistan, India and China.[4] She even adds: 'When it was shown in the Soviet Union ambulances had to be brought to carry those (who had fainted) because of the heavy congestion'.[5] Of all reviews, she cherishes a compliment by Jean-Paul Sartre who, according to her, wrote: '... when I saw this film ... I was greatly affected ... and I was moved by the young great actress ... who has torn tears out of us and made us forget our nationality'.[6]

* * *

In 1959, *Jamila* won the top award at the Moscow Film Festival, even though France had tried to stop it from being shown. Guerrasimov, the then dean of Moscow Film Institute, hailed Chahine for having founded, with *Jamila*, 'a film school comparable to that of Kazan and Logan in the United States'.[7] Yet Egyptian television for a long time did not show it. Asked why, Magda, producer and star, replies that they forbade 'showing the film on the pretext that it would harm our relationship with France. I find this a strange justification because the film was shown in France itself. Also, television shows films that are critical of British colonialism, yet our relationship with Britain has not been harmed.'[8]

Al-Ikhtiyar (*The Choice*, 1970)

Trauma of defeat

Of all the watershed calamities the Arabs have suffered during the twentieth century, none can compare with *al-zilzal* of 1967 – the earthquake, in the words of Naguib Mahfouz – that shook their world when Israel decimated the vaunted Egyptian army, occupied the whole of Sinai, the West Bank, southern Lebanon and the Golan Heights. In 1948 the Arabs were disunited, ill-equipped and utterly unprepared to meet the highly motivated

Zionists who pounced upon them, armed to the full. But the Arabs of 1967 were in a vastly improved position, or so they had been led to believe. They were constantly reassured that in the next confrontation with the enemy all their hopes and dreams would be fulfilled. Egypt's leadership since 1952 had been preparing to meet the challenge and recapture Arab land and restore Arab pride. Even before the dust of the Six Day War had settled, the Arabs found themselves enveloped in the worst nightmare in their history.

But no one had envisaged such a catastrophe. In 1973, Chahine dealt with the subject in the memorable *The Sparrow*. But in *The Choice*, three years earlier, Chahine and Mahfouz collaborated on the script which Chahine turned into dense and evocative film, indicting the Egyptian intellectuals for having betrayed the Revolution by failing to contribute to building the new society. Chahine wrote the first draft himself and showed it to Mahfouz. When he finished reading it, Mahfouz scribbled on the cover, 'This is the best script I've read in years.'

Precedents

Several critics have found the film confusing. Robyn Karney found it '[c]onstructed as a hall of mirrors, which reflects the hero's split personality' and consequently as 'far from commercial Egyptian cinema as one can get'.[9] Upon initial viewing, one might even find it contrived. To enter it properly one must be ready to suspend disbelief, which is not unusual in film history. *Sunset Boulevard* (1950) is told from the perspective of a corpse at the bottom of a swimming pool. In *The Seventh Seal* (1956) the Knight plays chess with none other than Death. What is important in a film is the totality of the concept. *The Choice* requires the viewer to accept that a psychopath can kill his imaginary identical twin in order to assume his personality.

Synopsis

The underlying diegetic structure of the film is the story of a writer who is going mad. Here we find Chahine importing modernist and reflexive themes and motifs. Chahine's protagonist in *The Choice* is schizophrenic, but this information is not conveyed to the viewer until well into the film. Here Chahine utilises an elaborate structure to dramatise the dichotomy in the Egyptian society, which led to the befuddlement after the 'earthquake'.

From the very beginning, the art work primes us to be disturbed. Behind and between the credits, it conjures up Jackson Pollock's wiry and entangled paintings. It is also reminiscent of Saul Bass's credit design for two of Hitchcock's films, *Vertigo* and *Psycho*, both of which deal with reality and illusion, just as *The Choice* does. The predominant colour Chahine uses is red: as though he were spilling buckets of blood on the screen. The music is equally discordant and foreboding.

In the opening scene the police discover an unidentified corpse. Soon all clues point to the death of Mahmoud. While looking for the killer, the two detectives assigned to the case become suspicious that Sayyid must have killed his brother. But Sayyid throws them off by always changing clothes and switching roles: with his girlfriend, Bahiyya, he is Mahmoud; with his wife, Sharifa, he is Sayyid. The mystery deepens, with the older, more realistic detective accusing Sayyid of killing Mahmoud, and the young assistant questioning whether it is a real crime and calling it instead an elaborate self-deception.

Sayyid and Mahmoud Murad are identical enough to be played by the same actor. But physical resemblance is the only thing they share. This is where the one-sided jealousy begins. Sayyid Murad is a playwright obsessed with fame and celebrity. We are not told what kind of plays he writes; all we know of him is that he is a humourless writer who indulges in his work to the dismay of his beautiful wife who begs for affection. He married Sharifa, daughter of a prominent cabinet minister, only to advance his career and social status. Selfishly and hypocritically, Sayyid finds nothing to write about except stories inspired by his brother's life. One of his priorities is attending international conferences or UNESCO events, or joining some prestigious literary society. When he hears about Mahmoud's death, he is untouched by sorrow. Instead of rushing to his brother's house to learn more about his death, he is worried that 'even in his death he's going to scandalise me'. All he can think of is how his brother's 'morphine-addiction and unsavoury past' would reflect on his own reputation. But his own wife, Sharifa, rejects all these accusations.

Sayyid's brother, Mahmoud, is his exact opposite. A sailor and a motorcycle rider, his only aspiration is to be happy. Neither vain nor deceitful, he enjoys life and is always surrounded by friends. He lives with vivacious Bahiyya who runs a bohemian studio-café-apartment where men and women come to paint, sing, romance, drink and have a good laugh. Mahmoud shows no signs of jealousy of his brother's social and cultural standing. Mahmoud's earthiness attracts his sister-in-law's attention, or so Sayyid imagines as he writes a new play about their flirtation or alleged affair. Sayyid's imagination proves to be partially correct, for Sharifa eventually declares her love to Mahmoud, who is not afflicted with Sayyid's detachment and self-absorption. Mahmoud returns the affection up to a point: he kisses her and then restrains himself out of loyalty to his own blood. Even in his agony over his unrequited love he emerges more human than his brother; he can feel whereas Sayyid is devoid of emotion.

Sharifa is eventually grateful to her brother-in-law Mahmoud for declining her advances

The detectives' visit to Bahiyya's studio sheds light on the twin brothers. The decor here is warm and inviting, with beautiful paintings adorning the walls and glass partitions. The entire place exudes energy, warmth and hospitality. The ambiance is in sharp contrast to that in Sayyid's house. There the walls are barren, the shelves nearly empty and the furniture looks plastic. Instead of being full of beautiful art objects befitting a humanist, Sayyid's house is as sterile and cold as his personality. When Sayyid learned of his brother's death he was outraged, fearing a scandal. But when Bahiyya and the other women at the studio read about Mahmoud's death in the papers they scream. When the older detective finally apprehends Mahmoud – or his double, for we are never certain – he takes him to the morgue to identify the corpse. There we see and hear simple peasant women immersed in black wailing over the loss of their loved one. And when the detective pulls out the drawer and uncovers the body, Mahmoud howls from shock. 'How can you do this to me,' he cries, 'he's my brother!' Chahine provides those moments of deeply felt grief to reinforce his loathing for the emotionally arrested Sayyid.

Indictment

Chahine's loathing for the shallow intellectuals becomes more apparent when Sayyid goes to the theatre to talk to the star/director who plans to direct his new play. A modern Egyptian classic is in progress, starring Yusuf Wahbi. Written by Wahbi himself, *The Confessional Chair* depicts a priest who violates his sacred oath and betrays the secrecy of holy confession. The instant Sayyid appears backstage to watch the performance from the wing, we see and hear Wahbi, as the Cardinal, 'thunder' his horror: 'Get out of here, O enemy of God. May God's curse be upon you.' The lines are doubly cutting. They are aimed at the fallen priest as well as Sayyid himself, for in Chahine's eyes both are equally despicable. By betraying his own nature, Sayyid joins the enemies of God. In the star's dressing room, Sayyid tries to justify himself: 'Who knows when illusion stops and reality begins. Are you Yusuf Wahbi or the Cardinal you've just finished playing? Or are you the image in that mirror?' Most artists occasionally grapple with such notions; Sayyid's split personality eventually leads to madness.

In his indictment of the Egyptian intellectual, Chahine does not spare himself. A scene at the ministry is quite revealing. When Sayyid goes to the ministry to inquire about his invitation to attend a literary conference abroad, an official is so impressed by his writing that he queries him about the sources of all the rich characters in his dramas. 'And Kinawi ... and that delicious Hannouma,' he asks, 'where did you meet such wonderful people?' Those familiar with Chahine's cinema know that Kinawi and Hannuma are the main characters in his film *Cairo Station*. In *The Choice* Sayyid is presented as the author of that screenplay; in reality Chahine is the film's auteur. By closely identifying himself with Sayyid, Chahine is suggesting that he too may be to blame just as much as the pseudo-intellectuals of his generation. Chahine identifies himself further with Sayyid by making their birth dates only three days apart: Chahine's is 25 January, Sayyid's 28 January.

Chahine confounds the viewer further by splitting his own personality in the same film. We have already seen him identify himself with Sayyid, and accept the guilt he is putting on him. Now we find him switching roles and identifying with Mahmoud, too. At the studio, the older detective and Mahmoud are talking about reality.

> 'What is reality?' the older detective asks.
>
> 'It's being faithful to one's self.'
>
> 'And what are the rules of the game?'
>
> 'He who has needs must be all right. It means he must know people. He who needs to know people must love people. And if you love people you must really know their true nature. You must forgive them the way they are ... People are always chasing after each other. That's not love. That's lust ... self-interest. After they have each other, the birds stop singing and the roses stop smelling like roses. We solve the problem of lust first. And then we relax. If afterwards there's understanding then it's real understanding. If there's tenderness then it's real tenderness.'

Knowing and accepting one's self, needing and wanting to know others, and forgiving them their weaknesses: these are primary Chahine themes. Mahmoud (or Chahine) is not advocating permissiveness as a general rule of behaviour; he is advocating self-awareness, forgiveness and tolerance at every level. Sayyid fails on all accounts: a hollow man, he is husband and not a husband, brother and not a brother, thinker and not a thinker. Unless he chooses to be who he is and to do the right thing, he will be doomed to be 'an enemy of God'. Unfortunately, God's curse will not be on him alone, but on society as a whole, for he is its ultimate peril.

Context

Ostensibly, *The Choice* is a film about conscience and identity, but it can also be read as a political statement. In the aftermath of the Six Day War, the Arab world was going through what became known as the period of 'No Peace / No War'. For a while people accepted the absence of shooting as an

Young and old detectives are part of a system of symmetrical pairings

alternative to peace. But as the period lingered, anxiety became unbearable. The stalemate was suffocating. Just as Sayyid had to choose, the nation had to choose: between courage or cowardice, victory or defeat, honour or shame. A state of limbo will only lead to madness.

Still, who killed whom? Did Mahmoud kill Sayyid because he needed money for his morphine and women? Or did Sayyid kill Mahmoud because of jealousy? By the intentional ambiguity, Chahine forces us to think. After Bahiyya coaxes him to surrender, in a scene of madness that recalls another scene of madness at the end of *Cairo Station*, the suspect is placed inside a car on his way to an asylum. The two women in his life bend down and look at him through the car's two windows: Bahiyya calls him Mahmoud; Sharifa calls him Sayyid. As we watch him wrestling with himself, from the point of view of the driver, we recognise that at the asylum he will either undergo a complete breakdown into madness or he will metamorphose into an organic whole.

Two clues to reading the subtext can help in decoding Chahine's intentions. The first concerns the system of symmetrical pairs that represent contrary qualities: two brothers, two women, two detectives and, ultimately, two roads in the fork that lies ahead. The touchstone of redemption also has two components: reconciling opposites and making the right choice. The second clue revolves around the use of names. Sharaf means honour. Sharif is an honourable man; Sharifa, an honourable woman. Here Sharifa, the frustrated wife who finally thanks her brother-in-law for having saved her marriage by declining her advances, is a good woman who almost slipped because of her husband's utter neglect. Bahiyya is a name for a lovely woman. She is also a mythical character in modern Egyptian culture, who is idealised in Chahine's *The Sparrow*. Sayyid is a title of respect. Here Sayyid is an elitist who is ironically misnamed. Mahmoud is a man who deserves gratitude. Not satisfied with the complexity of plot and richness of character, Chahine takes every opportunity to endow his film with a plurality of meanings.

* * *

Al-Usfur (The Sparrow, 1973)

Political and cultural context

Chahine's *oeuvre* includes no film more powerful than *The Sparrow* in which he incisively addresses the Six Day War. Non-Arab viewers can use it as an entrée into the Arabs' psyche following that watershed in their history. Their comprehension of the trauma of those fateful days will deepen were they to witness the transformation that occurs on the faces, in the voices and images that Chahine explores and explodes on the screen. To the Arab viewers, however, it is not a film but an encapsulation of their darkest memory. Here Chahine uses the full power of his medium to render a precise picture of the social and political conditions that caused such a tragedy. Without showing the battle itself, or lambasting foreign deception, or criticising the regime for its irresponsibility, he turns his camera inward and backward on Egyptian society at large to uncover the fissure in its foundation.

During the early 1970s Egyptian cinema and theatre went through another period of hardship. In 1972 Sadat's government imposed severe restrictions on what could be seen or heard on stage or screen. It lumped all foreign and Egyptian films together, permitting only those that were fit for audiences of all ages: children and adults were treated as if they had the same mentality and taste. Ironically, on that same day, 14 June 1972, the Egyptian film critics announced the establishment of their own society which pledged to defend freedom of expression. During the same period the film studios were producing five films that were destined to have their own battles with the censors. Most important among them was Chahine's *The Sparrow*.

Dramatic structure

The Sparrow eschews the conventional paradigm of a protagonist going through a crisis and reaching a resolution. Realising that an apocalypse is too big to be confined to one voice, Chahine relies on polyphony instead. At the outset we learn that a racketeer called Abu Khadr is being hunted. We neither see nor hear him, but we feel his presence everywhere. All those who are after him recognise that he is only an agent for a sinister group in high places. They still want to destroy him, each for his own reason. When his capture becomes imminent, and fearing exposure, his bosses arrange for his murder.

Foremost among those who are on Abu Khadr's trail is Youssef, an investigative reporter. The son of a former pasha who is now a wealthy businessman, Youssef is an idealist. His well-connected father tries in vain to dissuade him from attacking in print the monster who is responsible for dismantling and selling piece by piece a giant plant that was built to bring prosperity to an impoverished district. After six years, the plant, which was meant to employ 6,000 men, could not produce a toothpick. For six years Abu Khadr had every piece of equipment shipped out, with the threat of death hanging over the head of any informer. Then there is Ra'ouf, a young captain who still mourns his father's suicide. He despises his step-father and rejects any form of reconciliation. He too is looking for Abu Khadr for having killed an informer. Ra'ouf and his brother, Riyad, are two decent and patriotic young men, eager to perform their duty at home and at the front line. We learn more about Ra'ouf, for he is central to the story and brings us into contact with two other important characters. Shaykh Ahmad is an Egyptian *fellah* who had studied at al-Azhar and exudes goodness. He is frustrated because he wants to do his military duty but is always passed over by the army. Next time, they always tell him, and he gets drunk from not knowing when that will be. He wants to serve but cannot; and he certainly has no say in national policy. The only flaw in his character is his blind adherence to the time-honoured tradition of revenge. Obsessed with the idea that blood calls for blood, he plans to kill Abu Khadr for having killed his brother. But one of his wives informs on him, and even handcuffs him herself, because she would rather see him imprisoned than dead. That he is turned in by a woman insults his manhood. The fourth important character is Bahiyya, the living symbol of Egyptian wholesomeness. Her warmth and good nature cast a spell on us at first sight. In spirit, she is the same salt-of-the-earth Bahiyya whom we have encountered in *The Choice*. She is Chahine's favourite woman, and he calls her 'Mother of the world'.

Plot and texture

Kamal Ramzi quotes Chahine as saying, 'I made this film to deliberately open a wound we have been trying hard to conceal.'[10] The assault on our sensibilities begins from the first frame under the opening credits. The film opens with a song sung over the title, and repeated many times throughout the film: 'We are (companions) on a long and hard journey.' The camera pans over a newspaper rack crowded with dozens of newspapers stacked next to and on top of each other, the headlines of which scream of solidarity with the State. Anticipating a war with the arch enemy, Israel, they form a chorus of resolve and readiness. The revolutionary rhetoric and the declaration of unequivocal readiness to strike the enemy a fatal blow, all imbue the viewer with blinding optimism.

One minute into the film, Chahine unfolds a five-minute sequence of extraordinary images. After declining any help from his step-father, Ra'ouf drives his brother Riyad to a military post, where he is eager to participate in the impending war. While on duty, Ra'ouf heads a group of policemen in search of the notorious Abu Khadr. We are in a desolate area. Dressed in white uniform, Ra'ouf approaches a vast ancient compound and kicks the door open. Suddenly a burst of shrill laughter fills the air. Inside the four walls of the compound we see a tiny group of old women dressed in black hunched by themselves and cackling like a bunch of chickens. Every time Ra'ouf or any of his men moves they respond with mocking giggles. Suddenly a hauntingly tall woman, also dressed in black, appears on top of the wall in the background and starts shooting at his feet. Ra'ouf is startled, and the old women's cackles rise. As the woman atop the wall fires her rifle, she declaims, 'Too bad the sparrow has flown and the bullet has gone astray.' Ra'ouf retreats, and we see a wispy old man rocking with laughter. Then for a few seconds we glimpse several huts inside the compound, all looking like white snowmen with coal eyes staring at Ra'ouf. As Ra'ouf makes haste, the old women serenade him with a sarcastic song which says, '... they stole your hat, [you idiot], and you have returned bare-headed'.

After being unsettled by the surrealistic episode, we stay with Ra'ouf. The next setting is near a jail. We hear a prisoner behind bars saying that a few months earlier a fight erupted among men and two were killed for having looked at a woman. Ra'ouf turns around and spits at him. A few minutes later Zainab, who works in the kitchen, complains about men who cannot see a woman without undressing her with their eyes, item by item. She then bursts out crying and confides in Ra'ouf that her husband, Shaykh Ahmad, is planning to avenge the death of his brother by killing Abu Khadr. Sitting in an open field (out of the range of informers, but not Zainab), Ra'ouf and Youssef exchange information about the man they are both trailing.

Hope for the future: the dauntless boy

Back in the street, Ra'ouf listens as a skeptical old man sitting in the hot sun tells him that those who want to get rid of Abu Khadr had better plan carefully and prepare themselves for a lot of misery. Even a child under ten who is looking for someone (to give him a lift to visit a holy shrine) complains that 'in this town nobody knows anybody'. Thus, in staccato fashion, Chahine reveals grass-roots discontent.

Occasionally Ra'ouf receives letters from his brother Riyad at the front and we hear his voice narrating his own lines. In the first one he describes the agony of waiting in the remote desert. 'Why,' he asks, 'have we forgotten all about the desert? Why haven't we planted trees in it? Why haven't we covered it with factories? And why haven't we filled it with beautiful women? How are the women in Egypt, Ra'ouf, are they still beautiful? My mind is buzzing with questions.' And so does Chahine's. Egypt has been neglected far too long. Without jobs, security and a decent standard of living, soldiers will have nothing to fight for. Rhetoric does not fill stomachs; slogans do not win wars.

Bahiyya is a widow with a lovely young daughter. She rents rooms in her house and works as a part-time seamstress, sewing at home costumes for film studios. She is scornful of the films themselves, but she needs to make a living. Men love her and enjoy her company and good cheer. Once she was attracted to Ra'ouf's father and now she is attracted to Youssef whom, her daughter says, she will never marry because he is already married to his cause. Bahiyya is unavailable, for she is everybody's sweetheart and nobody's in particular. Though she moves in the company of men, she is above

Bahiyya ('Mother of the World') surrounded by friends

reproach. Hers is transcendent love. She is Egypt, or 'Mother of the world'.

Eventually Ra'ouf is brought to her house and is accommodated in her daughter's vacant room. Here we are treated to Bahiyya's singing and laughter and are smitten by her infectious smile. She is not gorgeous, but in her earthiness she is comfortably beautiful. Nor is she trouble free. Far from it: she toils and labours, with no support from anyone we can see. Her eyes become moist when she remembers a sister, who disappeared and was never found. She worries about her daughter, hoping that she will find a suitable husband. She worries about friends and neighbours. When interrogated about Youssef's whereabouts, she manipulates the police officer before he manipulates her:

> 'Didn't Youssef tell you that he's under observation and shouldn't leave the city?'
> 'Maybe.'
> 'What do you mean maybe?'
> 'Maybe he did and maybe he didn't. I can't remember.'
> 'You can't remember that he told you or do you mean he didn't tell you?'
> 'Of course.'
> 'Of course what?'
> 'Whatever you said.'
> 'I didn't say anything.'
> ' Neither did I.'

This circuitous logic is a means of survival. Bahiyya subverts the officer's inquiry to protect her friend. Like James Joyce, she is not above resorting to cunning if needs be. The song that bears her name and runs throughout the film says:

> Age grew old but you remained youthful
> He is leaving and you are coming
> Endless nights have come and gone
> But your endurance is still the same
> And your smile is still the same.

One of Bahiyya's friends is a likeable old drunkard, nicknamed Johnny, who had worked for the British occupiers and now misses 'the good old days'. He carries a bird cage that he wants to give to Bahiyya, but for some reason he never manages to leave it with her. He eventually lets the bird free, but we don't see that happen (perhaps due to the poor quality of the video tape we were viewing). His body misshapen and his tongue heavy, Johnny praises the British. He admits that from the Major on down they were all rascals, but everybody had money and everybody was happy. Johnny is a remnant of British colonialism in Egypt. He is jolly but cynical. The patriotic ballyhoo does not impress him. When he hears the news about the war or watches army vehicles full of soldiers passing by, he picks up an empty Coca-Cola bottle and starts firing mockingly. He is under no illusion. And when the bad news starts filtering to the street or when patriotism flares, he calmly sings a song to himself that sounds child-like but is so apropos that an Arab viewer must find it painful to hear: 'O where have you been, Ali, when your mother was looking for you?' Where, indeed, were Egypt's children when she was desperately calling for attention? Good

Last-minute bravura deserves Johnny's mockery, if not disdain

intentions are no substitute for sound policy. Last minute bravura deserves Johnny's mockery, if not disdain.

During the war, the theft at the industrial plant continues. The well-marked trucks carrying the stolen equipment zip through the city as usual. Youssef tries to get his articles published, but the editor is no longer interested. Disappointed but not discouraged, Youssef resumes his search for the truth, only to have his suspicions confirmed: his own father was a partner in the company that was buying and selling the stolen goods. The revelation might seem contrived, but we have been wary of this sleazy character who had tried to bribe his son to lay off the investigation, and who had intimidated the official in charge of public security to kill Abu Khadr overnight lest he become a liability to his superiors. Soon after the start of the war, we see him rushing out of his office, accompanied by a woman. He explains that while the people are in a state of confusion, and while waiting to see what the new regime would do, they needed to smuggle the goods without delay. Then he tells his chauffeur to light up his cigarette. When the chauffeur reminds him of the blackout, he replies: 'smoke and don't worry, it's all over.' He speaks with the confidence of a man privy to high secrets. Like a good traitor, he thrives on national disasters.

Throughout the film the viewer hears newscasters in the background, but once the war erupts Voice of the Arabs is foregrounded. In the early hours it announces the downing of twenty-three Israeli aeroplanes by the Egyptian forces; hours later, the number increases to forty-two. Euphoria engulfs the street. In retrospect the viewer knows this was a patent lie. But no Arab knew it at the time. Back in Bahiyya's room everybody is mesmerised by the television set to hear the news. Bahiyya herself is somewhere else attending to a neighbour in labour. The scrawny old husband wants a boy and is determined to give the newly born a boy's name regardless. Eventually his wife gives birth and Bahiyya breaks the good news to him. It is a girl and he ought to be happy. But the miserable father insists on giving her a boy's name. When one of the neighbours chastises Bahiyya for telling him, Bahiyya replies, 'The truth cannot be hidden.' Another truth awaits her in her own living room. There she joins her daughter, Johnny, Ra'ouf, and Shaykh Ahmad. Six days after the war had started, a

chastened President Nasser appears on television and admits that Egypt
had suffered a major 'setback', takes full responsibility, and submits his
resignation. From this point on the film ceases to be a film and dissolves
into a collective memory at the primordial level. The shock is emblazoned
on their minds and hearts. Bahiyya's sitting room is electrified. Suddenly
Shaykh Ahmad erupts bawling. 'What a black day!' he cries, his whole body
trembling and his face awash with tears. 'We lost and we didn't even know
it.' He is not acting, just an overwhelmed citizen.

Chahine cuts to Youssef at the newspaper office. He is in a fog of his own,
and we hear him tell a friend, 'Shaykh Ahmad is right. We think revolution.
We write revolution. But we don't do revolution.' He walks to the window to
watch the street below and this is the last time we see him. A decent human
being is marginalised by the historic event: but he is not dead. He is at the
window observing and absorbing.

As Nasser continues his appeal to the people to accept his resignation
and not succumb to despair, Chahine intercuts to the Nile river standing
still and then to the housing project that the Revolution had built for the
poor. It is a ghost town, for all people must be glued to their television sets.
Umm Kulthum's voice singing a rousing song about the glories of the
Revolution adds poignancy to the cruelty of fate. The irony is unmistakable:
the Revolution's reforms had not gone far enough.

Bahiyya is the most devastated. She breaks out of the house, hysterical.
She runs down the street, wailing, 'La'! Hanharib! No! We shall fight.' The
crowd is delirious. They join her screaming, 'We shall fight! We shall fight!'
Bahiyya is like a runner in a hundred-yard sprint. Her eyes are glazed, her
face is perspiring, and she is screaming at the top of her voice: hundreds
are running behind her, repeating her refrain. Her outburst recalls the
painting 'Liberty leading the People' by Delacroix, depicting a French
woman (also a seamstress) who played a heroic part in the French
Revolution of 1830. Bahiyya, the living symbol of Egypt, will settle for nothing less than freedom at all cost.

The Sparrow, then, is not just about the catastrophe or the immediate
causes that led to it. The Six Day War is the catalyst for examining a society
that seems to have lost its bearings. With social conditions being in disar-

ray, no leader and no army can hope for victory. Values and priorities had to be reassessed. Looking at a woman is not a crime; losing wars is a crime. Taking the law into your own hands is not a solution; defending your country is a solution. Shutting people out from national debate is not a cure; involving them in decision making is a cure. The touchstone is democracy. Gloomy as it seems, though, the film is not pessimistic. With Bahiyya's spirit alive, there is always hope. There is also hope in the new generations. With Ra'ouf insisting on honesty and Youssef rebelling against their culpable fathers, there is hope. And with the urchin clawing his way to where he wants to go, there is hope. This endearing little boy stands up to adults who refuse to give him a lift, hides in the pick-up truck, pelts them with stones when they break a promise, comes to their aid to win favours with them, curses them when they unload him from a bus, and finally squeezes himself into a crowded taxi – but, by God, he will reach his destination. His whole journey is to help a sick brother, and he must be applauded. This is the generation Chahine is counting on, the determined generation in whose hands the future of Egypt rests.

The surrealistic sequence at the beginning of the film now becomes clearer. The cackling women, laughing old man, and the lady shooting from atop the wall – they all know the futility of the captain's search. The criminal Abu Khadr is the tip of the iceberg: the roots of evil run deeper. Egyptian society is so disintegrated that even the mud huts are aghast. When the firing lady says, 'Too bad the sparrow flew and the bullet went astray', she uses the sparrow as a symbol of freedom that the Egyptians had lost. Later on we find the sparrow imprisoned in Johnny's bird cage. In both cases, freedom is misplaced. When Johnny releases it the people are freed. Unfortunately one strains to reconcile the two metaphors, an oversight in the screenplay which Chahine co-authored with Lutfi al-Khouli, another leftist.

The Sparrow is full of Chahine's distinctive compositions. One of the hallmarks of his style is conveying more than one meaning in every shot. One exquisite moment is captured at al-Azhar where a Muslim Shaykh recites verses from the Qur'an in support of the tradition of revenge. The scene is slightly overexposed and steam hovers over the believers. The

windows are in view and the effect could be attributed to the rays of the sun
that bathe the room. But this is not Chahine's intention. The steam is a
visual metaphor of the fog that clouds the Shaykh's head. But the most celebrated shot is that of Bahiyya running down the street screaming 'No! We
shall fight!' It is one of those images that remain indelible on a viewer's
mind. Looking back on it, Chahine says:

> I decided on the end of the film at the outset, because the end is the founda-
> tion of the film. It is my main idea. Everything in the story necessitates the
> last scene. Without it *The Sparrow* loses all relevance.[11]

Outside Egypt, Arab intelligentsia rallied on behalf of Chahine and his
masterpiece. Support came from one significant gathering in Lebanon.
Struck by the sheer power of the film (incidentally one month before Sadat
ordered his forces to cross the Suez Canal), the Film Festival officially
recognised the importance of the film, calling it 'an artistic event that
deserves the pride of every Arab, especially every Egyptian'.[12] The declaration appealed to the Egyptian authorities to rescind the order to have the
film banned. And it urged all Arab countries to exhibit it at their finest

The extraordinary and memorable outrage of Bahiyya in *The Sparrow* (1973)

theatres, 'particularly at a time when (we) Arabs desperately need freedom of self-expression so that we may face our reality with confidence, and look to the future with conviction and certitude'.[13] Now *The Sparrow* is considered a modern classic. After calling it 'politically explosive' and praising its 'imaginative language', one foreign historian proclaims that with it 'Egyptian cinema has found its voice'.[14]

Significantly, the idealist journalist is called Youssef, which is Chahine's first name. He is his alter ego: searching for the truth and ringing alarm bells against evil. In the last shot we see journalist Youssef (representing film maker Youssef Chahine) standing at the window (representing the film frame) and watching the horror below. The identification is total, and the role exemplifies Chahine's cinema.

* * *

Awdat al-Ibn al-Dal
(*Return of the Prodigal Son*, 1976)

Tragic roots
Having already made two films that directly or indirectly dealt with the Six Day War (*The Choice* and *The Sparrow*), Chahine returns to the same subject again in *Return of the Prodigal Son*. He was also to allude to it in *The Earth*, two years later. This preoccupation with one historical event is understandable, for it was a defeat like no other. Ahmad Fouad Nijm, the lyricist of the song about Bahiyya in *The Sparrow*, put it more emotionally when he said, 'Lucky is the generation that did not witness that period.' So deeply rooted is the agony that followed those fateful days that it will remain an inexhaustible source of material for future artists and scholars. One of those who are permanently wounded by it is Youssef Chahine. A song in this film touches a national raw nerve when it says, purportedly to the late Nasser, 'The promise was yours; the dream was ours.' The breaking of that enormous promise and the shattering of that beautiful dream constitute the heart of *Prodigal Son*.

Another Egyptian artist who felt the pain of those days particularly deeply was Salah Jahin. A gifted folkloric poet and a songwriter famous for his tenderness and range, Jahin idolised Gamal Abdel Nasser. He listened to Nasser's every speech and absorbed every thought and sentiment, and turned them overnight into songs that would stir the Arabs everywhere. For nineteen years after *al-zilzal*, Jahin lived a broken man. It is reported that when a play was staged in which Nasser's coffin was carried on the stage, a symbolic coffin was carried behind it, that of Jahin's. Knowing all this one is amazed that in 1976 Jahin still had the energy to collaborate with Youssef Chahine on *Prodigal Son*. Both he and Chahine are credited with the 'cinematic vision', and Jahin alone is credited for the lyrics and the dialogue. According to Samir Farid, while *Prodigal Son* is a Youssef Chahine film, it is also Salah Jahin's apology to the Egyptian people for the role he played in inflating their expectations.[15] His spirit was shattered after the war because his country was humiliated, his idol was crushed, his own dream was smashed and because he felt guilty for having made that dream appear within reach for millions of people.

Contexts

To fully appreciate this significant film the viewer still needs to situate it within two other contexts: one political, the other social. Under Nasser Egypt became a socialist country. The land reforms, and the nationalisation of industries were introduced ostensibly to make life fairer and better for all Egyptians. The theory might have been correct, and the intentions might have been good, but in reality the experience was disastrous. A tiny segment of the population got richer and the rest became poorer. Colonels and retired generals could not run industries; what they were good at was neglecting the factories they inherited and making appointments and granting concessions to those they favoured. Nepotism ran rampant and the public suffered. Following Sadat's 'corrective revolution', Egypt swung in the opposite direction, yet for the ordinary Egyptian things got worse. The replacement of socialism with capitalism continued to favour the rich and powerful at his expense. Under Sadat, Egypt witnessed the rise of a new class of multi-millionaires. Looking back at both periods, Chahine says, 'Socialism was for them, and capitalism was for them.'[16]

Even rural Egypt was not spared. Traditionally, villages and small towns are communities of great cohesion. The hardships of eking out a living were enough to occupy them. But with the successive wars and revolutions during the twentieth century, change was inevitable and it left no one untouched. The land reforms and the nationalisation of all industries produced convulsions everywhere. When nationalisation was reversed and the age of 'openness' arrived under Sadat, migration to the cities became a means for survival, and the stage was set for further destabilisation. Consequently attitudes shifted and traditions collapsed. But the scale of transformation that followed the cumulative political and military disasters was of such dimension that Egypt's equilibrium was endangered.

The good and the bad

As the bombs explode, societies implode. This is what Chahine shows us in *Prodigal Son*. The family he portrays is a microcosm of a deteriorating Egypt. The Madbouli family has a stranglehold on their community: it owns the farm, the factory and the cinema. Almost everybody in the village is employed by them. The family itself comprises an aging grandfather who runs the farm; a grandmother who meddles in everyone's life; a son named Tulba who manages the factory like a despot; a younger son, Ali, who spends twelve years in prison and emerges quite altered; a cousin, Fatma, who waits for Ali's return in hopes of marrying him; and a grandson, Ibrahim, who wants to study space science at a foreign university and who is in love with Tafida, a daughter of one of the workers at the factory. Together, they represent a dysfunctional Egypt.

There are only three good people in this family; the rest are 'stinking rotten', as Fatma ultimately calls them. The grandfather is a kindly old man who had studied engineering in Paris but returned home without a degree. As a student he pursued the joys of night life and showed great interest in the arts, particularly the theatre. He is ineffectual but totally sincere. He sees through his manipulative wife whom he calls 'Frankenstein.' When Ali is released from prison he throws a party in his honour and invites everyone, 'rich and poor, young and old, man and woman'. When he hugs his son and calls him 'you rascal' he beams and his eyes become misty. But he has no such affection for the older son, Tulba, whose heart is made of granite. After the party, Tulba corners his father and sternly instructs him to tell Ali to report to work at the factory next morning. His jealousy of his brother is so strong that it becomes obvious that he intends to break him down. The old man leaves the room and shuts the door behind him, only to re-open it and say, 'Tulba ....'. He never finishes the sentence. The subtitles translate him as saying, 'Tulba, go to hell'; on the soundtrack, however, we only hear the flushing of the toilet. The second good member in the family is Ibrahim, who is Tulba's son. A recent high school graduate, he dreams of following in the steps of Farouk al-Baz, the Egyptian space scientist who helped the Americans land on the moon. But the girl Ibrahim loves, Tafida, is opposed to the idea altogether. She wants him to study at a local university. Their argument is futile anyway because Tulba already has plans for him to become a veterinary surgeon and run the farm. Ibrahim's only hope to escape such a fate is to have

Uncle and nephew and a tangled web of emotions (*Return of the Prodigal Son*, 1976)

his uncle Ali intercede on his behalf. After having alienated all those around him, for reasons none of them can understand, Ali responds to Ibrahim's need and obtains a passport for him. Tulba, however, will have none of it. He tears up the passport and dashes his son's hope. When Ibrahim finally gets his wish and rides out of town with Tafida beside him, it is the grandfather who is in the street waving him goodbye. 'Go ... go ... with godspeed,' he says, again his eyes moist.

The third good person is Fatma, who is not an immediate member of the Madbouli family. Her sister was married to Tulba, and both are the grandmother's nieces. But her attachment to the family is based on financial and emotional reasons. She has loaned the Madbouli family a great sum of money, which Tulba has invested in his factory. More importantly, she is in love with Ali, the handsome and educated younger son who was framed by his bosses and ended up in prison. She waits for him for twelve years, suffering in her loneliness yet hoping that one day he would marry her. The waiting is compounded by the fact that Tulba, now a widower, wants her for himself. Jealous and depraved, he rapes her in the hope of forcing her to become his wife. The rape occurs before the film begins, but it haunts her and sours her attitude towards the whole family. When she demands her money back so she can leave, the mother tells her it is all tied up in the factory and untangling finances is not that simple. The old woman even tries to persuade her to settle for Tulba, reciting all the advantages such a marriage would entail, and forgetting that Fatma has no feelings for Tulba.

'Frankenstein' the mother may be, but she pales in comparison with Tulba. There is not a shred of decency or human kindness in him. His gruff manner and tyrannical control of his workers make them yearn for Ali who is everything that he is not. But Ali has been in prison ever since the contracting company he worked for sacrificed him as a scapegoat to escape financial ruin. In the meantime, they (the workers) have to slave under the tyrant Tulba who 'never bought a nail' for equipment maintenance, yet demands perfect performance of his technicians. Always walking with stick in hand, ready to smite anyone who might oppose him, he dismisses loyal employees at a whim and changes his mind only if compelled. His treatment of his family is just as beastly. From his abuse of his father, to his son, to Fatma – we glimpse a twisted man. Even his sarcasm is vulgar and mean-spirited. When Tafida, Ibrahim's girlfriend, defends her father in one of their many disputes, he turns to his son and says, 'What's the matter, Ibrahim? Aren't you satisfying her?' If Tulba, who can neither run his home nor his business, is representative of the new class of bourgeoisie, then Egypt is in serious trouble.

Fiction and reality

Allowing that *Prodigal Son* is rich with allusion and susceptible to multiple readings, Ali Abu Shadi suggests that Tulba might be perceived as a bitter Gamal Abdel Nasser. This is an inescapable assumption. He cites many similarities between the two, such as: their military background, their neglect of factories, love of cowboy movies and tyrannical style of management.[17] A scene in which Tulba is honoured is photographed in sepia colour as a parody of the recent past; and the accolades that Tulba receives and the way he moves summon Nasser to mind. Tulba is no Nasser, though. He lacks the one fundamental characteristic that is perhaps Nasser's primary source of political strength. Nasser's charisma was so dominant, his charm so appealing, that he seemed to hypnotise people. Their love for him exceeded the love for any human being in recent memory. Tulba is unsympathetic. A more likely scenario is that Tulba and Ali are the two sides of Nasser, representing him before and after the crushing defeat. Together they might be closer to who he really was. Ali is an idealist, handsome, patriotic – as Nasser was in his prime. Ali spends twelve years in prison and comes out changed. He is no longer recognised by family or friend. It is no accident that the duration between 1956 (the year of Nasser's triumph during the Suez War) and 1967 (the year of his fall from grace after the Six Day War) is a similar period – eleven years. In those eleven or twelve years Nasser lost his way; Ali confesses to his mother, 'I wasn't looking for glory. I was looking for my self. I found it and lost it.'

Other similarities suggest that Ali is the younger Nasser, and Tulba is the older Nasser. In one scene Fatma appeals to Ali to help Ibrahim in his ordeal with Tulba. Ali promises to do so, reminding her that one should use 'a little patience, a little wisdom and a little diplomacy'. Such stratagem could have been uttered by Nasser himself in his early days. Ali marries the daughter of the contractor for whom he works, but the two have no children. When one of the sloppily built buildings collapses, the unscrupulous contractor protects his company by accusing Ali of miscalculations, and he, Ali, is incarcerated. In the meantime he gets a divorce. This is political allegory. The truth is yet to be known about the behind-the-scene manoeuvres by the big powers prior to the Six Day War, but hints exist that implicate the Soviets for having provided Egypt with disinformation that led to the disaster.[18] A power game of the highest level was being played behind Nasser's back. Did the Soviets sacrifice Egypt for their own ends? Were they the father-in-law in the film who, for his own self-interest, 'framed' his son-in-law? Was the wedding to the contractor's daughter an analogy to Egypt's intimate relationship with Moscow? Certainly both marriage and political association were barren. Then there is the scene at the end of the film when Ali helps Ibrahim break out of jail to help him get out of the country and study abroad. Before he leaves, Ibrahim walks straight towards Ali, looks him in the eye and blurts, 'Look, if you're waiting for me to thank you for my freedom, forget it. My freedom is my right, not a gift from you.' This is not the language a teenager uses with his uncle who has just helped him escape imprisonment. This is Egypt's youth addressing Nasser and his regime: freedom is our birthright. Then, of course, Ibrahim rushes towards Ali and they both embrace. Even in their misery, Egyptians (and the Arab masses) cannot alienate themselves from Nasser.

Part of the complexity in Chahine's films stems from his investing the same character with different motivations. An example of this is the character of Fatma. The actress playing her says that Chahine prepared her for the part by explaining that Fatma is both a woman and a symbol of Egypt. Fatma, then, is not only a woman waiting for her lover but another Bahiyya waiting for her saviour: warm, loving, faithful, patient and rebellious. At the end, it is Fatma who kills Tulba. She invested in his business ventures, suffered from his physical abuse, but when he tries to destroy the whole family she is not above delivering the spear that kills him.

In Chahine's cinema, the good characters are usually the ordinary people. Besides the three already mentioned (grandfather, Ibrahim, Fatma), the good people in *Prodigal Son* are the factory workers and the family of one key employee: Hassouna. They are all decent human beings doing their job and minding their own business under Tulba's unbearable supervision. When they voice their grievances, they do so through their leader: a kindly smallish man with a non-Egyptian accent - he is Tafida's father. He and his family and the Madboulis are old friends. They rejoice as though they are blood relatives when Ali is released from prison. Baffled by Ali's indifference, they blame it on his need for a period of adjustment. But when he proves to be truly changed and unresponsive to their grievances, they stand up to him and demand their rights. Like her parents, Tafida is sweet and full of common sense. She even gets better grades than Ibrahim, the privileged son of the rich family. She loves him, wants him and will suck the poison out of his leg when a scorpion bites him — but she will not succumb to his flirtation or let him push her around.

Significantly, Tafida is played by a Lebanese actress / singer and Hassouna is played by an Algerian actor. Perhaps Chahine cast them to enlarge his audience in the Arab world. Perhaps they were the best talent available to him at the time, though unlikely, for Egypt's talent pool is considerable. By widening the scope of his film, Chahine is intimating that the social and political problems facing Egypt are also facing the Arab world in general. He is warning that the conditions are rife for widespread upheaval. His warning turned out to be accurate. While the film was still in production, Egyptian students stormed the streets, and a savage civil war erupted in Lebanon.

Prodigal Son, which Abu Shadi terms a 'satire on the Revolution and a eulogy for the Left',[19] cannot be mentioned without reference to its songs. Viewers are at first puzzled by their inclusion in a serious drama. Critics often accuse Chahine of mixing genres for commercial considerations. Yet a song in a Chahine film is rarely gratuitous: it is an integral part of the film's fabric. *Prodigal Son* would suffer immeasurably without Salah Jahin's lyrics, set to stirring music and superbly performed. They all add meaning and power to the saga of a nation on the brink of calamity. The song 'The street belongs to us', sharpens the division over the ultimate

authority in Egypt, for both government and the younger generation
appropriate the street to themselves.²⁰ 'The promise was yours; the dream
was ours' sums up the bond that once existed between Nasser and his people. 'What's gone is gone, and not much is left' echoes the feeling of incon-
solable masses. Yet the same masses do not lose hope entirely. In one of
the most poignant songs in the film, Majda al-Roumi (Tafida) projects
optimism despite all the misery around her when she sings, 'What shall we
do when we part our ways / Except look ahead at the sun of our dreams /
And find it penetrating the thick clouds.' And with a tear in her eye, she
adds: 'The birds still fly / The bees still buzz / The Child still laughs / Even
though not all people are happy.' Here again Chahine puts the song to its
optimal use, encapsulating an era and enlightening a generation.

Impact

To an Arab, the bloody denouement is inevitable. The horrendous state of
affairs, and the rising action within the film itself, point to one conclusion
– disaster. To a non-Arab, it is a concession on the director's part.
However, ending the film any other way would have been unsatisfactory.
This kind of resolution is crucial to the punch Chahine wishes to deliver:
unless social injustices are rectified, Egypt will be engulfed in a bloodbath.
Even the flourish with which the murders occur is not a concession to popular taste. It is part of the construction and the expressionist visual design
that Chahine chooses in telling his tale. A mere few shots and one stabbing
would be too limpid for the horror that Chahine envisions. Nor would a
pile-up of bodies communicate the outrageousness he strives to create.

The clown who frames the film does not mitigate the bleakness of its
reality. On the contrary, the ambiguity of his presence magnifies the problem and posits many meanings. As a laughing-crying commentator on the
proceedings, he articulates the viewer's inner thoughts or sheds light on his
or her misgivings. The fool or jester who is wiser than the wise is an old
archetype in world literature. As a Brechtian device, the clown reminds us
that we are watching a film rather than living a real experience. If Chahine
intends us to accept this alienation, it is only to say that the real problem is
too tragic to bear. The child protégé accompanying the clown gives the sit-

uation timelessness and universality. The biblical significance of the title becomes clearer. This, then, is a compression of the story of the prodigal son and that of Cain and Abel. The child clown will grow up to inherit the sins of his ancestors and to suffer without knowing why. That a metaphor can yield so many interpretations enriches *Prodigal Son*.

Five
Autobiographical Trilogy

> I am telling the same story over and over again,
> which is myself and the world.
> William Faulkner [1]

If Chahine's cinema is to be read as a microcosm of modern Egypt, Chahine himself must in turn be seen as a reflection of that image. As a major artist afflicted with insecurities and anxieties, he embarks here on a dual search for his own identity and that of his nation. By first understanding and liberating himself from his own demons, he emerges as a more credible observer of Egypt as she tries to recover her bearings.

What is startling about this trilogy, from an Arab perspective, is that it exists at all. It is unprecedented in the annals of Arab cinema for an artist to bare his soul for the whole world to see. Writers have written autobiographies, but only a few. But there is a vast difference between a book of modest sales potential and a larger-than-life film that will be seen by millions. Asked if his trilogy is semi-fictional, Chahine replies: 'No. It used fiction as little as possible and only in keeping with dramatic necessity. Most scenes were real and lived'.[2]

Though probably not contemplated in advance as a series, each film is instigated by some crisis in Chahine's life that leads him to psychoanalyse himself. In the process we are privy to illuminating information about three stages of his development as a man and an artist. By trailblazing cathartic cinema in the Arab world, Chahine made it possible for other directors to delineate their own personal experiences. Ali Abu Shadi cites the following examples: *Man of Ashes* by the Tunisian Nuri Bouzid; *Dreams of the City* by the Syrian Muhammad Malass; *Halfaouin* by the Tunisian Ferid Boughedir; *Houseboat No.70* by the Egyptian Khairy Bishara; *Summer Thefts* by the Egyptian Yousry Nasrallah; and *Stars in Broad Daylight* by the Syrian Osama Muhammad.[3]

al-Iskandariyya ... Leh? (Alexandria ... Why?, 1978)

Still considered one of Chahine's greatest achievements, *Alexandria ... Why?* is a complex film with five strands that span a period just before the battle of al-Alamein, in 1942, to 1947 when he left to study abroad. It is a mark of his creative power that he can sustain the labyrinthine narrative and weave the five subplots with each other without losing the viewer. And in so doing he creates a milieu, evokes a period and populates them with believable characters.

The film opens with documentary footage from Leni Riefenstahl's *Triumph of the Will*, celebrating the Nazi congress in 1935. Yahia and his friends are in a cinema watching a movie. A voice-over informs us that it is 1942, and Rommel is already in al-Alamein. We are in Alexandria, and the beaches are alive with vacationers who are totally oblivious to the battle raging at their western border. The idyllic scene is juxtaposed with some skirmishes between British soldiers and Egyptian youths and with footage from a Hollywood film showing Esther Williams swimming. From Esther Williams we cut to a close-up of Hitler, declaring 'Alexandria is mine'. Egypt, there-

Alexandria, Chahine's birthplace and favourite city

fore, is subjected to three western forces: British occupation, American cul-turalisation and German invasion. If the natives are not fighting soldiers in the streets, they are watching Gene Kelly singing 'Stairway to Paradise', and marvelling at Busby Berkeley's musical extravaganzas. The Egyptian soldiers in the audience are impressed. 'Those Americans are devilish,' one says. Another asks, 'Will the Americans help us get rid of the British?'

The threat of foreign intrusion, coupled with the absence of indigenous political leadership, finds most Egyptians adrift. As Egypt becomes a the-atre of possible identities, each casts his net in different waters. Those who prospered under the British still favour them. Others see salvation in the Americans, for one says, 'You can't go wrong befriending Roosevelt.' Still others are willing to welcome the Germans, if only to get rid of the British. A few even pin their hopes on Mussolini, for a coffee-house customer declares, 'Tomorrow Mussolini will come riding on a white horse and put an end to all this oppression.' This is followed by a montage of bombs and destruction. Families hasten to escape with a few pieces of furniture piled up on a wagon pulled by a donkey. As Mussolini's supporter is arrested and hauled off to prison, a fat woman makes an obscene gesture to express her opinion of Mussolini and his admirers. During all this chaos, some Egyptian ladies still make afternoon social visits for tea and cookies, with one of their parrot-like toddlers reciting a speech about the 'rights of man'.

The Egyptian youth are the first to rebel against such conditions. In a distant corner of Alexandria, young men are conspiring to assassinate Churchill who is expected to arrive in the city. A thug who stole a briefcase containing the itinerary and important maps, refuses to hand them over for an inadequate payment. 'Ten pounds to kill Churchill?' he asks, in disbe-lief. 'What a bunch of fools.' In another part of town, two young patriots meet with an old Muslim cleric at a mosque. They talk of armed struggle and he tries to convince them to join the Muslim Brotherhood. He also tells them that the Prophet had a high opinion of Egyptian soldiers because they were believers. At the end of the war, Eisenhower, Churchill and De Gaulle loom big on the screen. Westerners dance in the streets. To Chahine it is a western war over western interests. Why then is Alexandria made a stage for their battling armies?

A modest Egyptian family

Lawyer Qadri and his wife have two teenage children. The wife's outspoken mother lives with them. They live in a rented apartment above a nightclub. Qadri is a lawyer who is more interested in fishing than in practising law. Their daughter is pretty and of marriageable age. Yahia, her brother, dreams of becoming an actor. On the surface this is a bourgeois family. Qadri cannot be faulted, save for his excessive innocence. His attractive and much younger wife is always tastefully dressed. Except for the grandmother's caustic remarks, there is no blemish on this family. What binds them together is their love for each other.

Their apartment is small and overly furnished, but brimming with life. Men play cards and the women serve them food and drinks. Yahia tries to study but cannot concentrate on account of the loud voices. The poker players argue incessantly. Sirens blare down the street. Soldiers come to the downstairs door asking for girls, mistaking the apartment for a brothel. The women are shocked.

Qadri's scruples lead to a major financial crisis. A client came to him to handle her divorce case; instead of taking it, he told her to go home and make up with her husband. She left his office and headed straight to another lawyer who took her case and her money, lost the case for her and blamed it on the crooked judge. The landlord is threatening eviction. In their bedroom Qadri and his wife sit alone and discuss their predicament. 'And at a time like this,' he complains, 'Yahia wants to be an actor instead of pursuing a steadier profession.' His wife is less opposed, perceiving acting as an escape from poverty. Silence lingers. Qadri takes a deep sigh and asks, 'What have we done in life to come to this?' 'Perhaps we've lived beyond our means,' she answers, 'you've always had high standards.' She then holds up the letter from the landlord and he grasps the message. His immediate concern is the children. She assures him that they know nothing. When she mentions the word dignity, his eyes become misty. 'Where's the dignity when people see the furniture coming down the stairs?' At that moment, their two children burst into the room. Their parents engage them in banter and laughter. Warm feeling permeates the scene as the parents shield their children from worry.

Saladin (1963), Chahine's first epic and one of his most popular films

The kind father and scheming wife of *Return of the Prodigal Son* (1976)

In *Prodigal Son* (1976), Fatma longs for Ali's return only to find herself trapped at home

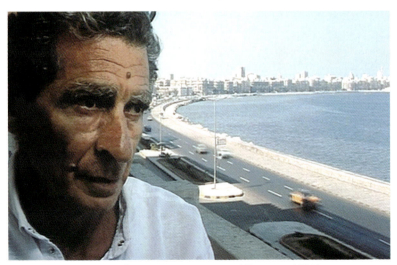

Chahine in Alexandria (*Alexandria Again and Forever*, 1989)

Beautiful and talented Yousra portrays a woman full of desire in *The Emigrant* (1994)

The gypsy tavern keeper and her poet/singer husband who is stabbed by the fundamentalists in *The Emigrant* (1994)

With *Adieu Bonaparte* (1985), Chahine embarked on a long line of co-production work with the French

A war profiteer ready to seize any opportunity that will satisfy his greed (*Alexandria ... Why?*, 1978)

An idealistic female journalist exposes a woman's scam after having fallen in love with her son (*The Other*, 1999)

A fabulously wealthy couple planning to defraud the public in the name of religion (*The Other*, 1999)

Twelfth-century philosopher, Ibn Rushd, believed that 'ideas have wings' and cannot be suppressed (*Destiny*, 1997)

After abandoning *Hamlet*, Yahia considered filming *Alexander the Great* (*Alexandria Again and Forever*, 1989)

Chahine's life on display, especially his love for the American musical (*Alexandria ... Why?*, 1978)

Financial difficulties and their son's determination to become an actor anguish his parents (*Alexandria ... Why?*, 1978)

Yahia (Chahine) recites a scene from *Hamlet*, with which he becomes obsessed for the rest of his life (*Alexandria ... Why?*, 1978)

A single beam of light penetrates Chahine's gloom in *Alexandria Again and Forever* (1989)

Fifty years of a distinguished career and still smiling

Impoverished as he is, Qadri remains ethical. When a young nationalist named Ibrahim is arrested, a friend of his comes to engage Qadri to defend him. They would not be able to pay anything except court costs. Qadri accepts, grinning and gesturing with his hand to indicate their mutual help-lessness. Mahmoud el-Milligi's performance is brilliant in its economy and precision of body language. Prisoner Ibrahim rejects Qadri's willingness to defend him. He is so bitter that he orders him out of his prison cell.

> 'Why?' Qadri asks, bemused. 'Are you afraid I might win the case for you? Let me assure you I won't. They'll sentence you to hard labor. The chances are 99 per cent I will lose it, and for the millionth time they'll say a jackass defends a jackass.'
>
> 'If you know all this,' Ibrahim asks, 'then why are you here?'
>
> 'To let off steam,' Qadri admits. 'You might say a nice word, a reporter might give us a kind remark, a judge might utter a word of courage. This will be a breathing spell for all of us. At a time when they decide to drop bombs on people's heads – people who have nothing to do with the war – and you expect me to win your case? At a time when they throw people in the ovens because their skin color is red or black or their eyes are slanted – and you expect me to win it?'

Qadri's sardonic speech reveals Chahine taking a broader view of suffering. Later on, when the judge pounds the gavel and says, 'The court has decided …' Qadri rises from his chair and starts to leave without even glancing at the judge. He already knows that he has lost the case. Verdicts are preordained.

Yahia and his dream

If *Alexandria … Why?* must be assigned a protagonist, then it is Yahia, although he is the main character in only one of the film's five segments. But he is a dominant figure, and his pursuit of his dream is endearing. Quickly scenes begin to etch Yahia's character. Inside the house he is prac-tising at the piano. His mother disapproves of what he is doing and asks him to concentrate on his studies. He leaves the living room in a huff and runs into his attractive teenage sister, whom he compares to Hedy Lamarr. The two dance to a Strauss waltz. His infatuation with the American musical is evident. At school, Yahia gives a powerful rendition of a scene from *Hamlet* in which the young prince confronts his mother. The British teacher is so impressed that he pulls him out of the classroom by the hand, takes him to the teachers' lounge and asks him to repeat his performance before the surprised teachers. Then we find Yahia and his fellow students putting on a play – a satire on Hitler's invasion of Italy. Swastikas are painted everywhere, and there is a pizza stand as well as a sign advertising Vino Rosso. Yahia is playing Hitler, and his foot soldiers are practising the goose step. In the audience is the British ambassador (with an Egyptian movie star inappropriately cast in the role). Before the curtain rises, the ambassador receives a note informing him that the British forces are pushing to al-Alamein to stop the Germans. Relieved, he whispers the information to the fawning pasha next to him.

The play includes a significant elliptical sequence depicting three different conceptual approaches to the subject at hand: documentary footage of an actual battle, a scene from a war film and then the play itself (about war) that Yahia is staging. This abrupt shifting from one medium to another shows the potency of manipulation. Chahine here gives us three ways of looking at the same event. His power to select and arrange the event and the interpretation of that event becomes a fourth way of looking at the same thing. Here two dramatic mediums are reflecting reality. The real battles are controlled by the generals; the film within the film is controlled by the film director; the stage play is controlled by the theatre director; and by his own power of selecting what to include or to exclude, Chahine is establishing the film director as a commander.

Chahine compounds his strategy by showing Yahia first playing Hitler and then a Saudi shaykh sitting on a sand dune, resting his elbow on a big cash register, setting oil prices and allowing the Egyptians 50 per cent discount because they are fellow Arabs. Germany's conflict with the Allies over Arab oil flashes before the viewer's eyes, but the implications resonate far beyond reel time. Such weaving of ideas and concepts enriches a Chahine film, yet at times renders it difficult to follow. Youthful Yahia could not have envisioned such an imaginative skit; rather, it is Chahine speaking from the vantage point of his fifty-two years. On the other hand, this sequence can be read as young Yahia's indulgence in fantasy: his dreaming of going to Hollywood; his comparing his sister to Lamarr; and now his interpretation of war – are all signs of his projecting himself as an artist.

Obsessed with becoming an actor, Yahia spends all his waking hours in pursuit of his dream. If he is not at the cinema watching yet another American film, he is at a palace trying to convince a nameless princess to sponsor his next stage production for a benefit. When she nods consent, he walks out of the meeting as though in a trance. Convincing a princess, however, is easier than convincing his father. When the boy encounters him while fishing, he finds no encouragement. His father tells him that he and the family are tired of being poor; therefore, he wants him to become an engineer and hold a steady job. Disheartened, Yahia replies that he wants to be an actor. The next scene reveals Yahia's callousness. His distraught mother returns from the Valley of Mercy where she pawned her wedding ring. Instead of sympathising with her, he boasts, 'And I have just come back from a meeting with the princess. She's going to sponsor my show.' He gets his comeuppance when his theatrical production proves to be a fiasco. The princess, the pasha and everyone else walk out in the middle of the show. Yahia's parents are mortified. But the show goes on with or without an audience. Though the production is too lavish for him to attempt at his age, it does project his dream into the future.

Suddenly Chahine re-opens a wound from his own childhood and recreates the death of his brother, Albert. We see the grandmother going around the house babbling that he died because 'he burned Christ'. Yahia even hears her saying, 'Why didn't the younger one die instead?' Magically rendered and emotionally felt, the scene stands comparison with the portrayal of childhood in Bergman's *Fanny and Alexander* (especially in the closet scene) or Fellini's *8 ½* and *Amarcord*. Chahine captures it with such power because its memory festers even now that he is older.

Then we are treated to Yahia's first effort as a film-maker: an 8mm home-movie about his school days at Victoria College. The footage is screened at school, and the rich pasha is in attendance. The latter's presence is neither explained nor plausible, but can be read as another mani-

festation of Yahia's fantasy. An attractive girl admires the film and gives
Yahia the idea of studying at Pasadena Playhouse, at that time a famous
drama school in the United States. His family objects - a family friend
secures for Yahia a job at the bank. Still dreaming of becoming an actor,
Yahia threatens to kill himself if he does not get his wish. When his mother
calls his last show an embarrassment he retorts, 'That's why I need to study.
I want to know *why* it was an embarrassment.' He seeks the advice of an old
actress, and she tells him, 'God gave you talent and you must take care of it.
It does not belong to you – it belongs to everybody.'

When the letter of acceptance finally arrives from Pasadena Playhouse,
family and friends contribute money to make his travel possible. The last
shot in the film is of the Statue of Liberty. Below is a crowd of Ashkenazi
Jews in their traditional garb and long sideburns. Suddenly the music
changes to a Jewish chant. Lady Liberty is toothless and painted like a
whore. She opens her eyes and winks at Yahia, 'laughing at the boy's lovely
dream'.[4] Here again the viewer finds himself wondering why Chahine
departs from the vivid recollection of his youth. So far the film has juggled
memories, but now it projects the future. This scepticism toward America

Who is mocking whom? The end of *Alexandria ... Why?* (1978)

is unwarranted, and could not have been felt by the boy on the ship's deck. In 1947, America had not yet tilted her might against the Arabs. There was no Israel to nurture and spoil at her neighbours' expense. This is the older and embittered Chahine speaking, and it is a moment that is gratuitously grafted onto his evocative memoir. Ella Shohat describes the ending as '... mocking the power that substituted European colonial power after World War II, the United States, seen from a seventies perspective'.[5] In truth, who is mocking whom is debatable.

For the 'love' of Egypt

In 1942, the western presence is felt in the clubs of Alexandria. The night-club Chahine shows is packed with soldiers. American and French music blares over the hubbub and clamour. Even Marlene Dietrich's voice is heard singing 'Lili Marlene'. A young British soldier, Tommy Friskin, is weaving between tables, waving a bottle of whisky and offering a drink to anybody willing to talk to him. This likeable youth from Dover is lonely. Aware that next morning he will be shipped off to the war front, he circles the cabaret singing, 'There'll be joy and laughter ...'. His desire for companionship is

The universal potential for wickedness and tenderness (*Alexandria ... Why?*, 1978)

rebuffed and his generosity repaid with a beating. Blood covers his face. The thug who stole the briefcase containing Churchill's itinerary gets an idea. He plans to kidnap him and 'sell' him to an Egyptian dilettante who likes to buy and execute British soldiers, presumably out of patriotic duty.

Adil, the Egyptian who 'buys' Tommy, is an icy young aristocrat. His sister is married to a war-profiteering pasha whom he despises. At a party at the pasha's palace, Adil borrows a hundred pounds from his sister to pay for Tommy. Next morning Tommy is discovered asleep in Adil's bed, but Adil is sitting on a chair pointing a pistol at him. Apparently Adil is gay and he had sex with Tommy during the night, but his victim cannot remember. Adil's younger sister passes by, grasps the situation and flees in horror. Abiding by his original intention, Adil drives Tommy to a secluded area by the sea to execute him. He takes him out of the car, dumps his limp body over a railing and returns to the car for his pistol. At that moment, Tommy wakes up and joins Adil in the car. When he realises that Adil has, in fact, bought and killed soldiers before, Tommy rebukes him. 'You should love them, not shoot them. They are as lonely as the two of us are.' It is an effective scene, primarily because of Tommy's wholesomeness. They embrace, and Tommy kisses Adil on the cheek.

Just before leaving for the war front, Tommy gives Adil all his money since he will not need it any more. Again, Tommy chides Adil about killing others. 'Go in peace, damn you,' Adil tells him, unable to hide his affection. Tommy returns to the car and tells him, 'I don't care what I'm called. I only care that I care. You're a son of a bitch.' Adil replies, 'And I care to tell you, you're divinely vulgar.' The encounter has turned into a warm relationship. At the end of the film, Adil looks for his British friend and lover: he finds his grave in al-Alamein War Cemetery. The visit to the cemetery is moving, with the camera lingering even on the tombs of German soldiers. Off screen we hear Adil sobbing; on screen we are offered a powerful montage of the ruins of war. Chahine's anti-war empathy is unmistakable, yet he does not rule out wars altogether. Though cruel and dirty, they are sometimes necessary.[6] Meaningless epitaphs abound on the grave markers.

This strand of the film is perhaps the most realised. Presenting the British in three different dimensions, Chahine gives us a chance to consider the range of human capabilities. Introduced first to Hamlet, then to Churchill and then to Tommy — we are being moved by culture, politics and love. Those we admire could become our enemies, who in turn could become our friends. The potential for wickedness — as well as tenderness — is inherent in all nations or individuals. What is often missing is the wisdom to choose properly.

Egyptian Jews at home

Until Zionism began clamouring for the creation of a national Jewish home in Palestine, Jews lived throughout the Arab world in peace and harmony. As the hostilities intensified, many Jews opted to leave. It is a prosperous and contented Jewish family that Chahine depicts in this segment.

We are at the Sorels' home. Worried about the brewing hostilities, the rich patriarch is reluctantly considering leaving Egypt. Sitting in his well-appointed living room talking to a friend, he says that the Americans have discovered an ocean of oil under the sands of Saudi Arabia. They will need a local policeman to guard their interests. Their solution is to give Palestine

A prosperous Jew bemoans having to leave Alexandria and Egypt

Religion was not an issue between Jewish Sarah and Egyptian Ibrahim

to the Jews. Then he declaims like an Old Testament prophet: 'O, Jerusalem! O, Holy Land! You have allowed brother to kill his brother. O, Jerusalem! You are the killer of prophets and the innocent.' The role is suitably played by the grand old man of Egyptian theatre, Yusuf Wahbi, whose forte is such rhetoric.

The Sorel family is not trouble free. The widower patriarch has a young daughter, Sarah, and a son, David. Both are in their late teens. Sarah is in love with Ibrahim, an Arab her father admires. She visits Ibrahim in prison and informs him that she is pregnant with his child: he tells her not to abort and that she should name the baby after him, even if it is a girl. In another scene, the father tells Sarah that he has decided that they should all leave for South Africa, but eventually settle in Haifa. Sarah replies that she cannot leave for she is carrying Ibrahim's child. Her intimacy with an Arab does not seem to bother him.

Of the five strands in the film, this is the least realised. The characters are one-dimensional and we never see them grow. The drama happens off screen. In one scene, they are on the deck of the ship. Over a close-up of his weary face, we hear the father lamenting:

Alexandria has become for me all my life. It's not because my relatives and my people have lived here for centuries. My childhood and all my thoughts spring from here. And your mother, my darling, is buried here. And what's being asked of me is to throw away my life and all of my memories behind me and roam the world.

After spending a few years in South Africa, Sarah again visits Ibrahim in prison. With her is their little son, Ibrahim, who is fair like his mother. When her lover comments on the baby's complexion, she smiles and assures him, saying: 'Believe me, Ibrahim is from Ibrahim.' Then she talks about how she has missed Egypt, adding, 'Egypt is all goodness and her people are gentle and kind.' Upon hearing that Qadri had defended Ibrahim without pay, she goes to pay him for his services. But Qadri declines to take her money. Had she come a day or two earlier, when they were scrabbling for money to send Yahia abroad, he might have accepted. Now he does not need it. Touched, she tells him that she had always hoped to find a man who would say 'No', and he was that man. Qadri talks to her about needing to keep one's head high.

Hostile reaction

No sooner had the film been shown, than a fresh controversy erupted and made its release impossible throughout the Arab world. But it was timing, not complexity, that seemed to conspire against it. Because the film's release coincided with President Sadat's trip to Jerusalem, '... the film was banned by several Arab countries, even though it was approved by the Palestinian organizations'.[7] Questioning whether the time was ripe yet to speak of tolerance and forgiveness (supposedly between Arabs and Israelis), Chahine replies:

> I started writing this script four years ago, and began making plans to pro-
> duce it a year and a half ago .... My film has nothing to do with [recent] polit-
> ical developments. In all my life I've never been prejudiced. Anyone who
> looks carefully will find the roots of my new film in my earlier film, Saladin.
> Ever since I've been advocating tolerance. I am for peace [but it has to be]
> just peace.[8]

Some authors parcel parts of their life experiences over several books, in hopes of saving enough material to sustain a literary career. Chahine does the exact opposite. He pours everything he has to offer into each of his films, as though it might be his last. Besides the cinematic mastery, what drives *Alexandria ... Why?* and gives it richness is his apparent need to unburden himself. The film's complexity recalls a remark Chahine (playing himself) makes in *Alexandria Again and Forever*. Preparing an actor to play a part, he uses the colloquial word *tirkeebah*, which means layered or mounted. Using perhaps his own multifarious personality as a model, Chahine succeeds in re-creating his youth and Egypt's political and social mosaic in the 1940s, by endowing each of his *dramatis personae* with a montage of conflicting emotions.

Hadduta Misriyya (An Egyptian Story, 1982)

If *Alexandria ... Why?* can be described as an external look at the early stage of Chahine's life, *An Egyptian Story* is an internal look at him as an artist besotted with a need to confront the demons in his past. Chahine himself plays the role of a film director named Yahia Shukri Murad. Like Chahine,

Scenes from a marriage: Yousra and Nour el-Cherif in *An Egyptian Story* (1982)

he is an inveterate smoker and an indefatigable task master, sometimes working his actors and crews till three o'clock in the morning. Estrangement from his wife and the onslaught of a heart attack do not come as a surprise. At the age of fifty-two Chahine did have a heart attack which gave him time to meditate about his life and accomplishments.

From the beginning Chahine insinuates that this is not merely an account of his life, but also a premonition about Egypt's future. Between takes and just before he collapses from the heart attack, he auditions a new singer. The lyrics are explicit:

> We don't accept letting people crush each other
> Who is sane among us, and who is crazy?
> Who is the victimizer, and who is the victimized?
> Who sells his conscience and buys destruction?
> I care about the human being.
> Egypt, I am worried about you.
> O bewildered masses!
> This is the story: the Egyptian story.

Yahia the child swims out of his mother's womb to confront his older self

The trial

Several scenes stress that Yahia is Chahine himself. Although he goes to London for medical treatment, Yahia opts for an Egyptian surgeon. The decision is consistent with Chahine's loyalty to Egypt. In the doctor's waiting room, a young boy from Saudi Arabia recognises him. 'Your best film is *Cairo Station*,' he tells him. While under anasthesia, and facing imminent mortality, Yahia puts himself and his family on trial. The film provides a series of extended flashbacks to a court room, designed to look like a chest cavity, with the rib cage and all the arteries. The science-fictional 'delivery' sequence reminds us of Woody Allen's parody *Everything You Always Wanted to Know About Sex but Were Afraid to Ask*, in which a sperm travels throughout a woman's reproductive system.

The only witness to emerge out of Chahine's innermost thoughts is a handsome but feisty boy of about ten. Taking the stand, he tells the judge that he is Yahia at that age. Asked why he is there, he answers, 'I want to kill him in order to get rid of him. He's been trying to kill me for fifty years.' The boy is followed by a humourless elementary school teacher who fashions himself after Hitler. In a flashback within the flashback the teacher slaps Yahia in class and goes on to rotate a large globe as Chaplin does in *The Great Dictator*. Here Chahine treats us to some Christian iconography: from a crown of thorns to a nail being driven into the palm of a hand. Echoes of Fellini's *8 ½* and Fosse's *All That Jazz* are again unmistakable.

The women in Yahia's life

Fellini returns to mind when we are introduced to Yahia's women, only to discover their claim on him. His mother is an attractive and well-dressed woman in her early forties. Another flashback within a flashback takes us to an earlier scene in their life. At a birthday party for him, little Yahia watches her flirting with a man. When he confronts her she accuses him of lying and in turn he calls her a liar. She storms out of the room, saying, 'I'm sick of all of you.' Later on she tries to justify her behaviour. By the age of eighteen she already had two children and nothing else to look for in life. She was married to a man thirty years her senior, whom she respected and admired but did

In a flashback Yahia confronts his mother

not love. On their wedding night she was ignorant of the facts of life. What transpired between them in bed was nothing short of rape.

Back in court, we see the first clash between Yahia's wife and sister. When the wife tells the court that the teacher's slap had scarred her husband, the sister cannot keep quiet. 'Your husband?' she sneers. 'He's just a provider for you. My brother didn't need a wife, he needed a mother. You're his mother.' His real mother is shocked. 'You put her in my place?' she protests. The three women get into an argument. As they raise their voices and point fingers at each other, little Yahia drops a crystal in one of the many tubes before him. He will do this throughout the film, illustrating that these quarrels are what is clogging his arteries. As the argument intensifies, Yahia's condition on the operating table worsens. The sister senses it and screams, 'My brother is going to die.' The mother screams, 'May I die before him.' What Yahia is suffocating from is too much love.

Yet the women continue with their recriminations. Once more the mother tries to defend her past actions. 'I was a mother twice by the age of eighteen,' she tells them. 'Is it right for life to end when a woman is only eighteen? Is it right for a woman to be deprived of her desires and feelings

Yahia (Chahine) is suffocating from too much love

when she is only eighteen?' The confession prompts her daughter to ask, 'Why didn't you learn from all this? Why were you in such a hurry to get me married off?' Her sister-in-law explains in answer: 'Because when the mother is thirty-four and the girl is eighteen, they need to be separated so they won't compete with each other.' True or not, the mother rushes her daughter's wedding to a rich but much older man, only two days after his father's death. She cannot wait for a respectful mourning period lest he change his mind. Her haste makes the daughter's complaint over the years more biting.

Almost absent from *An Egyptian Story* is Yahia's father. We never see him in a family setting, nor with any of the women around him. He has abdicated his role as the head of the family and withdrawn to himself. We only see him in two brief scenes with his son: in one, he says that he used to be the first in class and tells Yahia to excel in school; in the other, he mentions the circumstances of his daughter's wedding. Polishing a hunting gun, he adds that the well-off groom is able to supply her with all the nylon stockings she needs. 'Are nylon stockings everything in life?' Yahia asks. His father glares at him, then says, 'Ask your mother.'

Political echoes

Like most of Chahine's films, *An Egyptian Story* touches on politics. Even when the three women argue in flashback, Chahine injects his low opinion of the legal system. As the judge tries to silence the women, young Yahia objects to his objections. 'Who are you,' he asks, 'to keep telling us what to do?' The boy's effrontery shocks the caricature-like judge. 'This is what the State wants,' he fulminates. 'The State decides. The State's word is final. The State gives directions. All of you are *nothing*.' Incredibly, those in the court-room break out in applause. Another politically charged moment arrives when adult Yahia appears in court. He tells the judge that he is there to explain the plaintiff's case, for he knows him best. Then he turns to his mother once again, and asks, 'Do you want to keep certain behaviour of yours hidden even from your son?' Again she speaks of her youth, of her marriage at the age of sixteen to a man thirty years her senior whom she respected like a father. For ten years she did not step outside her house. When the sister again raises the question of her arranged marriage, Yahia reminds her that at eighteen she was old enough to have made her own decisions. When he was seventeen...! But his sister interrupts him. 'You're a boy,' she replies,

The finger of suspicion is pointed at the judge himself

During a political demonstration, Yahia is chased by soldiers

'and I'm a girl. They were worried that I might be raped by some English soldier.' To which Yahia retorts, 'At that time wasn't the whole country being
raped?' Suddenly the film cuts to stock footage of discredited King Farouk in
a crowded street. This is followed by a demonstration in the street. Army
officers stand on the balcony watching. One of them, fat and smug, looks
through his binoculars and gives orders to soldiers on horses to fire on and
club the demonstrators. Injured, Yahia hurls a stone that hits the commander on the balcony. He then runs into hiding, only to be seduced by a doctor's wife who happened to be watching the scene from her own balcony. On
the street and in the bedroom, the Egyptian was prey to predators.

Yahia's quest

Chahine denies that the family in the film is his family in real life. In many
respects this is true. In life Chahine does not have any children; in the film
he does. The relationship between his real wife and sister is close; here they
are constantly bickering. Chahine is a devoted husband, and married to the
same woman for half a century; in the film he cannot wait to be away from
her. In life his wife is not a producer's daughter; in the film she is. Apart
from these changes, Yahia is Chahine. Chahine unmasks himself at the out-

set. His name and credit appear on the right side of the screen. On the left side he himself enters the frame to give directions to an actor. His half smile is beguiling: it identifies him with Yahia, yet reveals his apprehension about the viewer's reaction to his 'confession'. This becomes clearer as soon as the film begins. The director who is the subject of this film is directing *The Sparrow*, one of Chahine's best films.

To dispel any doubt that *An Egyptian Story* is autobiographical, Chahine includes earlier experiences in film festivals. In 1952, Yahia takes *Nile Boy* to Venice where it does not win. But an exchange between Yahia and a festival official disappoints him. He, the young enthusiast, is discussing art and ideas, and she bluntly brings him down to earth. Shocked, he tells her, 'Then it's a *souk*'. Nonplussed, she replies, 'Yes, it's a *souk*'. The mentality at Venice is no different from the mentality in Egyptian studios: cinema is an industry, film is a commodity and a festival is a marketplace. However, in 1959, the treatment he and his entourage receive in Moscow is heartwarming. Because *Jamila* condemns the French brutality in Algeria, the French government tries to suppress it. The film is shown nevertheless,

In Moscow, Langlois warns Yahia that France is trying to block screenings of *Jamila*

and the Soviets (still wooing the Arab world) shower Yahia and his entourage with so much attention that Abdel Hadi (in his friendly days) remarks, 'They're spoiling us'. But in Moscow a revelatory moment distinguishes Yahia from commercial cinema. He notices that the film's star and producer is wearing a red chiffon dress. As she rides in an open car and waves her red cape to the cheering Russians, he asks her why is she wearing a red dress. She stares at him then says, 'They're communists, you fool.' She, the producer, aims to please the crowds; he, the creator, aims to satisfy his own personal needs. Finally, Yahia concludes that for a film to win, artistic merits and international politics must complement each other. That same year, the Berlin Film Festival devastates him by denying him, due to an unfortunate stroke of misjudgment, the best actor award for his extraordinary performance as Kinawi, the cripple in *Cairo Station*.

An aspect from Chahine's life resurfaces: here he is a young man who aspires to be an actor and wants to study abroad. A second issue concerns his true identity. In this film we hear an exchange between Yahia and his mates that troubled Chahine throughout his career. Two of Yahia's friends come to class to inform him of the demonstration they are a planning to join. 'Come on,' one says to him, adding, 'Are you one of us or aren't you?' Yahia's face discolours. The other cajoles him to prove that he is an Egyptian. Of course he will join. Chahine, the son of Lebanese immigrants, desires above all else to be accepted as an Egyptian. And as we have seen, in London he chooses an Egyptian surgeon to operate on him.

Yahia's obsession is twofold: commitment to film art, and the pursuit of international recognition. He refuses to succumb to the demands of the marketplace, insisting that he is more than an entertainer. At one point he complains, 'You spill your guts out and no one wants to listen. Not here nor anywhere else.' Another time he explains, 'All my life I've tried to do the decent thing.' Even when he pitches a story to a producer he presents it in commercial terms, fully aware that he will turn it into something else. He does not want to 'sell dreams like Hollywood'. His is personal cinema – and a tool for social change. Even when the Algerians invite him to make films for them, he hesitates. 'How can I make films about a society I don't know,' he replies. Lesser directors would have jumped at the chance, but not Yahia.

Wife and children

Beautiful, loving and always supportive, Nadia still cannot please her husband. We never see her doing or saying anything wrong, yet he emotionally alienates himself from her. Even before they were married, she attended a film festival with him to cheer him on, to commiserate with him for not winning, to agree that Nasser's regime is neglecting the cinema industry and to boost his morale. Too poor to rent a car, they go sightseeing on bicycles, like two youngsters on a day out. By the road side she asks him, 'Are you going to marry me?' '*Allah yikhrib baytik*,' he answers, affectionately. 'Darn you, you took the words out of my mouth.' But he warns her: he is burdened with complexes, he is a nervous creature, sometimes thinks like a child, and desperately needs people to spoil him. She accepts him as he is. That night they attend a glamorous party given by a foreign movie star, and dance cheek to cheek. Wearing a chequered cap, like a Parisian, she holds on to him, dreamy and happy.

Her support of him over the years never wanes, even when she pricks his obsession with recognition by the West. 'For how long are we going to be preoccupied with the Germans and Americans?' she asks, hoping to disabuse his delusions. He responds by blaming her father for not winning the

Yousra as Nadia in *An Egyptian Story*: a demanding role

best actor award, and includes her among all those who are holding him back. The first time we see them together, he accuses her of causing the marriage to deteriorate. 'Is this the way things come to an end?' he snaps, putting all the blame on her. 'Can you let twenty years melt away just like that?' By the end of the film we know it was all his fault.

In that same scene his adolescent daughter tells him 'I need you', but he ignores her. The only time we see the children is as babies being powdered by their mother. Years later, we are shocked to see the daughter grown up and in jail with her boyfriend, on charges that are never explained. When Yahia tries to break up her relationship with the stranger in the cell with her, she resists, telling him that she values her love for her boyfriend more than his consent. He slaps her and literally pulls her out of jail, but fails to change her mind. Then, for the first time, we glimpse a haughty side of Nadia that brings Yahia's mother to mind. Furious at her daughter's 'affair' with a lower-class young man, she slams the car door, threatening, 'Tomorrow she's going to be married to her cousin, a doctor's son.' At a calmer moment, Yahia is reminded that in *Cairo Station* he was sympathet-

Adult and child, finally reconciled (*An Egyptian Story*, 1982)

ic with the young lovers who could not even say goodbye to each other prop-erly because of the social gap between them. Has his attitude changed? Yahia avoids the tricky issue, content to remark, 'I failed my children the way my parents failed me'.

Reconciliation

Curiously we do not see Yahia resolve his differences with any of the three squabbling women in his life. We must assume that a harmonious relation-ship with them is concomitant with the healing of a deeper emotional wound. His main problem has always been within himself, but its origin rests with the thorny relationship with these women. One of his friends tells him, 'You always alienate the ones who love you the most.' However, this is not true, for it absolves all those who had scarred his psyche. But now he seems unburdened.

Back at the hospital, ten-year-old Yahia takes his place in bed next to his older self. In a dream-like superimposition the two bodies merge. The nurse enters the room to inform Yahia that it is time for her to go home, saying that she hates to leave him alone. 'I'm not alone – not anymore,' he tells her, smiling. After the final fade-out, 'The End' is replaced by 'The Beginning'. Unencumbered, Yahia is ready to start life anew.

The question remains: how does Chahine correlate his personal drama with Egypt's, for he calls his tale *An Egyptian Story*. The song with which the film begins (snippets of which are heard throughout the film) makes it clear that this is not just a story of a troubled artist. The troubled artist is the offspring of an Egyptian family which is, as in most literatures, a micro-cosm of society. If Yahia is to live a normal life, he must be unshackled first. The tensions, the bitter quarrels and the deception that can be so crippling to the individual can also be crippling to a nation. Yahia's father should have been more assertive. His mother should have been less vain, and more sensitive to the feelings of a noble husband. 'I worry about you, Egypt,' the song says. One should, indeed, if there are many Yahias around, with emo-tional wounds begging for a healer.

* * *

al-Iskandariyya ... Kaman wa Kaman
(Alexandria Again and Forever, 1989)

Alexandria Again and Forever is perhaps Chahine's least accessible film, yet he himself says: 'I think it's my favorite.'⁹ While quirky and fantastical, its importance lies in the revelation of many key facets of Chahine's complex personality. In *Alexandria ... Why?* he deals with his youth and the pursuit of a dream. In *An Egyptian Story* he reviews his life as death becomes imminent. Here he is an internationally acclaimed film director, yet still shadowboxing his own demons. Thus, *Alexandria Again and Forever* is more like Fellini's *8 ¹/₂* than either of the other two films in the trilogy.

Synopsis

In *Alexandria Again and Forever*, Chahine's obsession with *Hamlet* is pronounced. The film begins again with a song, but this time it is a startling rendition of 'To be or not to be ...'. *Hamlet* sung in Arabic is a definite clue that we are embarking on a bizarre journey. Hamlet's problem is all too clear; Chahine's is yet to be gleaned. On the sound stage Yahia is directing *Hamlet*, which is more Egyptianised than adapted. A confused actor asks a fellow actor, 'Why is he so obsessed with Bahiyya? Why is he shedding tears and breaking his heart over her?' Again this recalls Hamlet's lines upon seeing tears in the player's eyes: 'What's Hecuba to him or he to Hecuba / That he should weep for her?' ¹⁰

As we have seen earlier, Bahiyya in Chahine's films is a romanticised symbol of Egypt. Here he is combining two of his obsessions, Hamlet and Bahiyya – obsessions that are central to this film. Because Chahine is 'writing a film and not a script',¹¹ *Alexandria Again and Forever* meanders in and out of subplots to the near confusion of the viewer. Its artistry is in the interweaving of incidents, cumulative effect of allusions, inner tempo of the telling and visual style. The basic story line depicts middle-aged Yahia, a prominent film artist. Though married, he has an attachment to his main actor, Amr, who suddenly decides to ditch both him and *Hamlet*. Yahia is confounded. Under pressure from his wife and his producer, he considers making a film about Alexander the Great instead. Some even suggest Cleopatra as a suitable subject. 'It's about time you had a woman play the

Chahine as actor

lead in one of your films,' his wife chides him. To fill the void that Amr has created in his life, Yahia flirts with Nadia, a spirited young actress. But his attempt is not entirely successful, for she senses his cynicism about love. In the meantime, the actors' union is on a hunger strike because of oppressive intrusion by the government. The film ends when the strike is over and Yahia and Nadia are reconciled.

One man and two women

Yahia is married to Gigi, a handsome lady with a winning smile. She is scarcely seen, but her presence (or absence) is acutely felt. We meet her at a difficult moment in Yahia's life. Amr is the most important person in his life. But Amr is disenchanted and wants out. 'People are talking,' he tells Yahia. 'People are jealous,' Yahia retorts. Amr is adamant. The thought of losing him renders Yahia apoplectic. Having eavesdropped, and now sensing that her husband might do something rash, Gigi walks into the room frowning. 'If you run after him,' she warns calmly, 'I will leave the house.'

Shaken by Amr's exit from his life and by the collapse of the *Hamlet* project, Yahia rushes to Alexandria. There he meets with his producer, a sympathetic young man who urges him to forget about *Hamlet* and to start thinking of another subject. Obsessed with the actor and the play, Yahia is unyielding. Then two men arrive to tell him that his wife has been hurt in an accident. He rushes to Cairo and to the hospital: Gigi is lying in bed, her leg in a cast. Yahia is attentive and loving. She urges him to attend the upcoming film festival abroad and not to worry about her. 'Take the boy [Amr] with you,' she tells him, 'and come back with an award. Go on.'

Thereafter, she rarely appears, being marginal in Yahia's life. Enter Nadia, the beautiful actress who fills the void Amr's departure left in his heart – if only temporarily. Eventually she too is dissatisfied, refusing to be 'an apartment for rent'. Yahia is in love with Amr, Nadia and Gigi all at once, and in this order. It is an unhealthy situation.

Song and dance

Some of the most delightful, yet baffling, moments in the film revolve around an operetta that Chahine stages in a film that is a hybrid of straight-

One of the largest musical scenes in cinema history: Chahine's *Alexandria Again and Forever*

forward narrative, *cinéma vérité*, formalism, expressionism and some animation. He slides in and out of each style with relative ease, but not always
to the viewer's satisfaction. The result is stimulating, its style fresh and
original - amazingly it all works.

Urged to stop thinking about *Hamlet*, Yahia turns his attention to
Alexander the Great, the founder of magnificent Alexandria from which he
himself hails. We are treated to a fantasy that covers a space considerably
larger than any sound stage on which Busby Berkeley, Vincente Minnelli or
Gene Kelly ever worked. In lieu of a spacious sound stage, Chahine is using
Alexandria's seashore and its environs. It is one of the largest musical
scenes in cinema history, as though to confirm Shakespeare's notion that
all the world is a stage.

Actually Yahia is not making a film about Alexandria, only contemplating the possibilities. Like Guido in Fellini's *8 ½*, Yahia is searching for an
idea that might tie up all the loose ends in his life. What we have here, then,
is a germ of a story. It is like watching a scene in an opera without knowing
the plot. We can guess but we cannot be sure. We see a great number of

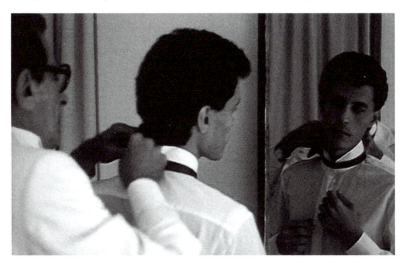

In happier times, when Yahia and his star were intimate (*Alexandria Again and
Forever*, 1989)

extras dressed up like Greek soldiers and generals; we see a large number
of actors dressed up in caps and gowns; we see the same people dressed up
like batmen; we see Yahia wearing a mask and dangling his feet in the
Mediterranean sea. And we are enchanted by lovely songs, yet we are not
certain what it all means. We see the actor playing Alexander (with his
plumes, shield and two horns) raised higher than the statue of Ramses. A
debate ensues as to Alexander's nature. Was he a god, demi-god or just a
conqueror? One character sings of his 'miracles' then quickly replaces it
with 'achievements' to escape the abuse of those around him. A robust
Egyptian *fellaha* sings a solo which includes the word 'mafia'. The diversity
of opinions is perplexing. Does the presence of the academics in the film
insinuate that the issue of Alexander's true nature is still unresolved? As
viewers we only know that Alexander is partially responsible for Yahia's
being what he is: for he had built a magnificent city which became a cradle
for many cultures which in turn had helped shape Yahia's character. 'If we
were wrong about him,' Yahia sings, 'then we've been had.'

The narrative is also augmented by three elaborate dances. The first is a
celebration of winning the Golden Bear at the Berlin Film Festival a decade
earlier. Those were the good days when Yahia and Amr were intimate. As

A homage to the American musical

A dance for every mood, here full of pain

they walk out of the theatre with their awards in hand, they break into a stylised dance, a homage to Fred Astaire and Ginger Rogers. It is pure Hollywood, as they dance to 'Walking My Baby Back Home'. Chahine has always fancied himself as a dancer and was enthralled by the MGM musical, – here he exhibits his considerable talent. The next dance is a solo by Amr, after having failed to win an award at another festival. By now his homo-erotic relationship with Yahia is at an end, and we find him alone twisting and turning on an outdoor floor, this time to the beat of a plaintive Egyptian song. The dance is erotic, for while he is writhing on his back a dozen foun-tains erupt in the background. The third number takes place in the heart of Cairo. Yahia is now courting Nadia. They are in a crowded bazaar where a carnival is in progress. Reminding him of his dictum that an actor must be able to dance, shoot, sing and ride horses, she coaxes him to practice what he preaches. He tells her, 'I danced in *Cairo Station*' (yet another proof that this is Chahine's story), but she is not satisfied. She wants him to dance now. He complies. Before he leaves the dance floor he is challenged to a stick dance, which is comparable to but more strenuous than fencing. Yahia's skill and physical strength are tested against those of a young and virile-looking man. It is a draw. Yahia has acquitted himself in Nadia's eyes. The dance sequences serve Chahine well on three levels. One, they demonstrate his love for the art of dancing. Two, they acknowledge his indebtedness to the Hollywood musical. Three, they dovetail with a convention in the Egyptian cinema. Like songs, dance is an intrinsic part of the tradition in most of the Egyptian films. By adhering to local taste, Chahine demonstrates his idealism and a pragmatism at the same time.

Fantasy and farce

While preparing for the film on Alexander, Yahia visits a plaster workshop where statues of ancient deities are on display. He has to choose a prototype for the Greek conqueror. Suddenly some of the statues come alive. One of them kicks a worker, another knocks him down, and a third pierces him until his blood spouts. In another scene Nadia climbs a huge statue and stands in a strikingly dramatic pose: one leg sticking out behind her, her golden hair highlighted like a halo and her flimsy costume blowing. Gigi is on the sound stage and Yahia turns to ask her opinion. She replies, 'It's inspired, but where does the wind come from?' 'We've installed a fan,' he answers, smiling. The flippancy is telling about Yahia's irreverence for things divine. Is cinema a sleight of hand? Is life itself an illusion? No matter, his cynicism is all embracing.

Disillusioned himself as a result of the break-up with Amr, he no longer believes in love. Most people, he thinks, make love with their groins rather than their hearts. This is conveyed in a plaster workshop when Yahia and Nadia copulate in the background behind a scrim screen. Utilising acceleration, Chahine simulates copulation at a record speed, with the makeshift bed zipping on coasters from left to right and right to left, as if driven by a machine. They laugh, tumble and satirise loveless sex. There is animation here too, for the climax is achieved when an electric garland on someone's forehead lights up like fireworks.

At one point in their relationship, Nadia suggests that he make a film about Cleopatra. Yahia is not interested. She calls it a great love story; he says it is not. She praises Cleopatra; he calls her a harlot. In a flashforward, Nadia plays Cleopatra. Elaborately costumed, she is about to make the ultimate sacrifice for her lover. Finding life unbearable without Antony, she

Nadia decides to run for her life

lets a viper poison her with a bite. Back to the present, Nadia questions
Yahia about the meaning of all this devotion. 'After all she did – this is not
love?' Yahia scowls. He argues that she committed suicide, because she was
afraid of being dragged through the streets of Rome as a harlot, not because
she was in love. 'Love!! It is a carousel that grinds you and moves on to grind
the next victim.' Nadia watches his tirade with trepidation. In another
flashforward Yahia treats us to his interpretation of the same play. Over
spectacular views of Alexandria's blue sea, we hear a well-known song
depicting the legendary couple. The singer intones, 'I'm Antonio ... and I
cannot live without love.' In the last shot of this musical episode, we see
Yahia, playing Antony, swimming towards a male swimmer. He surprises
him with an embrace and a kiss on the mouth, then calls him 'Cleopatra!' By
intimating that Antony was either capricious or bisexual, Yahia reduces the
legendary couple's love story to sheer lust. After listening to all this, Nadia
sobers up. Convinced that his cynicism is pathological, she tells herself,
'Escape!' And she runs for her life.

Occasionally we see a man dressed like Dick Tracy snooping around a
museum. He is a Greek archaeologist from Alexandria. Like all

Alexandrines, Yahia says, he is obsessed with love. Having discovered Alexander's empty tomb, the archaeologist is obsessed with finding the body. In a way he is like Yahia (or Chahine) who is obsessed with Hamlet and with the actor who was supposed to portray him. Each is searching for the one he loves. At the museum Omar is lying in a casket encased in glass. He is wearing Alexander's costume and helmet. Suddenly the ceiling splits, an auger descends and crashes into the encasement. It pierces Amr/Alexander until blood fills the screen. Samir Farid concludes that in this scene Chahine expresses his derision – even hatred – for Amr.[12] In truth, Yahia's impulsive reaction upon sensing danger is to jump in the casket to shield the one he loves.

The strike as metaphor

The longest subplot is a re-enactment of the general hunger strike of 1987. In protest against the government's unilateral decision to change the laws governing their own union, the actors barricade themselves inside their building for several weeks. They bring their suitcases, mattresses and fans, and demonstrate a solidarity unique in their history. They take shifts in

At the actors strike, Nadia and Yahia come to terms with their feelings for each other

going on hunger strikes, debate the principles of democracy, and exhibit solidarity. When a cabinet minister comes to discuss a recent decision, a famed actress and dancer, herself a respected nationalist, sneers at him, 'You mean the decision you've cooked behind our back.' And when the minister tries to persuade them to end the strike, promising that their grievances will be taken into consideration, cynical Yahia tells him, 'I guess we'll stay put where we are.'

Having herself given up on Yahia, Nadia seeks Amr in the hope of reconciling the two. She finds him working on low-rate television programmes, and still resentful of his relationship with Yahia. He informs her that he is married, has a family and owns a car. He admits that he still loves Yahia, then adds, 'Does he love me as I am, not as an image he is obsessed with?'

At the end of the strike, a large number of film stars, actors and professionals are assembled in a huge auditorium. Suddenly they all break out singing the national anthem. They are out of tune. Most of their voices are discordant. Operating the camera himself, Yahia is filming the unusual gathering. He spots Nadia and focuses on her. She slithers towards him, oblivious of all others. Her eyes locked on Yahia, she sings:

> I want to live the way I am
> I have my own personality
> My own identity
> I am free to do with my life as I wish
> Only love can overpower us.

Yahia responds with a song of his own, snatches of which we have heard early in the film:

> Look at him through my eyes
> You will find him to be the beautiful one.

We hear three songs sung simultaneously by the general assembly, symbolised by a shaky old actor struggling with words, and by both Nadia and Yahia who are embarking on romance. Their lyrics are different, their tunes

Reading the pulse and capturing the images of Egyptian society: Chahine in
Alexandria Again and Forever (1989)

are different, but in essence they are all singing the same song – it is about
a yearning for individual freedom. Thus the setting becomes a microcosm
of an Egyptian society that is decaying, regenerating itself and yearning for
love. Significantly, it is the motion picture camera, with Chahine himself at
the helm, that captures the nuances.

It is difficult to classify *Alexandria Again and Forever*. Rife with fantasy
and farce, straightforward narrative and stylised dances, it also posits a
large dose of realism. The strike sequence is *cinéma vérité* down to spraying
insecticide and picking up cockroaches. Samir Farid calls the film more of
a reconstructed memoir than a story.[13] Yet it is not even a conventional
memoir, but a blending of fact and fiction. Novelist Edwar Kharrat speculates on the subject of writing the self: 'I am only wondering whether these
imaginings of a writer are perhaps more authentically "biographical" than
what actually had "really" happened.'[14] Bearing this broad definition in
mind, we accept Chahine's trilogy as autobiographical, despite his departure from the known data of his life. Psychological disposition is the foun-

dation of one's character. Stripping Chahine of his thoughts, passions and musings would render him a mere shell of his true self.

Alexandria Again and Forever is a classically structured story of a dynamic character who goes through a crisis and emerges altered. In *Alexandria ... Why?* Yahia is a flat character in that he does not change. His only devotion is to become an actor. In *An Egyptian Story*, he does change in that he confronts his past and reconciles the differences between himself and the boy within him. And here too, he finally accepts Amr's desertion and embarks upon a new relationship. Yet the question of his wife remains unresolved, for she represents the one strand in the story that is open to speculation.

* * *

The issue of interiority in this autobiographical trilogy recalls many of Bergman's films and particularly Fellini's *8 ½*. The intimation of mortality is the driving force behind Fosse's *All That Jazz*: John Boorman's *Hope and Glory* also comes to mind, for it is explicitly autobiographical, with the young Boorman experiencing World War II. Chahine's trilogy differs from all these confessional films in that it casts a wider net. Chahine and Egypt are centre stage. By baring his soul, Chahine is inviting Egyptians to come to terms with themselves. Without being didactic, he appeals to Egypt to recognise that pluralism, variety and nonconformity can be vibrant and positive. The mix produces healthy individuals, without whom a healthy nation cannot exist. For Egypt to restore her equilibrium – if not her glory – Egyptians should be diverse in personal pursuit but united in national spirit. The welfare of the nation and that of the individual are inseparable.

Six
Historical Films

The past is never dead. It's not even past.
William Faulkner [1]

The controversies that surrounded Chahine's historical films were as incendiary as the attacks Oliver Stone received following his two films, *JFK* and *Nixon*. In response, Chahine seemed to defend himself by implicitly asking: whose version of history is to be trusted? Who is the custodian of the truth? Whereas lawyers can argue on both sides of an issue, historians can argue from a considerably broader perspective. Whose interpretation should we accept? Some historical facts are unassailable, but when do we stop reassessing the new evidence which each generation seems to uncover? The passage of time does not mitigate matters or guarantee veracity. Excavating biblical times is no less accurate than excavating recent past. Objectivity cannot always fill a gap or overcome a slant. The terrain is often slippery. Multiply these oppositional forces, and you will have a mosaic of personalities and events that contradict and vilify each other. In the end, it is folly, if not sheer hubris, for everyone to think that he or she has a monopoly on what actually happened. History is a construct devised by people, and we all have our motives and prejudices.

A number of contemporary historians have finally concluded that there is no purity in their profession. Even if the most scrupulous historian cannot hope to plumb its depth, why then should not film-makers project history according to their perceptions and not be chained to what some other 'authority' deems correct. Filtering the 'facts' through an artist's sensibilities cannot only be compelling but also revealing. Picasso's 'Guernica' depicted the horror of war better than all the histories written about the Spanish Civil War.

Chahine does not distort history as much as view it subjectively. His perspective, as it were, occasionally differed from those of others. Regarding history as a continuum rather than sequential episodes, he turned to the distant past to shed light on the immediate present. Like an endless but well-structured novel with interwoven tales, history foreshadows or triggers subsequent actions. Against this backdrop, Chahine focuses on the roots of many problems that plague modern Egypt. To understand contemporary Egypt, he draws parallels between then and now. Not surprisingly, he finds many pitfalls and shortcomings. Thus the collision with those of different persuasion.

Tentative steps

The history of the Egyptian historical film is slim. Ironically, one of the oldest civilisations on earth left it mainly to Hollywood to explore its glorious past. From the beginning Hollywood was eager to send her crews around the world to 'thrill' her audiences with exotic lands – and she found nothing nearly as dazzling as Egypt. Not even the love of ancient Rome could compare with her love for the Pyramids, Sphinx, mummies and the Valley of the Kings, not to mention Cleopatra. Ever since *The Sheik* (1921) starring Valentino, Hollywood lavished her attention on the region and tarnished the image of its people forever. For nearly a hundred years Hollywood has been portraying the Arabs, first as ignorant and lecherous and now as rich, decadent or fanatical people.

Certainly it was beyond Egypt's capabilities to put right this imbalance. Until the collapse of the monarchy in 1952 and the evacuation of the British in 1955, the authorities clamped down on the freedom of expression, particularly in the cinema. The Ministry of the Interior, which was then in charge of censorship, and the British officials would tolerate no film that hinted at the public's dissatisfaction with their rulers or was deemed to be threatening to the stability or the security of the country. The repressive climate during the 1930s and 40s obliged film-makers to eschew politics altogether. No one needed the aggravation, especially the commercial producers who were in the business for the money. Yet, there were a few attempts at using history as a source material. Marginal as they now seem, such films demonstrated that even then there were those who saw the potentiality of the historical film as a new genre. Three such films from that period are worth mentioning.

Shajarat al-Durr (1935) told the story of a legendary Egyptian queen who was married to the Ayyubi ruler of Egypt in the thirteenth century. In 1249, during the preparation for a battle against yet another Crusade, her husband died. Later on she 'was chosen by the army to rule over Egypt until her infant son was old enough to rule in his right'.[2] But when the Abbasid ruler (who, while in Baghdad, could appoint or dismiss Egypt's rulers) objected because she was a woman, she married a general to be her ruling partner. Before long, she had him killed for wanting to control the treasury.

There are good reasons for an Arab to be attracted to the story of *Salah al-Din al-Ayyubi* (*Saladin*), the twelfth-century hero who is still admired as much for his chivalry and magnanimity as for routing the Crusaders and liberating Jerusalem. Unfortunately, the cinematic treatment he received in 1941 was crude. The film was produced by Ibrahim Lama and starred his brother Badr Lama, who fancied himself as Rudolph Valentino. Concocted by a minor poet, the script bore no resemblance to historical facts. The standard of production hit a new low when it was discovered that the film-makers had bootlegged footage from Cecil B. DeMille's scenes of the same battles, which gave the Arab soldiers 'foreign features'. When the Lama brothers read this criticism they deleted the heisted scenes, which, according to the editor of *Radio* magazine, made things worse and added to the fiasco. When the panoramic battlefields appeared on the screen there were exactly twelve knights on their way to do battle. This led the editor to muse: 'Are they on their way to liberate a city or to open a shop?'[3]

The third and best historical film from that period is *Lashin* (1938). Though excellent for its time, *Lashin* still has some lapses: credible blending of classical and colloquial dialogue that occasionally sounds stilted to the modern ear; stereotypical characters; amateurish acting on the part of minor players; beautiful sets that look too 'fresh'; and a predictable ending that was imposed on the producers by the censors. In many ways, however, *Lashin* looks and feels like an interesting German film from the 1920s, because the director Fritz Kramp and many of the technicians were German. The lighting is expressive, the compositions often arresting, and the camera work smooth and unobtrusive. The handling of the crowds is imaginative, particularly in the scene where a hungry crowd fight over a piece of a palm date. The film even boasts an actress in the leading role who bears a striking resemblance to Garbo. Her soulful expressions and languid body almost carry her through, despite her inexperience. It was edited by Niazi Mustapha who became one of Egypt's finest directors. He bridged two scenes using dialogue rather than the technical dissolve, which was the norm at the time.

Abu Shadi considers *Lashin* a classic because of the script's complexities and the film's artistic merits. Above all, he praises it for its political sophistication and daring, finding in it many beneficial lessons. Indeed the film touches on loyalty, palace intrigue, conflict among the centres of power, treason, sedition, assassination, reconciliation and triumph. It shows the sultan as a pawn in the hands of traitors. It depicts his weakness for women and his inability to rise above mixing the affairs of state with personal jealousies. Furthermore, it illustrates two methods of governing. Rulers have a crucial choice in how to handle a rebellious populace: brutality or understanding.[4]

Alarmed by the film's message, the Minister of the Interior tried to ban it. To protect the monarchy (and his own job), he chose to ignore the *fellahin*'s starvation, repression and exploitation. Though in the 1930s Egypt seemed relatively stable, the revolution was palpable. By declaring on the screen that 'The events of the story took place around the twelfth century', the producers hoped to conceal the true intentions of the film or to minimise its impact on the audience, particularly the censors. Audiences were shocked to learn that the scenes showing the storming of the storage depots had been deleted. They wrecked the seats because they subconsciously knew that the film foreshadowed the storm to come.

* * *

Al-Nasir Salah al-Din (Saladin, 1963)

Political background

By the end of the 1950s, Chahine was in the ascendant as a director, primarily on the strength of *Cairo Station* and *Jamila*. So it was not surprising then that when another director, Izziddine Zulfiqar, realised that he was terminally ill, he decided to turn his cherished project over to Youssef Chahine. The film was still in the preparation stage and he chose Chahine to make it, even though his own brother was also a director. Such was the faith and trust other film-makers had in Chahine, though still in his thirties. The film was *Saladin*. Juxtaposing Nasser and Saladin in the title was intentional. By 1963 Nasser had achieved several milestones: peaceful evacuation of the British from Egypt, victory over Suez, and forging the Treaty of Non-Alignment with Nehru and Tito. Even the dissolution of the union between Egypt and Syria did not affect the people's love for him, for they blamed it on others. No longer was he simply the titular head of the Arab nation, or just a head of state of consequence, but a paradigm for the rest of the Third World leaders to emulate. To the Arabs he was the reincarnated Saladin. If anyone could liberate modern-day Jerusalem, Nasser could. And so it fell upon the shoulders of thirty-seven year-old Chahine to depict the idealised hero of old, not for the sake of nostalgia, but as an inspiration for a nation yearning for salvation.

Total commitment

With *Saladin*, Chahine gave Egyptian cinema its first epic. Written by the original director and three other writers (including Naguib Mahfouz), filmed in Eastman-color and widescreen, starring a number of Egypt's finest actors, heavily supported by Nasser's regime, it was produced by Assya who was by now as meticulous as Chahine himself. Two years in the making and with thousands of Egyptian soldiers as extras, the film was earmarked for distinction and success. It might not have been, though, had it not been for the dedication of its youthful director. Chahine's enthusiasm and total devotion must have been contagious, for the same approach was evident in all those who worked on it. There was a trend in the late 1950s and early 1960s for making costume dramas, a trend the Egyptians could not have missed. Many of the scenes in MGM's lavish *Cleopatra* (1960) were shot in Egypt. And in 1961, Anthony Mann made his epic, *El Cid*. By 1963, *Lawrence of Arabia*, which had been shot two years earlier in the nearby Jordanian desert, was so popular that it must have been on Chahine's mind as he embarked on his own spectacle.

Synopsis

The film opens with Saladin receiving emissaries from Jerusalem telling him of the dire situation in Jerusalem. Arabs in the holy city are starving, and the occupation is brutal. Having already unified Arab kings and rulers in anticipation of an assault on the aggressors, Saladin rises to the challenge. He marches with his army to liberate the beleaguered city. What infuriates him about the Crusaders is their attack on pilgrims while on their way to Mecca. That they violated a code of honour banning such behaviour made him vow to teach them a lesson. The script develops two conflicts; one personal, the other political. On the personal level we find Isa, a Christian Arab soldier, falling in love with Louise, a blonde from the enemy camp whom he has rescued during a battle. Political treason is rampant on both sides. On the Arab side there is the *wali* of Akka betraying his people, in hopes of becoming king of Akka and Jaffa. On the Crusaders' side treason is pervasive. European Kings are constantly squabbling and deceiving each other. The main instigator for all the in-fighting is Virginia, the widow of the former king of Jerusalem. Adamant that Jerusalem must not fall, she travels to Europe to rally all the kings for fresh supplies of men, arms and money. She even plots the assassination of King Richard the Lion-Heart for having concluded a truce with Saladin. But he is only wounded, and ironically it is Saladin who administers his recovery. The film ends with Arab rule restored to Jerusalem, and with Isa and Louise united in love.

Echoes from the distant past

As a film, *Saladin* resonated throughout the Arab world because the analogy between Jerusalem of the twelfth century and Jerusalem of the twentieth century is inescapable. In both cases, the perception was that under the

guise of religion, a sacred Arab city was descended upon by waves of outsiders who, unprovoked, proceeded to dispossess the rightful owners and
inhabitants and to wreak havoc in their life. The fragmentation of the Arabs
in their city-states during the time of the Crusades, however, was far worse
than the fragmentation of the Arabs in modern times. At that time there
were dozens of Arab city-states, each ruled by an independent and often
paranoid prince or a sultan, always envious or fearful of the others.[5] Thus it
was easy for the Crusaders to decimate most of them and to establish a
foothold, some of which lasted nearly two hundred years. It took a brave and
wise Saladin to unite the Arabs and liberate Jerusalem. This is how the
Arabs in the 1960s saw Nasser – in reality or in hope. To listen to some of
the dialogue from the film itself is to imagine how it must have replayed
itself between Arabs and Israelis. Saladin's message of strength in unity,
tolerance, and the necessity to defend one's country coincides with
Chahine's political philosophy.

Satisfaction and dissatisfaction

Chahine is proud of two technical innovations introduced in *Saladin*. First
to simulate a split screen, he built two contiguous sets and alternated
between them by turning the lights on and off: the same effect, however,
could have been achieved at the laboratory. But some of the editing in this
sequence is worth noting: on the right side of the frame is Saladin interro-
gating the treacherous *wali* of Akka; on the left side of the frame is King
Richard the Lion-Heart accusing Virginia and her co-conspirator of having
tried to kill him. But the editing is such that in large close-ups Saladin and
King Richard seem to be opposing each other. The tension within the original two separate scenes spills over to a higher level. This effect could also
have been achieved at the laboratory. The point remains that Chahine is
always experimenting. Second, he is particularly proud of having photographed a battle scene impressionistically. To portray the enmity
between Christians and Muslims during the Crusades, and yet to avoid a
renewal of hostility among Christian and Muslim viewers sitting in the
same cinema, Chahine relied on musical crescendos and red paint splat-
tered on a disk rotating before the camera. He explains that 'by intercutting

Two Christians (one Arab, the other European) fall in love during the Crusades

fragments of the disk shots between the combatants who were charging against each other on their horses I was able to create the impression of violence without showing actual violence.'

Chahine succeeds both on the large and the intimate scales. His deployment of the large number of troops on a vast scale is a considerable achievement for someone who had not attempted such feats before. Overcoming logistics alone must have been daunting, and he meets the challenge credibly. But there is a small scene that does not call attention to itself, yet it registers well on the viewer's mind. When Isa, the Christian Arab, is about to be shot by a firing squad, Chahine cuts to a long shot of white pigeons taking flight in the distance. Such a visual metaphor is almost a cliché, but Chahine does not linger on it, resulting in a subtlety one wishes there was more of in this film. Towards the end, there is another scene that is problematic because it could not have happened, yet it delivers a punch. The celebration of Christmas Eve in Bethlehem becomes a symbol of peace and tolerance, both of which are expressed in the voice of the *muezzin* calling the faithful to prayer, immediately followed by a choir singing a Christmas song. As one critic pointed out, such things do not happen in real life, for the *muezzin* never chants at midnight.[6] Dramatically and emotionally, however, the moment reverberates.

Reservations

Though *Saladin* was hailed as a triumph for Arab cinema, Yousry Nasrallah, a protégé of Chahine's, raises a valid point. 'The problem with *Saladin*,' he says, 'is that he is presented as an ideal human being. We start with him as a good man, and then he becomes a great man and then he turns into a legend. Up ... up ... up. There's no room for him to grow and develop as a well-rounded character.' [7] Another German critic, who is an admirer of Chahine's work, does not like the film. But he finds in it a moment of great poignancy:

> Once in this film an astonishing picture surfaces: on the side of the path two boys sit near their houses, several animals graze not far from Saladin's troops marching in endless rows, but the two children remain sitting. They don't allow themselves to be disturbed because for them the war is a normal part of life. This scene in its objective clarity, in its naïveté becomes in this historical mosaic a vision of another view of the war. It remains here a seedling that certainly is supposed to grow strongly.[8]

Throughout his career Chahine has shunned official history, or what Napoleon defined as 'a lie agreed upon'. What concerns him more is conveying how the past informs the present. For instance, there were no binoculars at the time of the Crusades, yet he uses them. And as historian Donald S. Richards points out, women were not admitted to the Templars Order, yet here we find Louise not only a Templar but a captain too.[9] Chahine would justify the anachronism by reminding us that he is making a theatrical film, not a documentary. One critic explains further: 'Historical epics are not simply used by Chahine to illustrate historical events, but as a lens on the present. In this sense, his epics emerge as national allegories.' [10]

But the film has more serious flaws. As a character, Saladin is too noble for his own good. Although the film is a hymn about him, he should not be

presented unblemished. Also, the dialogue is unnatural: written in classical Arabic and highly pleasing to the ear, it reaches for eloquence at the
expense of believability - ordinary conversations do not occur in the film,
only political discourse. Even the romantic moments are charged with politics. The fencing is perfunctory and the acting is occasionally unconvinc-
ing. To wear a foreigner's costume does not make you a foreigner. Many of
the Egyptian actors playing Crusaders look and sound alien to the characters they are portraying. As Saladin, Ahmad Mazhar shines in some scenes
and lapses into exaggerated facial expressions in others. The two women,
however, Laila Fawzi and Nadia Lutfi, give the two liveliest performances in
the film: furthermore, they are strikingly beautiful – in the Hollywood tradition.

* * *

Al-Wada' ya Bonaparte (Adieu Bonaparte, 1985)
The circumstances during which *Adieu Bonaparte* was made are worth considering. Having, in 1984, signed a cultural treaty, Egypt and France decided to co-produce a film on Napoleon, then both independently invited
Chahine to direct it.[11] Consequently it would have been impolitic and
counter-productive to flaunt the cruelties of Napoleon's invasion in the
face of the French. Chahine shows enough of the military campaign, but
stops short of embarrassing a new friend.

Synopsis
The plot line is non-linear. Instead of a traditional protagonist going
through a crisis and finally emerging either happy or unhappy, we are
offered a bigger canvas and many more characters. The film's complexity is
appropriate for such a gigantic clash between two peoples and two cultures.
Adieu Bonaparte tells a story with many strands and many subplots. On the
Egyptian side, we see a family composed of two parents and three sons, each
representing a segment of Egyptian society. The elderly, obese father is a
baker with a fixed expression of resignation. From the beginning he sens-

es the futility of any Egyptian effort to resist the mighty fleet and contents himself with baking bread for the French, defending his action by saying, 'I've always worked and I'm not going to spend a day unemployed.' He is conditioned by his own unhappy experiences and burdened by Egypt's long history of invasions and defeats. As he watches and hears young men clamouring to fight, he cynically remarks under his breath, 'They want to make bread before they learn how to make dough.' In other words, Egyptians need years of preparing and training before they can do battle.

A controversial view of Napoleon's expedition into Egypt: *Adieu Bonaparte* (1985)

The father's docility brings him into sharp conflict with his oldest son, Bakr, who accuses him of collaboration with the enemy. Bakr is an intense Muslim cleric who sees the invasion for what it is and becomes a leader of the resistance. The second son, Ali, is a likeable fellow who writes poetry, speaks French and has a smattering knowledge of French literature. He befriends one of Napoleon's generals, Cafarelli, and this relationship brings him too into conflict with his older brother, Bakr, who, in a moment of anger, tries to take a swing at him. But Ali catches his arm in time, threatening, 'You know your way and I know mine. None of you had better raise a hand. Understand?' Their eyes lock, and the brothers become enemies. The youngest boy is Yahia, a lanky teenager who is in love with a sweet girl his age. He is killed by an explosion in a French ammunition warehouse. The mother is the eternal sufferer: over the alienation between her husband and her children; over having to uproot her family and move to Cairo; over the tragic death of her son, Yahia; and over her failure to reconcile her two remaining sons, Bakr and Ali. When she sees that the two do not even speak to each other even after Yahia's tragic death, traditionally a time for healing, she tries to mediate. 'He's your brother and he still loves you,' she pleads with Ali as she embraces him. But Ali shakes his head.

On the French side, the focus is on Napoleon's three-pronged strategy to occupy Egypt: befriend, dazzle and brutalise. Belying the title, *Adieu Bonaparte*, Napoleon does not dominate the film. He is there to proclaim himself a friend of Islam, to watch his scientists launch a gigantic balloon (which to his embarrassment bursts in the air), and to let his cannons thunder and smoke in battle. The most prominent Frenchman in the film is Cafarelli, a general with a wooden leg and a warm smile. He is the one who humanises the French campaign and gives it a cultural dimension. Whereas Napoleon comes as an invader and remains an invader till the end, his pretension about loving Islam notwithstanding, charismatic Cafarelli befriends the Egyptians – first Yahia and then Ali. The spectator is put in a position to draw a distinction between the hardcore military and the humane individual. Cafarelli laughs with the Egyptians, argues with them, smashes things in front of them, yet enjoys their company in his private quarters. Off screen he is injured, supposedly in a battle at Acre, and on his death bed he still banters with Ali. Cafarelli's congeniality is endearing.

Two perspectives
One of the controversies surrounding Napoleon's invasion revolves around whether the resultant contact between Egypt and the West was indirectly beneficial to the average Egyptian. Even if it was, one is apt to ask: at what

price? There is no denying that ultimately benefits were reaped on both sides, though the scales were always tilted in favour of the conqueror. Equally, had it not been for the invasion Egypt would probably not have made the advances it did. Yet again: what price 'progress'? Abu Shadi is adamant on this point: 'One can say, and with great enthusiasm, "Damn the printing press if it's going to sacrifice so many lives."'[12] Napoleon's invasion slaughtered thousands of innocent Egyptians. Edward Said attributes the beginning of imperialism in the Middle East not only to the magnitude of Napoleon's conquest, but to the spirit and racism with which it was undertaken:

> And the Napoleonic expedition, with its collective monument of erudition, the *Description de l'Egypte*, provided a scene or setting for Orientalism, since Egypt and subsequently the other Islamic lands were viewed as the live province, the laboratory, the theatre of effective knowledge about the Orient.[13]

Obviously Napoleon relied on his experts' extensive knowledge of Islam to further his ambition to possess and control Egypt. Only a naïve observer could have believed that his 'love of Islam' was genuine. Yet there were some who succumbed to his flattery at the time. Napoleon 'tried everywhere to prove that he was fighting *for* Islam, everything he said was translated into Koranic Arabic, just as the French army was urged by its command always to remember the Islamic sensibility'.[14] He did indeed establish a *diwan* – a body of notables to act as consultants – and 'appointed sixty members, Shaykhs of the Theologians, Shaykhs of the guilds, Copts, and the French'.[15] Once he even 'dressed himself in the Mahometan [*sic*] costume'. [16] His deception seems continual. He urges the 'ulama, Sharifs, and Imams' to support his expedition, then claims in a proclamation 'directed to all the inhabitants of Egypt of all ranks' that 'since the beginning of time God has decreed destruction of the enemies of Islam and the breaking of the crosses by my hand'. [17] French historians, including Napoleon's private secretary, have long admitted that Napoleon's use of religion was no more than a stratagem.

Violence minimised

Recognising that one should not indict a whole nation (in this case the French nation), allowing that nations should not hold a grudge forever against an old enemy, and firmly believing that an artist has the right and the freedom to express his or her own point of view, Ali Abu Shadi nevertheless takes strong issue with Chahine over *Adieu Bonaparte*. He complains that Chahine's 'vision was not accurate; maybe incorrect'. He points out that the film fails to show the 'fantastic Egyptian resistance' as it should have done. The relationship between the Egyptians and the French was not as gentle as it is depicted on the screen. In the film, the young cleric Bakr appeals to one of the senior shaykhs for support against the invaders and the old shaykh is unmoved, calling Napoleon a friend of Islam. This contradicts what the historian al-Jabarti had to say about the desecration of the mosque by the French.[18]

An Islamic cleric describes Napoleon as a friend of Islam

According to Abu Shadi, the negative reaction to the film was so extensive that the Minister of Culture sent a committee to the Cannes Film
Festival to listen and observe everything pertaining to the film. Eventually
the committee gave permission for it to be shown. Farid Samir shares Abu
Shadi's misgivings and refers to Chahine by saying: 'Every race horse has its
fall'.[19] He attributes the film's poor reception to the fact that 'although the
film is about invasion, it lacks a single drop of blood because, in reality, it
is a film about love. Its problem is that it appears at a time when love is not
known, and addresses people who are surrounded by enemies on all fronts
and at all levels ...' [20]

Technical mastery

Chahine's films are known for their pictorial beauty. Even viewers who
might not be versed in the dynamics of visual configuration, instinctively
find something pleasing or necessarily jarring in his images. At the outset
of *Adieu Bonaparte* we learn about the cosmopolitan nature of Alexandria.
We are introduced to three characters: a Greek girl speaking Arabic with a
foreign accent and trying to seduce an Egyptian boy; and a French merchant
conversing with the same Egyptian boy in French and sharing with him his
excitement about the opportunities the French fleet, which has just been
spotted on the far horizon, would be bringing with it. With remarkable
brevity and clarity, Chahine sketches a morning in the life of Alexandria
where languages commingle and ethnic minorities live, love and do business together. He also sets for us the style and texture for the rest of the
film, and invites us into a world saturated with nuances that demand close
reading. In the same expository sequence, the Frenchman points his finger
to the sea as he speaks of the arriving fleet. Chahine refrains from showing
us what the man is referring to, and we long to see what he sees. Moments
later, however, when the Greek girl and the Egyptian boy make love in a
deserted building, we see a ship through a window. It is small and distant—
like a little cloud that is portentous of the storm to come.

Yahia's tragic death is also rendered in a visually symbolic and effective
scene. As Yahia tries to open a box, unsuspecting that it is full of ammunition, the frame explodes with tremendous flashes of fireworks.

Superimposed images amplify the nastiness of war and the victimisation of the boy at the hands of French pyrotechnics. What is remarkable is that Yahia is not shown as a shattered corpse. We do not see his body flattened or charred. Rather, he remains standing in the midst of all this carnage. His expression is that of bewilderment, not defeat. (Significantly, his name means 'to live' in Arabic.) Yahia's defiance in the face of death is reminiscent of another memorable scene at the end of Dovzhenko's *Arsenal* (1929). In it a Russian revolutionary is riddled with a fusillade of bullets fired at him from the guns of the Czar's army. But the revolutionary bares his chest and dares them to kill him. They continue shooting but, to their disbelief, he refuses to collapse. He will not die because the revolution will not die. Here too, Yahia will not die. To borrow from William Faulkner, he will endure as Egypt had endured for centuries. It is a scene of pure cinema. The scene of the wake after Yahia's death is emotionally wrenching. Here the impact of the horror of war on this Egyptian family is evident. With a few dense shots, Chahine reveals that the fragmentation is irreparable. Another visually compelling shot shows Ali walking down an empty road. It is late afternoon and he is alone. His isolation is total. The shadow of the long wall fills half the road, and he is walking along a line separating light and darkness. By now this is a bit of a cliché, yet it works because visual metaphors are the essence of cinema. And on the soundtrack we hear *ana al-masri* (I, the Egyptian), Sayyid Darwish's patriotic and haunting song.

* * *

Al-Muhajir (*The Emigrant,* 1994)

The controversy that surrounded *Adieu Bonaparte* pales in comparison with the rupture that followed Chahine's production of *The Emigrant*. The new clash was not over history but over something considerably more sensitive: religion. Since it is purportedly 'forbidden' in the Qur'an to portray any prophet visually – and *The Emigrant* is, in the eyes of Muslim fundamentalists, a retelling of the story of Joseph in the Qur'an and the Old Testament - it follows that Chahine must be guilty of a major offence against Islam.

Dangerous climate

To understand why by the time *The Emigrant* was made Chahine had already been viewed as a subversive, one must not overlook a little film that he had made following the Gulf War in 1991. It was a twenty-two-minute documentary of extraordinary imagination and boldness he called *al-Qahira munawwara bi ahliha (Cairo ...as Told by Chahine)*. Unfortunately, Cairo's residents were outraged. Expecting a film that would glamorise and honour their city, they stared at the film in disbelief. The images parading before their eyes included: congestion at its worst, minarets everywhere, sewage system flooding the streets, hustlers preying on the innocent, husband and wife on a movie screen discussing official schemes to exploit the poor, hundreds of men prostrating themselves in prayer on the pavements and multitudes of idle youths staring blankly into space. The living conditions are ghastly: families huddling on rooftops, married couples not finding a square foot for privacy, university students demonstrating against the Americans, a mother lowering her young son's lunch in a basket from the tenth floor. The boy opens the pitta bread only to find some red paste at the bottom, yet he and his mother exchange loving winks and smiles and she brags about what a money-maker her son is going to be. This irritates a crusty old man reading a newspaper, who lifts up his eyes and admonishes her, saying, 'He'd be better off reading a book.' Juxtaposed with the abject poverty and dire conditions are the high fashion shoes and golden purses which are prominently displayed in shop windows and yearned for by a young woman whose beautiful face is half-veiled. In one 'staged scene' we see Chahine's assistant observing life on the street. He eyes and admires a blonde, but he himself is being admired by a male foreigner trying to pick him up. A few feet away is an old hag singing a jingle while squeezing a plastic Coca-Cola bottle. In the meantime, a bearded Muslim youth is watching while he himself is being watched. The characters in the scene are watching each other, Chahine behind the camera is watching them watching each other, and we are watching him watching them too. It is a cinematic nugget on spectatorship. We are privy to layers of commentaries that expand and underscore each other. We see conflicts brewing. We see external influences clashing with internal suspicions, and we can only hold our breath.

Cairo is rich with exquisite moments. One sequence consists of a collage of old Egyptian men. Their faces are as ravaged as the face of the Sphinx itself, and they seem almost as ancient. It is terrible to watch human misery at this level and to know that those blinded eyes mask still deeper scars, yet it is beautiful to see an artist capture their dignity and pain with such compassion. Over this quiet montage we hear a woman's low and haunting voice singing: 'I have trusted my affairs into your hands, O God, for other than you I have found no one.' For these trodden old men God is literally their only refuge. Also mitigating against Chahine was the fact that in 1991 he had been invited by the French to direct a play on their national stage. The French 'connection' was suspect, even though he had chosen to do Albert Camus' *Caligula*, a play against tyranny. In the view of Muslim orthodoxy, Chahine was a man straddling two continents.

Synopsis

The Emigrant revolves around Ram, a young man from an unnamed country 'north' of Egypt. He is the youngest of seven brothers and his father's favourite. As a clairvoyant, he foretells impending storms and is accused of possessing the ability to change the sex of an unborn child. Predicting famine, he pleads with his aging father to let him travel to Egypt to study their agricultural methods. His jealous brothers conspire to dispose of him. They take him on a trip, gag him and dump him in the bottom of a boat. The boat's owner discovers him and sells him to Amihar, Egypt's Army General. Amihar is a sexually impotent man who once saved a beautiful foreigner, Simhit, who out of gratitude agreed to marry him. Sexually deprived for ten years, she is now ready to romance the handsome Ram. But out of loyalty to her husband, Ram declines her advances even though he is attracted to her. Ram's intelligence and ambition earn him the respect of Amihar who grants him a remote piece of land to test his newly acquired knowledge. With the help of fellow Egyptians, particularly the young girl who sought him out and married him, Ram discovers fresh water and is able to cultivate the land. But his crops are destroyed by his adversaries who regard him an outsider. Towards the end of the film Ram's earlier prediction about famine is fulfilled. His brothers arrive in Egypt seeking help for their starving families.

Ram, the emigrant who travels to Egypt seeking knowledge

Ram recognises them but they fail to recognise him. After feeding them and then rebuking them for the way they had treated him, he returns with them to his country where he is united with his grateful father.

A call to the young at heart

Chahine is renowned for feeling the pulse of Egypt. His important films are a result of agonising about the problems that are bedeviling ordinary citizens. He has repeatedly shown an uncanny ability to sense the malaise around him and to anticipate dire consequences, if they are left unchecked. He made *The Emigrant* because he wanted the Egyptian youth to be like Ram: energetic, brave, curious, ambitious and willing to sacrifice. This is the story of Joseph in the bible and the Qur'an. This is Ram in *The Emigrant*, or Chahine himself. This is why he calls his film a story of hope. This is why he proclaims: 'I am Ram.'[21]

In many ways *The Emigrant* is a sequel to Chahine's autobiographical trilogy. The four films dovetail and complete his odyssey in Egypt and in Art. Here he models Ram's mission on his travel to Pasadena Playhouse to study, and his return to Egypt to benefit his people. The reversal of movement is interesting. Chahine *left* Egypt; Ram *came* to Egypt. The stranger's arrival from abroad allows the film to hold up a satirical mirror to Egyptian attitudes, which Chahine has dated to antiquity. During the time of rivalries between religions, foreigners were not welcome in 'the land of light'. Chahine warns that Egypt could harm herself if she reverts to such practices.

In *The Emigrant* Chahine casts a disapproving eye on institutionalised religion. It is set in the fourteenth century BC, when Egypt was in a transition from the worship of Amun to Atun, the sun god. Akhnatun, whose followers set out to demolish the temples of Amun, is believed to have started monotheism. The struggle between the two camps leaves Chahine convinced that they were all, as the religionists of today are, after *al-sulta* (authority). They are all schemers and manipulators. It is a blunt indictment from a man who draws parallels between past and present.

Foreigners are suspect - even Simhit the wife of Amihar, the head of the army. She is also the priestess of the new religion, that of Atun. When the chief priest of Amun's religion learns of her holding ceremonies and dancing in celebration of the sun, the symbol of rival Atun, he fixes her with his eyes, warning: 'The punishment of the commander is easy – execution. But the punishment of the foreigner whom we embraced and whom we allowed to enter our best places, and who betrays us – we will crush her bone by bone.' Justice depends on your place of birth. Towards the end of the film, Ram's father-in-law says: 'We Egyptians must decide that.' The camera freezes on Ram's face, capturing his disappointment. Under his breath he repeats: 'Ah, we Egyptians ...' He had cultivated a remote and arid piece of the desert and provided grains to feed the hungry, yet he is made to feel the outsider.

The archetypal outsider

The Emigrant must be seen as a story of a stranger who comes to a new place, remains in it for a while and leaves it altered. The Egypt to which Ram comes is not the same Egypt he leaves. New energies are released and new attitudes are struck. One cannot predict whether or not Simhit will remain satisfied to be unsatisfied. She could continue to be the suffering but faithful wife, or she might take on lovers, or seek a divorce. And the husband, Amihar, the proud general — what will become of him? Will he close his eyes to her infidelities or will he seek revenge on her and her future lovers? Perhaps he will experience pangs of conscience for having robbed her of happiness for the last ten years of marriage. He might even commit suicide rather than face shame and ridicule.

The resolutions of all these problems are a matter of conjecture. The fact remains that the Amihar and Simhit relationship will never be the same. Other issues go beyond the personal. Will Simhit's sun-worshipping sect openly stage a revolt? Will they triumph or will the priestess, the foreigner, be crushed 'bone by bone'? The question of borders and collaboration between nations smacks of utopia. Surely everyone can see the benefit of exchanging knowledge. Green fields, abundance of crops and fresh water are all desirable. The benefits of the exchange of ideas might translate themselves into state policy, or they might be regarded with suspicion. Chahine poses the dilemma for society to consider. Ram does not instigate unrest, except in the viewer's mind. Nor does he consciously cause an eruption between husband and wife. Morally circumspect, he cannot be held responsible for the consequences that flow from his entering the country. As a catalyst for change, not simply an emigrant seeking knowledge, he becomes an archetype.

Imitations and weaknesses

One does not know whether Chahine had read or was aware at the time of making his film of Thomas Mann's novel, *Joseph and His Brothers*, a moral fable set not in historic times but in mythic times. But he must have been aware of Hollywood's epics on Egypt. Howard Hawks's *The Land of Pharaohs* (1955) comes to mind, for the conflict between the followers of Amun and Atun is an obvious parallel to the court intrigue at the time of building the Pyramids. Then there are Cecil B. DeMille's *Cleopatra* and *The Ten Commandments*, not forgotting Joseph L. Mankiewicz's later version of

Cleopatra. To be sure, Chahine's *The Emigrant* is never as stilted or banal as DeMille's, nor as lavish or meandering as Mankiewicz's. Nor is it as compelling as Hawks's, the script of which was co-written by William Faulkner. What it does have in common with these Hollywood extravaganzas is a variation on the history and the setting of ancient Egypt. But whereas these foreign productions were made with the intent of marvelling at the glory or debauchery of one of the first civilisations on earth, Chahine's intention is to learn from the past lessons that modern Egypt could use. More important, none of the Hollywood directors put part of his own life on the screen in any of these films as Chahine does in *The Emigrant*. But Chahine's film does emulate aspects of these foreign films, especially DeMille's dances by scantily dressed women. Simhit's dance at Atun's temple does advance the story line in revealing her attraction to Ram; it makes explicit her pent-up sexuality; and it fulfils the expectations of the Egyptian audiences. Nevertheless, it does seem an intrusion in a serious film.

More problematic is the episode showing Ram in the remote area of the

With the help of his beautiful Egyptian wife, Ram turns barren land green

desert trying to test his knowledge of agriculture. The marriage to the young girl who proposed to him provides some humour in the desolate desert, and dispels any doubt about Ram's sexuality. The episode's main weakness, however, is in failing to deliver on its premise. Except on one or two brief occasions, we never see Ram tilling or planting. Suddenly fresh water is discovered, barren land turns green and the crops are plentiful. The whole enterprise is playful, and the good fortune is not a reward for hard and thoughtful work. Magic has its place, but not here.

Serious threats

Because in the eyes of some radicals Chahine 'offended' Islam, *The Emigrant* was banned and Chahine himself was prosecuted in a court of law, charged with blasphemy. The day the verdict was to be rendered, the scene in front of the courthouse was one of uproar. While hundreds of people were stampeding to get in, two scholars were holding a cross-fire debate of their own about the *Poetics* and Aristotle's theory of art on the steps outside. Suddenly a sinister-looking man stretched his neck and threatened in a calm but chilling voice: 'Anyone who dares to touch our religion will be dismembered.'

Inside the courtroom, Chahine defended himself, saying: 'Yes, I was *inspired* by the biblical story of Joseph. But aren't these stories given to us as *qudwa* – as paradigms? Aren't they there to guide us and teach us?' He further explained that he 'was attracted to *sayyidna* Youssef [Joseph] for a number of years. Maybe because my name is Youssef, I don't know. But also because [his character] embodies what I want to say today [about] strong will ... and love of work.'[22] Chahine was acquitted, but the ramifications will continue. Egyptian intellectuals predict that the verdict will be studied for years to come in law schools because it constituted a landmark for the rights of the Egyptian artist.

Thou shall not offend

Chahine's ordeal with the Islamists has precedents. Traditionally tolerant, Islam is inflexible on matters concerning religious taboos. In the late 1920s, the literary giant Taha Hussein was dismissed from Cairo University

on account of a book he had written that, in the eyes of the Islamists, undermined the linguistic roots of the Qur'an. In 1959, Naguib Mahfouz stirred
up emotions upon the serialisation of his novel *Giblawi's Children*, in which
he allegorically suggested that God is dead. The ultra pious never forgave
him even after he had won the Nobel Prize for Egypt and the Arabs. In 1994
(one week before Chahine's legal problems began regarding *The Emigrant*),
Mahfouz, who was already over eighty and in poor health, was stabbed several times in the neck. The Salman Rushdie affair, six years earlier, had
already poisoned the air. The western world's outrage at the severity of the
Ayatollah Khomeini's judgment against the author only fanned the fire of
resentment in the Muslim world, which viewed *Satanic Verses* and the
acceptance of it as a sign of conspiracy on the part of the West and the
Zionists to demean Islam. The retribution against the Muslim world always
seemed harsher than against anywhere else. This hypocrisy and double
standard justified their anger.

Perhaps the most unfair criticism levelled against *The Emigrant* is the
one that sees in it a Zionist message. After pointing out the many similarities between the film and the story of Joseph in the Qur'an, one reviewer
accuses Chahine of advocating normalisation with Israel.[23] On the same
page others fulminated against Chahine, accusing his cinema of reflecting
'The American Dream and the Hebrew Redemption via French Channels'.
To those critics, the direction from which Ram came cannot be but Israel.
To them, snippets of dialogue such as 'we need each other' and 'turning the
soldiers into farmers' and 'borders' are proof enough that Chahine's message on the screen negates his disavowals. One's first reaction is to agree.
On second thoughts, one begins to doubt the charge. Those familiar with
Chahine's films and politics would know that Chahine – speaking as citizen
of the world, if you will – is casting a wider net: the open borders he advo-
cates are among all nations, and not just between Egypt and Israel. So long
as Israel occupies Arab land and denies the Palestinians the right to form
their own State, he would oppose normalisation with her. Chahine is a sig-
natory on a manifesto signed by leading Egyptians, all opposed to any normalisation with Israel. A director who in *Jamila* and *Saladin* made the case
against injustice and occupation is not likely to abandon those ideals. The

most despicable character in *The Emigrant* is the effeminate artisan who is willing to change sides at a moment's notice. He would serve Amun as well as Atun. Some might call this being pragmatic; Chahine would call him unprincipled.

* * *

al-Masir (*Destiny*, 1997)

Often a Chahine film evolves out of its immediate predecessor, or from the need to crystallise Egypt's psychological reality at that particular period. In *Destiny* he succeeds in warning that Egypt is veering in the wrong direction. Stabbing a writer or suing a film-maker in a court of law simply because they hold views that are contrary to someone else's is not the way for a free society to behave. Intolerance is unacceptable and is bound to lead to repression. The role of the artist is not to satisfy popular taste, but to shake lethargy and dispel fogginess; not to conform to the mould, but to shatter it.

While reminiscing about his first experience at an international film festival, Chahine talked about the day he had shown his film *Nile Boy* at Venice in 1952, and how he and a group of Egyptians ended up at a café where one of the Egyptian singers in the crowd was persuaded to play the *oud*. He was joined by the café musicians and soon a memorable night of music and singing began to unfold. The discussion soon centred on how in al-Andalus, Arabic music, Spanish dancing and Jewish chanting blended together to create a wonderful musical heritage. There was a time when the Arabs lived harmoniously with other ethnic groups. Chahine was immediately taken with the idea of making a film about Arab Spain. Researching the possibilities, he and his collaborator came upon the character of the twelfth century Arab philosopher Ibn Rushd (Averröes) who was at once a renowned physician, Grand Judge and a philosopher whose brilliant commentary on Aristotle had an influence on the Renaissance. But his claim that there was no conflict between faith and reason made him a heretic in the eyes of the Islamists. Ultimately he was banished by his friend and supporter, the caliph, and his books were burned in the public square. The parallel between the distant past and the immediate present was eerie. Were elements of this not reminiscent of what happened to Naguib Mahfouz, and to Youssef Chahine himself?

Synopsis

While Europe was still languishing in the Dark Ages, the city of Cordoba in the twelfth century, under Arab rule, was the centre of civilisation. In the film's prologue we see a Frenchman burned at the stake for having translated the works of the 'heretic' Ibn Rushd. The episode is juxtaposed with a lively street scene in Cordoba. The marketplace is crowded and outdoor tables are laden with rare books that shoppers haggle to buy.

The sultan al-Mansour has two sons, al-Nasser and Abdullah, both of whom he considers decadent. He particularly disapproves of the younger one, Abdullah, who loves to dance and spends his evenings at a dance hall owned by a gypsy family. There Abdullah falls prey to a group of religious extremists who want him to renounce his immoral lifestyle and join their

A sharp contrast between Dark Ages Europe and Arab Cordova

austere sect. Already feeling rejected by his father, Abdullah is lured to a training ground in a remote area of the desert where they inculcate in him Qur'anic verses and almost brainwash him into believing that his own father is evil and that he should kill him. One of the radicals even stabs the gypsy man, for as a poet and singer he represents for them everything unholy in their society.

When we first meet Ibn Rushd he is sitting at his dinner table at home. His family and the sultan's brother are around him and they all seem relaxed. The scene is enlivened with the arrival of Abdullah on his way to the dance hall. Here Ibn Rushd strikes us as a happily adjusted man, not a hermit as philosophers are reputed to be. He laughs, tells jokes and approves of Abdullah's dancing. 'When I was his age,' he admits, laughing, 'I used to dance all night.' His humanity is endearing. Throughout the film he is a beacon of integrity. He sits on the marble floor of the school's portico, surrounded by his students, one of whom has travelled from France to study under him. Ibn Rushd sees no conflict between faith and intellect. His approach to life is tolerant; his demeanour unaffected. His sincerity is soon tested when the gypsy poet/singer is stabbed. The sultan orders swift punishment by death, but Ibn Rushd counsels patience. First he wants to know why the boy committed the heinous crime, and who drove him to do it. To determine the real villain, he visits the boy's home, sits with him and his family. Convinced that the youth was only a stooge of a sinister group out to wrest authority from the sultan, Ibn Rushd sentences him to prison rather than death. This infuriates al-Mansour who feels disobeyed. The youth is summarily hanged, and the relationship between the sultan and Ibn Rushd begins to deteriorate. When Ibn Rushd warns of the enemy within the kingdom, the sultan dismisses his warning and distances himself from him.

Anticipating reprisals against him, and fearing that his books might be lost, Ibn Rushd's followers embark on the task of copying all his books and hiding them in places as distant as France and Egypt. This proves to have been a wise move, for the attackers do set Ibn Rushd's house on fire. Eventually truth triumphs. The extremists are exposed as having collaborated with the enemies of al-Andalus, the sultan is reconciled with his sons, and Ibn Rushd's honours are restored. The reconciliation comes too late to save his books from the public bonfire, but Ibn Rushd is undaunted, for he knows that his followers had copied them and stored them in safe places. He even tosses one of his books into the blazing fire, implying that 'ideas have wings' that can never be destroyed.

A stern warning

The prologue, which occurs during the Inquisition, is a chilling parallel to what could happen in modern Egypt. A man is burned to death because the Catholic Church was opposed to Ibn Rushd's 'radical' ideas. Providing a sharp contrast to this episode, the rest of the film shows the Arabs at the zenith of their civilisation, living in luxury and in harmony with all their neighbours. Their scientists, poets, musicians and architects were at the height of their creativity. Yet in the midst of that society there were ominous symptoms of a disease that threatened to destroy it. The deadly disease took the form of an attack on the brilliant Ibn Rushd who had translated Aristotle, written excellent commentaries on his works, and has

Son escorts his mother after the burning of his father at the stake

been acknowledged as a contributor to the birth of the Renaissance. The West learned from Ibn Rushd, but his own people exiled him and burned his books, which were his and the Arabs' pride. Chahine's warning is forceful: unless today's Egyptians allow free exchange of ideas and respect their artists and thinkers – and unless they reconcile reason and revelation – one day they might find themselves engulfed in their own Dark Ages.

Arab viewers left the cinemas feeling exhilarated as well as unsettled. The beautifully mounted *Destiny* evoked for them one of the finest chapters in their history. Cordoba shone because of its natural beauty and architectural splendour, and because of Ibn Rushd, the symbol of enlightenment. Here, and for the first time, Egyptian film-goers came in 'contact' with the historical figure, and they were delighted. Ibn Rushd is presented as a warm, decent, fair human being, not a stuffy thinker immersed in his books at the expense of living. He is brilliant, yet normal. He has a sense of humour and enjoys watching people sing and dance. He enjoys humming a pretty tune, is courteous with family and friends, and lets his daughter poke fun at him. As the caliph's counsellor, he advises vigilance against the flatterers who, in the name of religion, are scheming to usurp his power. As the Grand Judge, he pronounces a mild sentence against a boy the criminals used as a pawn.

Arab viewers were even more unsettled when they became conscious that things had not changed. Extremists were still recruiting innocent youth and brainwashing them to do their evil work. As the film unfolds, the viewers' attention is focused on four parties to the conflict: the caliph, who is beginning to grow arrogant and insensitive; the clerics, who are more political than religious; the youth, who are too naïve to know right from wrong; and the poet, who brings joy to his listeners and is felled with a butcher's knife. The voice of reason is Ibn Rushd who sees that those obsessed with the assumption of *sulta* (authority) will, in the name of righteousness, ally themselves with the enemies of their own people just to gain control. The game is power – not religion. The stabbing of the poet reminds them of the stabbing of Naguib Mahfouz. The burning of Ibn Rushd's books parallelled the banning of Chahine's films. The sporadic violence in Cairo

Focusing on the ancient past, Chahine draws a parallel to the present: filming *Destiny* (1997)

cannot be but at the urging of some ambitious and wily men such as Shaykh Riyad, the chief conspirator against the caliph.

All artistic works are intended to stimulate thought, but *Destiny* strikes a raw nerve. Instead of posing a rhetorical question, it raises ideas with disturbing implications. Though the viewer enjoys the film's artistry, he or she leaves the cinema feeling challenged and with a desire to read Ibn Rushd as a reminder of the history of al-Andalus, to see how internal conflicts eroded that golden age. This is precisely what Chahine must have hoped his audiences would do: stop being complacent and start thinking.

Critical response
No sooner had the film been released than Egypt was plunged once again into a new controversy. Chahine's admirers hailed him for his brilliance, and used superlatives that, according to an unimpressed economist-cum-

film critic, transformed him into a 'mythical and sacred character'.[24] But Chahine's enemies were on the attack with almost the same refrain. The economist accuses the film of offering the viewer an unworthy choice: 'to be a terrorist or to dance with Laila Elouie,'[25] referring to the gypsy café owner portrayed by the movie star. In another foray he accuses Chahine of spending an inordinate time showing or talking about sex. Then he asks: 'Who ever told Chahine that God is love? This is a notion that is alien to Islam and must be rejected.'[26] Others complained about the film's 'undignified' representation of the venerable Ibn Rushd. How absurd, Law Professor Hassan Shafii thought, that the great philosopher who had taken only two days off from his studies, the day his father died and the day he got married, would sit around humming a tune.[27] They also objected to the use of colloquial Egyptian rather than classical Arabic which, surely, the eminent scholar must have spoken. How shameful it is to show that on the day of his banishment his wife would only remember the bench on which they consummated their marriage.[28] One critic who castigated Chahine's earlier films for having been highbrow and enigmatic, now makes a u-turn and denounces Chahine's plainness and accessibility when Chahine deliberately simplified his message in order to reach the youth who are being preyed upon by the extremists.

Colloquialism is one of the means that Chahine uses to mediate between the past and the present. Arab playwrights and novelists have had to deal with diglossia for the last fifty years, to no one's satisfaction. Because film is aimed at predominantly semi-literate masses, the dilemma becomes more acute. In *Destiny*, sustained classical Arabic would have presented the past at a remove Chahine sought to avoid. Shadi Abd al-Salam's much admired film *The Mummy* is visually arresting and thematically profound, yet its dialogue does not ring true to the modern ear, especially when spoken by actors not trained in elocution. Using a simplified language with an occasional slip into colloquialism is Chahine's deliberate ploy to pull the viewer into the vortex. He presents history as a continuum and allows complete identification between the viewers and the characters on the screen. The parade goes on and the continuity is unbroken: one people, one language, one destiny.

Chahine's reliance on song is by design. Besides symbolising a joyous epoch in Arab history, it demonstrates Ibn Rushd's zest for life. The Andalusian *muwashahat* and the Arabic *'oud* have had a lasting influence on Spanish guitar and flamenco, and are essential to any depiction of that period. No celebration of the grandeur of al-Andalus would be complete without music and poetry. Long before the birth of Islam in the seventh century, Arab poets were revered and their odes hung on the walls of the temples. Stabbing the poet in an attempt to silence him is one of the ghastliest crimes in the film. Chahine would have been remiss had he not paid tribute to the artists and poets of al-Andalus.

Chahine has struggled throughout his career to have his films distributed in America. When *Destiny* finally fulfilled that ambition, one Arab critic viewed it with suspicion:

> Given Chahine's depiction of the Islamists as a fantastic mix of Protestant puritans, ruthless assassins, evil mafiosi, and obstructionist cultists − an image that does not fit even the most extreme among them much less the majority − it seems hardly coincidental that this is the only film of Chahine's that has ever been picked up by a US distributor.[29]

While the distributor's motive may be suspect, the innuendo against Chahine is misplaced. It is axiomatic that blaming the part is not the same as blaming the whole. Any sect has its own hierarchy of honourable or dishonourable members. Generalisations usually pervert the truth. Without implicating *all* religionists, Chahine only vilifies the minority that used religion to usurp authority for themselves, and in so doing contributed to the decline of the golden civilisation in al-Andalus. His warning of a similar malignancy spreading throughout today's Egyptian society is a patriotic act. That the portrayal of a certain segment of Islamists happened to conform to the foreign distributors' stereotypical impression of them is unfortunate. On the other hand, not to have exposed the extremists for what they are would have been feckless.

Destiny is an important film because it '... expresses a deeper reverence for books than any film since Truffaut's *Fahrenheit 451*'.[30] Enough praise has come Chahine's way from the right places, not just the foreign audiences as the local cynics sneer, but from Egyptian audiences as well. And it comes from Naguib Mahfouz himself, who is too feeble and home-bound to go to the movies. Informed by a reporter that by including the stabbing of the poet / singer in *Destiny* Chahine is reminding Egyptians of his, Mahfouz's, ordeal with his own assailant, the Nobel Laureate answered, 'May God grant him plenty in return.'[31]

CONCLUSION

Chahine's *oeuvre* rests on the bedrock of concern for the deprived or victimised. Most of his films are fraught with tensions and anxieties that verge
on pessimism. In his quest for solutions to the problems of the individual
and national identity, social justice, political integrity and freedom of
expression, he has created a body of work worthy of such ideals. He has sur-
vived as an artist for half a century, often at loggerheads with repressive
institutions. Yet through his provocative cinematic narratives that synthe-
sise varied genres and styles — all rendered in radical *mise-en-scène* — he has
articulated his generation's angst, and provided a portrait of contemporary
Egypt in search of her identity.

   Although the praise that surrounds Chahine's name and the approba-
tion he is accorded are often impassioned, we cannot discount entirely
these opinions, for they illustrate the hold he has on some of his audiences. One critic has called him 'the pharaoh of the Egyptian cinema'[1]
and another echoes many in calling him 'brilliant ... audacious'.[2] French
critics have also waxed lyrical, with Serge Daney referring to him as the
'champagne d'Egypte'.[3] And in April 2001, the magazine *Rose al-Yusuf*, lavished honours on him in an artcle entitled 'Human Treasure'. Despite
this adulation, Chahine remains as uncompromising in his seventies as
he was in his early twenties when he embarked on his career in the cinema. This final chapter seeks to give an altogether more dispassionate
assessment of this original and transgressive artist who is not easy to fit
into a facile category.

   Chahine's insistence on tolerance, harmony and love is a hard line to
pursue in modern Egypt. The prospect of reconciliation between all opposites is utopian. Even in his idealised Alexandria, not all ethnic groups
mingled with and tolerated each other to the extent that he suggests. The
Greek poet Cavafy retained his ethnic roots and culture till the very end,
even though he was born in Alexandria and lived there for over seventy
years. Only a few scattered lines in his voluminous poetry even mention the

word Arab or Egyptian. Chahine's memory of his upbringing in Alexandria is perhaps more idealistic than realistic. Human nature, being what it is, drives minorities to cluster together. The French, Italians and Greeks who lived in Alexandria had their own schools, churches, banks and magazines; they went to their own doctors, hired their own lawyers and were tried, until the Revolution of 1952, under the law of capitulation in their own courts. Compared to Cairo, life in Alexandria must have been far more congenial. Chahine would like to see this sort of situation throughout Egypt: indeed, his scope stretches further than Egypt.

Chahine wants understanding and respect among all nations: no more domination, no more exploitation, no more flexing of military muscle, no more 'Other'. Too intelligent and pragmatic not to know that this is an elusive ideal, he is committed to doing his share of attacking ignorance and bigotry, and celebrating love and understanding.

Controversy

Chahine is critical of any authority, religious or otherwise, that interferes with the artist's right to express himself; and for him the freedoms of speech, religion and self-expression are paramount. 'I hate rituals,' he says, 'whether Christian, Muslim or Jewish. One of the things I like about Islam is that you have a direct relationship with your God. I hate intermediaries.' No one in the Egyptian press openly raises the question of Chahine's Christianity, although it has been considered partly responsible for the controversy surrounding him. One of his closest friends suggests that one of the reasons his film *Alexandria ... Why?* was rejected by the public was the discovery that 'Youssef Chahine, the symbol of progressive Arab cinema, was a Christian'.[4] Asked to comment on the issue, Chahine answered: 'I'd rather keep away from such rotten and backward circles and distance myself from anything that is racist'.[5]

A tangled web of emotions contributes to Chahine's complex personality which, inevitably, finds its way into his films. Besides his Lebanese origins, his love for Alexandria (whose culture is considered more Mediterranean than Egyptian) and his 'problematic' Christianity, there is a curiosity about his sexuality. One only finds polite and oblique references to some of his

Symbols of Christianity appear in several of Chahine's films

characters' undefined inclinations. Christian Bosséno singles out Chahine's courage when he writes that Chahine 'has not hesitated to implicate himself personally in two films which lay him open to the risk of mockery or misunderstanding by a macho Arab society that considers indecent any evocation of tenderness in male homosexual love'.[6] Alluding to the same topic, David Kehr has written: 'Watching Chahine's work, it is impossible not to be struck by his rapturous appreciation of human beauty of both sexes. Here is a continuum of desire to please the most fervid postmodernist.'[7]

And Bérénice Reynaud echoes this viewpoint: 'It doesn't matter whether this love was phantasmic or consummated (or whether Chahine is gay, straight or bisexual) because the love that shines for all his actors – male, female, young and middle-aged – is love for the cinema.'[8] A career that may have started as a means for Chahine to assert his individuality and to overcome multiple insecurities, led to a massive obsession with the cinema and a source of pleasure and valuable insights for future audiences. Yet his search for self-identity and for an enlightened Egypt, has often brought him into direct conflict with those who are not like-minded.

Cinematic style

In 1961, Chahine made *Lovers' Complaint*. Though otherwise inconsequential, it contains a remarkable shot that illustrates his obsession with the power of an image. The son of a small factory owner is in love with a dancer who has run away from Cairo and is hiding in the countryside. He wants to marry her, but she tells him that she is already married. As soon as he recovers from the shock he pleads with her to divorce her husband for his sake. They embrace and the dissolve moves us to the morning after. The two lovers have spent the night on a platform covered with hay. In a double movement the camera moves downward and tilts upward, giving us a view of the lovers from a low angle. We see them looking dishevelled, but we also see two boards of the platform's floor separated, and the window pane behind them broken as though by a fist. Sex, separation and violence are compacted in one shot, the density of which is pure cinema. Since his first film, *Daddy Amin*, finding the exact visual metaphor to convey meaning has been a passion with him. His painterly eye is what prompted Hind Rustum to call him 'a mad man with a camera' and led Kehr to say, 'What registers in this vast body of work … is Chahine's sheer love of his profession: this is a man who lives to lay out shots, to cut film, to huddle with actors.'[9]

Stylistically, Chahine does not shy from utilising every element in film syntax. If at times some of his shots seem ostentatious or mannered (as in framing the head of a person with the back of a wooden bench or under the arm of another), they serve to benefit the eye and not just the ear. Diagonal lines cut the screen to indicate tension; jagged lines mean aggression; curves intimate tenderness; doors offer opportunities or a means of escape; corners denote entrapment or isolation, and staircases denote rising or falling.

The fashion of relying on these techniques is cyclical. Some of the old masters such as John Ford and Howard Hawks shunned them; others, from Josef von Sternberg all the way up to Martin Scorsese, have relished them. Chahine is happy to layer them on top of each other. Over the years they have become second nature to him. An extreme long shot means loneliness or insignificance or freedom; high angle means a diminished stature; low

Chahine's painterly eye is evident in almost every scene

angle means empowerment; a spiral staircase means vertigo. Distances between characters and proximities between characters and camera are chosen to illuminate attitudes and reveal relationships. Camera movement, of which he is very fond, plays a major role in unfolding his narrative. His camera probes, attacks, encircles and indicts – but rarely stands still. All the elements of film-making can be found in each of his films: light and shadow, colour, music, song, dance, costume, flashback, montage, vigorous *mise-en-scène* – are all on the screen in all their variations and aspects. What is often missing in a Chahine film is the quiet moment, the lingering silence that can also be eloquent. While not an 'action film director' in the pejorative sense, Chahine directs with gusto until the viewer's mind and senses seem bombarded. Kehr has identified this sense of richness: 'Even the least of his films gives off a sense of physical pleasure and sensual engagement ...'[10]

An Egyptian critic, writing in French, focused on the structure of a

The psychology of the moment determines the composition of every shot
(*Alexandria ... Why?*, 1978)

Chahine narrative. Though his frame of reference is *The Earth*, what he says
applies to almost all of the films that followed: 'In place of apprehending
the situation from a single point of view, he brings onto the stage a succession of characters whose distinct points of view he adopts temporarily,
passing from one to the other ... so he arrives at a richer sort of multifaceted
vision.'[11] The same critic then isolates a sequence in *Alexandria ... Why?* to
demonstrate how such method is developed. The young boy has just
received an acceptance to study abroad:

> At first Yahia isn't sure he has understood; then he breaks the silence of the
> bank with a cry of joy. The rhythm suddenly becomes very rapid. He leans
> toward the next desk to tell his friend the news. Then, amid general stupe-
> faction, he climbs onto his desk and heads towards the exit, jumping from
> desk to desk ...[12]

Yahia leaps for joy at being accepted by the Pasadena Playhouse (*Alexandria ... Why?*, 1978)

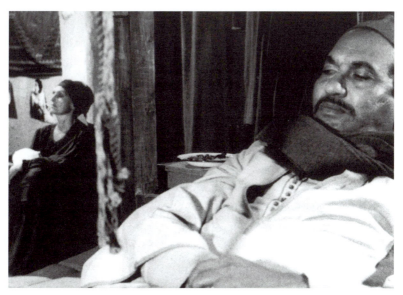

The quiet desperation of the bed-ridden husband in *The Sixth Day* (1986)

Chahine takes great care in selecting his faces, voices, eyes and the right demeanour, for he loves the acting profession and respects the actor. Even the stars, such as Mahmoud el-Milligi and Hind Rustum, stretch their talent better under his direction than under any other director. Chahine lavishes the same devotion on the bit player as he does on the star. Ram's vivacious bride in *The Emigrant*, and the melancholy husband, as well as the stoic boatman in *The Sixth Day*, remain vividly etched on the viewer's mind even though they only appear in a minor part and a cameo. Laila Elouie, who starred in *Destiny*, says 'Chahine spoils his actors'.[13] This is not surprising from an artist who was originally attracted to the cinema because he wanted to be an actor. A cinema built around celebrating life and living cannot be credible if the actor is not at its heart.

Chahine mixes genres not to be flamboyant, but to ensure that his message is properly communicated. He explains:

> There's an interplay between everything. That's why, in the same film, you might see a scene that is totally fantastic and two seconds later, they're dancing, and six seconds after that they're doing something else. This happens to me every day. This is life.[14]

Chahine's films benefit from the fact that Egypt is a cultural and linguistic crossroad to the world. For centuries it was the target of many invasions and is now the home of multi-racial communities. Because it is one of the greatest tourist attractions in the world, one is apt to hear a cacophony of languages in hotels, restaurants, marketplaces, and in Chahine's own offices. Similarly, one finds actors of diverse backgrounds in Chahine films: some are English, others are Scottish, French, Russian, Italian, Greek, Nubian, Iraqi, Algerian and Lebanese. *People and the Nile*, *Return of the Prodigal Son*, *Alexandria ... Why?*, *Adieu Bonaparte* and *An Egyptian Story* are some of the films that utilise foreign actors. Furthermore, Chahine himself is multi-lingual. He says that writing dialogue in different languages has taught him the usefulness of knowing more than one language lest he become its prisoner. As he consults many foreign dictionaries to express the exact meaning, he relies on different film styles to communicate his exact intentions.

The question of cinematic influences on Chahine can be misleading. He adopts whatever technique or genre is necessary to maximise his impact. The two decisive influences on him have been Julien Duvivier's *The Great Waltz* and, perhaps surprisingly, the American musical, particularly the fantasy-ballets of Gene Kelly. But there is even an element of neo-realism across his work, most evident in *Nile Boy* and *Cairo Station*, and three decades later, in a segment of *Alexandria Again and Forever*. For a Third World film-maker, neo-realism of some kind is perhaps an inevitable phase, but in Chahine's case, he has moved on to embrace a wider range of genres — as did many of the original Italian neo-realists, including Visconti, Fellini and Rossellini. Roy Armes, in fact, finds Chahine comparable to Fellini,[15] perhaps due to the discernible similarities in their autobiographical films. More pointedly, Armes compares Chahine with the most famous Indian director: 'Chahine's career makes a fascinating contrast with that of his contemporary Satyajit Ray, in that it shows an artist formed and educated under colonialism coming enthusiastically to terms with a postrevolutionary society.'[16]

One can also detect a similarity between Chahine and Jean Renoir. In content they both stress humanism, and in technique they both rely heavily on the moving camera. Ultimately, however, Chahine is not an emulator. By combining different styles he has created a style of his own. He is neither a Fellini nor a De Sica, but there is in him an element of both. He might not have reached the height of beauty one finds in a Fellini film, or the warmth often associated with a De Sica film; but then, Chahine is more emotionally scarred, and more inclined towards polemics.

The sun and the sunflower

The national cinemas in the Middle East, North Africa and in sub-Saharan Africa — and perhaps the Third World — testify to the awakening of people everywhere after the crumbling of colonialism. In the post-World War II era — a period of intensified struggle for liberation — progressive film-makers disavowed cheap entertainment in favour of cinema of ideas. In their hands cinema became a weapon for change. A cultural historian writes:

> The principal characteristic of Third Cinema is really not so much where it is made, or even who makes it, but, rather, the ideology it espouses and the consciousness it displays. The Third Cinema is that cinema of the Third World which stands opposed to imperialism and class oppression in all their ramifications and manifestations.[17]

In another provocative essay, the same historian sets the parameters of Third Cinema's aesthetics along the following lines:

> In fact the manifesto of Palestinian cinema, as the original manifesto of 'Third Cinema', explicitly calls for 'the establishment of cadres capable of using a camera on the battlefield as a gun'. In such instances, Third Cinema is a soldier of liberation.[18]

As the recipient of the Cannes Film Festival's 50th Anniversary Lifetime Achievement Prize, Chahine belongs to the world of other recipients: Welles, Fellini, Visconti, Bergman, Kurosawa and Hitchcock. In the eyes of some critics, however, this award has more to do with the fact that he himself laboured under disadvantages the others did not have, such as low budgets, technical inadequacies and more stringent censorship. Others find his achievements the more deserving precisely because of this 'handicap'. Of the seven members in this elitist group, Chahine shares with Bergman more than anyone else the sense of being identifiable with the national cinema of his country. Yet, Chahine has a clearer affinity with Ousmane Sembene of Senegal, for the two share a passion for political and social change. Born in the same decade, they came to cinema from disparate backgrounds: Chahine is a bourgeois who dreamed of becoming an actor; Sembene is a dock worker turned novelist. Their orientation is relatively dissimilar: Chahine is a lapsed Christian and a socialist; Sembene is an atheist and a communist. Sembene's *Borom Sarret* (1963), marked the beginning of film making in sub-Saharan Black Africa. It was twenty minutes long and cost $4,000 dollars.[19] During that same year, Chahine was already making *Saladin*, the first Egyptian epic and in full colour. Sembene was starting from scratch; Chahine was operating within a sixty-year-old cinema industry at its zenith. When the Egyptian industry began to deteriorate in the 1970s and 80s, both film-makers faced the same dilemma. In reference to his accepting money from the French Ministry of Culture, Sembene said, 'I am ready to join up with the devil knowing that I won't renounce any of my political conviction.'[20] Nearly twenty years later, and angered by an implicit accusation – (levelled at him in an interview with an Arab scholar living in the United States) – regarding his co-production with France, Chahine said almost the same thing: 'The money can come from Hell if it wants to.'[21]

In addition to challenging the systems within their own countries, one finds a parallel between Chahine's and Sembene's wrestling with the difficulties that are endemic in the postcolonial era. The title of Chahine's film on the subject of globalisation – *The Other* – reveals his resentment of the

Postcolonial aesthetics and political conviction: Sembene's *Xala* (1974)

pejorative label imposed on his world. After having shown that it is prefer-
able for a Senegalese woman to commit suicide than to be a servant for a
French family (Black Girl, 1966), and after having depicted the president of
independent Senegal as sexually and politically impotent (Xala, 1975),
Sembene affirmed: 'Let us make one thing clear: my future does not include
or depend on Europe. You can put Europe and America together in Africa
and there will still be space. Why be a sunflower turning toward the sun? I
myself am the sun.'[22] Despite this self-aggrandizement, one can understand his sense of pride and need for self-assertion. The idealistic and
cerebral Chahines and Sembenes of former colonies seem bent on raising
their voice in anger, often against their own people. Chahine is explicit: 'My
enemy is sometimes my government – most of the time it is my government
– and people who are behind my government.'[23]

The issue of audience

Two complaints are often levelled against Chahine: his films are either too
obscure for an Arab audience, or too parochial for western comprehension.
Sophisticated Arabs see his films in the same framework as foreign films;
Arab masses prefer less convoluted entertainment. This raises the question
of the acceptance of avant-garde art in Arab cinema, which, to his credit,
Chahine spearheads at the risk of alienating the masses with the hope that
one day they will catch up with him. Chahine is known and respected in
Europe, particularly in France, and to a lesser extent in Australia, Japan,
South Africa and Latin America. But in the United States and England he is
hardly known. Perhaps Chahine himself is partially to blame. His penchant
for synthesising genres within his films, and for subjecting foreigners to a
history and a culture to which they cannot easily relate, seems at times
bewildering. Kurosawa succeeded in doing it, but he is not as burdened with
political baggage as Chahine. On the other hand, the Anglo-Saxon world
can never be accused of being friendly towards the Arabs or receptive to
their culture. Those who are demonised (especially by Hollywood) will not
be given a chance to look respectable. Jack G. Shaheen has identified one
thousand Hollywood films that depict the Arabs unfavourably.[24]

Asked to define his audience, Chahine replied:

> I owe everything to those who are around me. I make my films first for myself. Then for my family. Then for Alexandria. Then for Egypt. And if the Arab world likes them *ahlan wa sahlan* [welcome]. And if the foreign audiences like them – they are doubly welcome.[25]

This personal approach to film-making is the most important quality that differentiates Chahine from other Egyptian directors. Some of his peers are competent and have worked longer and produced twice as many films as he has. Each of them can lay claim to a number of distinguished films of his own; none, however, has Chahine's breadth, depth or sustained vision. When, in 1996, the Egyptian film community named the top hundred films in the history of Egyptian cinema, Chahine came first with thirteen listings; Salah Abu Seif came second with eleven. And if international recognition is another yardstick by which to judge him, then Chahine has no rival in Egypt. One of the measures of his worth, however, rests on the technical and artistic excellence of his films, the consistency of his vision and the constancy of his theme: the welfare of the human being. Another measure is the number of disciples he has inspired throughout the Arab world. In Egyptian cinema alone, the directors with the greatest promise are already following his path: Yousry Nasrallah, Radwan al-Kashef, Khaled Youssef, Atef Hatata and Asma al-Bakri.

Finance and production

Problems faced in Egypt are typical of most countries. In Egypt, however, the universal problem of film financing seems even more acute. A number of factors have contributed to the disarray that now exists: television has distracted viewers from the cinema and paid little for the films it broadcast; video piracy robbed film-makers of huge profits; almost two-thirds of the 400 cinemas closed; high taxation took its toll; and Hollywood blockbusters crippled competition. Furthermore, the Egyptian government, which seems to view cinema as a troublesome medium, deliberately ignored any calls for reform. Another major problem was the disappearance of film studios, such as Studio Misr in the 1930s, which provided fully equipped stages and covered all production costs. Ever since the nationalisation of the cinema in the 1960s under Nasser, Egyptian film-makers have had to struggle to find backers. Consequently a situation developed that recalls the so-called 'quota' production in Britain in the 1930s and the 'straight to video' sector in current US production.

Typically, Chahine has had his own share of financing problems. Except for *People and the Nile*, the Egyptian-Soviet production, he has relied on collaboration with Lebanese, Spanish, Tunisian, Algerian and Palestinian backers, with varying degrees of satisfaction. Then, in 1985, his financial worries seemed to subside. In that year he met the French producer Humbert Balsan who provided him with new opportunities. The co-production of *Adieu Bonaparte* with France became possible because the president of the main French television channel was interested in the Middle East and the Arab world.[26] Since then, a co-production arrangement has been maintained between Chahine and France. Film production money is now packaged from different sources: from his own company, Misr International Films; from French cultural organisations, television stations in France and other European countries; and in the form of advances from cinema chains and video distributors. The relationship has been both satisfactory and problematical for Chahine. It has sustained his ability to make films, but created some political difficulties for him among detractors, who view his professional dealings with France as a sort of 'collaboration' at Egypt's expense. The accusation which began with *Adieu Bonaparte* in 1985 and surrounded *Destiny* in 1997, never ended.

That France supports Chahine largely to maintain the cultural / diplomatic sphere of influence in the postcolonial world does not explain Chahine's immense popularity with French critics and audiences. Furthermore, when there are so many Egyptian film directors, why does France limit her support to Chahine and his protégés? Chahine's cosmopolitan upbringing, education at western schools and fluency in five languages (including French) render him more sympathetic than other directors who are less privileged. He also espouses values France respects: he insists on the diversity of the human condition, freedom of self-expression, tolerance and separation of church and state – all values that the French hold dear. Above all, they share with him his *joie de vivre*. Not to be

discounted is the fact that the French cultural elite have their own distinctive taste in artistic matters, and pride themselves on having created film
art in the first place. In short, they recognise an affinity with Chahine, and
he serves as a suitable interlocutor between East and West.

There is, of course, a more critical point of view. To the Egyptian and
Arab populace, who suffered enough under western colonialism, speak one
language and are less travelled and educated, Chahine is suspect – especially when, as a Christian, he dares to present Islam to the West. That he is
secular and a product of both Christian and Muslim cultures does not seem
to redeem him in the eyes of the 'guardians' of the faith. For Chahine,
working with France is a mutually beneficial enterprise and a commercial
salvation. 'Without French support,' he admits, 'even I could no longer
make films [in Egypt].'[27] Considering the impoverished condition of the
Egyptian cinema industry, it is therefore an ideal opportunity for Chahine
to continue making films without having to compromise his integrity or to
lower his standards, as would be the case if he were to accept financing from
the ultra conservative Gulf States.

In the end, two types of audiences watch a Chahine film: Europeans who
are charmed by his exotic yet accessible cinema, and discerning Arabs. That
he stays afloat is quite an accomplishment in itself, considering that the
Arab market is shrinking due to growing home production (in North Africa
and Syria, for example) and the absence of reciprocity between Arab countries. Statistics reveal that '... between 1980 and 1989 the share of the
Egyptian films in Morocco did not exceed 3 per cent and in some years like
1988, not one film was imported from Egypt'.[28] As to Chahine's fortunes in
this financial morass, his niece (who is also his business partner) says, 'We
break even, but we don't make money. Our productions cost a lot, relatively speaking, and the returns are what they are.'[29]

Even under ideal circumstances, film-making is an ordeal and a gamble.
But undertaking ambitious projects on shoestring budgets with little support requires a genius or a miracle. As explained earlier, Egyptian cinema
has declined from its heyday in the 1940s and 50s, to the point that film-
making has become a hazard attempted only by the reckless or the brave. To
minimise risks, most Egyptian films today are modest and inconsequential,

costing a mere $250,000. Chahine's large-scale productions cost $3 − 5 million, which makes the likelihood of their going into profit that much slimmer. It is a credit to the film-makers' ingenuity that they have been able to transcend all of the limitations that they have had to face. Hind Rustum observes: 'One must see the dilapidated conditions of our studios to be able to appreciate what we're doing.'[30]

The song in Egyptian cinema

A hallmark of Chahine's cinema, which further divides his admirers and detractors, is his use of songs. To be sure, the song has always been a staple of the Egyptian cinema, à la Yusuf Wahbi's dramatic *Romance and Revenge*. Yet this feature in Chahine films has proved to be disconcerting to western audiences who only expect performed songs in musicals. Egyptian films are not all musicals, but many songs continue to be present in a range of Egyptian genres − as it once was in western theatre. Some of Egypt's finest musical examples have been staged by Chahine himself: one memorable duet is in *Farewell, My Love*, and there are many others in *The Ring Seller*, considered by Jean-Marie Sabatier 'the finest musical comedy of the Arab cinema ...' and often compared to Jacques Demy's *Umbrellas of Cherbourg*.[31]

But these were full-scale musicals that benefited from Chahine's love for the art of dance. In the middle part of his career, however, he began to use songs in films that cannot be classified as musicals. From *Prodigal Son* to *Destiny*, almost all his films include musical numbers which at times seem to intrude on the dramatic flow and make his films look old-fashioned. But, again, Chahine is a trend setter and not an imitator. Upon first viewing, *Prodigal Son* seems bizarre. A social tragedy is unfolding and yet adolescent Egyptians break out into the street, singing and dancing. The idea came to Chahine when he saw the Parisian police chasing students down the street.[32] Since then he has relied on the song to crystallise an idea or underscore a point. After labelling *Prodigal Son* a 'musical comedy', he tells Samir Farid, 'Songs have made me say what I want to say more forcefully, with greater clarity and better effectiveness.'[33] The resultant disparity between realism and fantasy no longer bothers him.

He illustrated his point by referring to *The Earth*, and in particular to one of the most vivid shots in all of his cinema:

> It is realistic to see Abu Swaylim fall and be dragged forcibly by a horse, but it is not realistic to see him plough the earth with his fingers. When the idea occurred to me I used it and didn't think of anything else.[34]

Remarkably, Chahine's use of song in his films and his penchant for blending genres form a strong connection between him and the two greatest icons of popular Egyptian culture: Muhammad Abd al-Wahhab and Umm Kulthum. At first sight there is little in common between the avant-garde film-maker who refused to pander to popular taste in cinema, and the two legends from Egypt's musical world. But upon closer inspection, one discovers that they do, in fact, have certain things in common, especially in their attitudes towards their respective arts and the innovations they introduced. Both Muhammad Abd al-Wahhab and Umm Kulthum starred in several separate films, but none by Chahine. From the beginning of his career in the 1920s, '... Muhammad Abd al-Wahhab and others advocated the invention of new musical genres ...'.[35] As a 'self-proclaimed modernist, he evinced extensive interest in new instruments and commanded a wide variety of styles, Arab and Western'.[36] By the 1960s, his robust compositions required that his *firqa* [ensemble] expanded again as musicians were hired to play electric organ, piano, saxophone, accordion, electric and acoustic guitar and various percussion instruments'.[37] Here we see that Abd al-Wahhab was a forerunner to Chahine in his desire to break the old mould in favour of establishing a new form. The similarity between the two artists' approach to their mediums becomes manifestly clearer when Danielson tells us that 'Juxtaposition of styles distinguished his [Abd al-Wahhab's] composition from others.'[38] A similar charge regarding 'juxtaposition of styles' is often made against Chahine's cinema by foreign critics as well as discerning Arabs.

Chahine can also be measured up against Umm Kulthum. Hind Rustum says that a Chahine film cannot be absorbed in one viewing, then adds, 'I compare a Youssef Chahine film to an Umm Kulthum song which you need to hear once ... twice ... or three times before you can get its full impact.'[39]

Chahine also shares Umm Kulthum's populism, patriotism and, to a much lesser degree, impact on audiences. After the Revolution of 1952, most of her songs were decidedly patriotic, celebrating the new regime and reflecting the mood and sentiment of the masses. Another fundamental characteristic binds Chahine to Umm Kulthum: affinity with Egypt's peasants. In spite of her celebrity, the exquisite gowns and jewels she wore during her concerts, and the wealth and glory that surrounded her, Umm Kulthum never lost touch with her humble roots. She often reiterated her pride in her peasant stock and identified wholly with her compatriots. Similarly, if one theme is to be isolated in Chahine's cinema, it is his concern for ordinary Egyptians. Though not of humble roots, Chahine never wavered in his empathy with *al-nas al-tayyibin*, the decent people.

Friendly competitor

For another dimension of Chahine's standing in the culture and industry of Egyptian cinema, one must compare him to director Salah Abu Seif,[40] his friend and putative 'rival' for prominence. In an opinion poll conducted among Egyptian artists, Chahine was voted the best Egyptian film director of the twentieth century, with his *The Earth* as the best film; Abu Seif followed in second place.[41] Both were committed socialists who used cinema as a weapon for social change. Both have been recipient of local, regional and international awards, and both took pride in teaching at the Higher Cinema Institute. Their careers diverged sharply when, in the early 1960s, Chahine chose to leave Egypt for Lebanon, in search of work and in protest against the anarchy that engulfed the cinema industry following its nationalisation. In contrast, Abu Seif accepted the governmental appointment as head of the General Organisation of Egyptian Cinema to oversee the transitional period.

Though in many ways alike, they were also different. Abu Seif, who died in 1995, was *misri ibn balad*, born to Egyptian parents in a poor district in Cairo. Chahine was born of a father who was a Lebanese emigrant and of a Greek mother, who lived the life of the 'aristocrats'. While in reality of modest background, Chahine's family life and social standing were privileged compared to his friend's. It was Abu Seif who in 1948 first lured Naguib Mahfouz to the cinema, and the Nobel Laureate admits to having learned screenplay writing from him.[42] The two worked together on ten film adaptations of his novels. Chahine also worked with Mahfouz, but never on adaptations of the novelist's works. Abu Seif was a translator of other writers' works; Chahine is a storyteller who originates ideas but is not above seeking other writers' help. Abu Seif's cinema can be described as sober, conventional and impersonal; his forte straightforward narrative. In contrast, Chahine is a ceaseless innovator. His cinema is eclectic, demanding and sometimes avant-garde.

Their collaboration on *Death of the Water-bearer* in 1977 reveals much about Chahine's commitment to film art. Over many years Abu Seif had failed to find financial backing for a film he wanted to make. Because the script dealt with the subject of death, no producer was interested. But when Chahine, who had recently formed his own production company, suggested the same project, Abu Seif informed him of all the previous rejections and warned him that the project could lose money. Chahine astonished him by saying, 'It's not important that I make a profit off this film. What's more important to me is that we make a good film, even at the risk of a financial loss.'[43] This answer typifies Chahine's attitude throughout his long career: making money has never been his top priority. Yet Abu Seif could also be critical of his friend. After praising Chahine's earlier work, and after admitting that Chahine is the best known Egyptian film director outside Egypt, he explained his reservations in that some of the scenes in Chahine's latest films 'seem peculiar to [Egyptian] society', and that his films are often elitist.[44]

Chahine's imprint

An Egyptian film director visiting a Hollywood studio would be analogous to a youngster visiting Disneyland. The only common ground he would share with his American counterpart would be that both tell stories on the screen. But the process and the rules that govern that process are vastly different. Can the two be considered *auteurs* in the same sense? What criteria does one use to judge who is and who is not an *auteur*? Since *auteurism* has a special meaning in cinema lexicon, it is prudent that we bear in mind its origin and evolving ramifications.

Ever since François Truffaut and his colleagues at *Cahiers du cinéma*, in the 1960s, championed Hollywood's old masters such as John Ford, Howard Hawks, Alfred Hitchcock and lesser-known directors such as Sam Fuller, film theorists have not ceased embellishing the meaning of *auteurism*. To Truffaut and the other disciples, these directors, by the sheer power of their personalities and strong track records, imposed their visions on the studios and shaped their films to their own satisfaction. Orson Welles and Eric von Stroheim may have lost their battles with the philistines, but it is undeniable that they left their mark on every shot they had staged. Film may be a collaborative art, but ultimately it takes one intelligence, one creative mind, one persuasive individual to override any pressures and see the project through to completion. That individual is the director whom Truffaut anointed as the film's *auteur*. Since Truffaut's initial pronouncement, one of its major proponents has been Andrew Sarris. The *auteur* theory caused a major controversy among his fellow critics and a furore in Hollywood itself, where indignant producers defended their status as the real power behind the screen. Sarris defined *auteurs* as 'directors whose careers showed the consistency and individuality that made them artists worth serious attention'.[45] Suddenly the phrase 'a film by' gained currency to the point of absurdity. The usual credit 'directed by' was no longer sufficient. Every egocentric director began to assume authorship as well. Chahine seemed to have succumbed to the temptation, for the phrase 'a cinematic vision by Youssef Chahine' started to appear above his titles. Such a phrase, however, might not have been out of vanity so much as an attempt to deflect any criticism that might be lodged against him for not having replicated the period he was covering 'exactly' as it was.

According to Sarris's definition, Chahine is a genuine *auteur*: and by Geoffrey Nowell-Smith's 'structural approach' and Peter Wollen's 'structural oppositions', Chahine also passes the test.[46] Almost all his films are patterned on the clash of opposites: rich and poor, ruler and subject, foreigner and native, cosmopolitan and provincial, city and countryside, rebel and conformist, democracy and dictatorship, sectarian and secular, individual and community, past and present, memory and forgetfulness, East and West. All these motifs and many others, coupled with Chahine's conscious development of them, entitle him to claim *auteur* status. But this is measuring him up against directors working in a system entirely alien to his. In Third Cinema, the issue is not a matter of *auteurism*, for these film-makers are *auteurs* by necessity. The issue is that Chahine's brand of *auteurism* bears little resemblance to its counterpart in the West, especially Hollywood. Chahine is unequivocally an *auteur*, for he is the final arbiter on all the creative decisions that go into making his films. Though autono-my comes in degrees, he is autonomous, responsible only to himself and to his vision, without infringing his moral and social commitment as a com-mentator. So *auteur* theories tell us little about Chahine; less perhaps than the theories of Third Cinema, already invoked. By having such a powerful hold on his films, however, Chahine risks becoming self-absorbed. Replacing conventional film aesthetics with one's own aesthetic mode must be exhilarating, but there is a strong sense that the cost may at times be high: turning dialogue into didacticism, drama into schematisation and character into a mouthpiece. Chahine achieves balance in his films by suit-ing form to content, but as a result of his passion for his subject he occa-

Post-modernist framing. Chahine casts an eye backward at his own youth in *Alexandria ... Why?* (1978)

sionally foregrounds one at the expense of the other, as in *Alexandria Again and Forever* and *The Other*. Apparently this shortcoming was unheeded by the organisers of the Cannes Film Festival, who selected *The Other* for the opening of the 'Un Certain Regard' section in 1999. Yet the inversion of the elements of dramaturgy, according to Teshome Gabriel, is the norm in the works of postcolonial directors: 'If Third Cinemas are said to have a central protagonist, it is the "context" of the film; characters only provide punctuation within it.'[47] As an individualist and innovator, however, Chahine cannot be pigeonholed or compartmentalised. His robust and thoroughly entertaining cinema is rife with revolutionary concepts and ideas, yet it is instinctively driven by an artist challenged by his own need for fulfilment.

* * *

In the final analysis, Chahine's cinema does represent modern Egypt. He seems to be honour- and duty-bound to bear witness to his age. His films are visual chronicles or indices of Egypt's social and political fabric. Naguib Mahfouz has methodically set on the page the tone and tenor of his times; Chahine does the same, only using the screen. In *An Egyptian Story*, the second film of his autobiographical trilogy, the singer / commentator informs us from the outset that the story is an allegory of Egypt's modern history. The lyrics are worth recalling, for they encapsulate the artist's total identification with his nation:

> We won't accept letting people crush each other.
> Who is sane among us, and who is crazy?
> Who is the victimiser, and who is the victim?
> Who sells his conscience and buys destruction?
> I care about the human being.
> Egypt, I am worried about you.
> O bewildered masses!
> This is the story: the Egyptian story.

NOTES

Introduction

1. Derek Hopwood, *Egypt: Politics and Society 1945–90* (3rd edition) (London: Routledge, 1991), p. 196.
2. Afaf Lutfi al-Sayyid Marsot, *A Short History of Modern Egypt* (new edn) (Cambridge: Cambridge University Press, 1996), p. 56.
3. Ibid., pp. 56–7.
4. P. J. Vatikiotis. *The History of Modern Egypt*, (Baltimore: Johns Hopkins University Press, 1991), p. 74.
5. Ibid.
6. Muhammad Mandour, *Al-Masrah (Theatre)* (Cairo: Dar al-Ma'arif bi-Misr, 1959), p. 30.
7. Ibid.
8. Ibid., p. 66.
9. Ibid.
10. Ibid., p. 29.
11. Ibid., pp. 49–52.
12. Ahmad al-Hadari, *Tarikh al-sinema fi-misr: al-juz' al-awwal min bidayat 1896 ila akhir 1930* (Cairo: Matbou'at nadi al-sinema bi-l-Qahira, 1989), p. 19.
13. Ibid., pp. 230–31.
14. El-Charkawi, 'History of the U.A.R. Cinema', in George Sadoul, *The Cinema in the Arab Countries* (Beruit: Interarab Centre of Cinema and Television, 1966), p. 69.
15. Ibid., pp. 69–70.
16. Ibid., p. 70.
17. Muhammad Kamil al-Qalyoubi, *Ra'id al-sinema al-misriyya al-awwal* (Cairo: Akadimiyyat al-funoun, 1994).
18. Personal communication. Interview with al-Qalyoubi. Cairo: March 1997.
19. al-Qalyoubi, *Ra'id*, pp. 65–8.
20. al-Hadari, *Tarikh*, pp. 163–74.
21. Ibid., pp. 166–7.
22. Ibid., p. 170.

23. Ibid.

24. Mustafa Darwish, *Dream Makers on the Nile: A portrait of Egyptian Cinema* (Cairo: American University of Cairo Press, 1998), p. 15.

25. Muhammad Karim, 'Qissati ma' Zainab', *al-Hilal*, January 1969, pp. 59–70.

26. Ibid., p. 59.

27. al-Hadari, *Tárikh*, p. 352.

28. Ibid., p. 351.

29. Ibid.

30. El-Charkawi, 'History of U.A.R Cinema', p. 77.

31. Abd al-Mun 'im Talima, (ed.), *Al-howiyyah al-qowmiyyah fi al-sinema al-Arabiyyah*, (*Arab Identity in Egyptian Cinema*), (Beirut: United Nations Centre for Arab Union Studies, 1986), p. 21.

32. Jan Kassan, *Al-sinema fi-l-watan al-Arabi (Cinema in the Arab World)* (Kuwait: al-ma rifa, 1982), pp. 48–9.

33. Ibid.

34. Ibid., p. 82.

35. Mohamed Khan, *An Introduction to the Egyptian Cinema* (London: Informatics, 1969), p. 34.

36. Ibid., p. 33.

37. Personal communication. Interview with Marianne Khoury. Cairo: January 1997.

38. Ibid.

39. Personal communication. Cairo: January 1997.

40. Personal communication. Cairo: February 1997.

41. Miriam Rosen, in John Wakeman (ed.), *World Film Directors: Vol. 1* (New York: H.W. Wilson, 1988), p. 202.

1. The Formative Years

1. Personal communication with Gibran's friend and biographer Mikhail Naimy at his home. Biskinta, Lebanon: September 1961.

2. Chahine's trial is a historic event. I watched the newsreel footage of the court session.

3. Robin Waterfield, *Prophet: The Life and Times of Kahlil Gibra* (London: Penguin Press, 1998), p. 51.

4. Personal communication with Youssef Chahine. Cairo: January 1997. Unless

specified otherwise, all of the quotations in this chapter are from the cited interview.

5. 'Le spectacle et la vie: Entretien avec Youssef Chahine', *Cahiers du cinéma*, October 1996, p. 9.

6. Ibid.

7. Roy Armes, *Third World Film Making and the West* (Berkeley: University of California Press, 1987), p. 243.

8. Ibid., p. 187.

9. Labib Fumil, 'Youssef Chahine yaqul banaitu al-najah', *al-Kawakib*, 13 October, 1959.

10. Ibid.

11. Ibid.

12. Ibid.

13. Cahiers du cinéma, October 1996, p. 10.

14. Fumil, 'Youssef Chahine yaqul banaitu al-najah'.

15. Personal communication with Khaled Youssef. Cairo: January 1997.

16. Personal communication with Youssef Chahine. Cairo: February 1997.

17. Miriam Rosen, in John Wakeman (ed.), *World Film Directors* Vol 1 (New York: H.W. Wilson, 1988), p. 200.

18. Fumil, 'Youssef Chahine yaqul banaitu al-najah'.

19. *Cahiers du cinéma*, (October 1996), p. 10.

20. Joan Dupont, 'Reason and Revelations: The "Destiny" of Youssef Chahine'. *International Herald Tribune*, October 17 1997, p. 28.

2. Chronicle of Chahine's Career and its Context

1. Doriyya Sharaf al-Din, *Al-siyasah wa-as-sinema fi-misr* (Cairo: Dar al-sharq, 1992), pp. 13–14.

2. Ibid., p. 15.

3. Samir Nassri, *Muhawarat Samir Nassri ma' Youssef Chahine* (Cairo: Samir Farid, 1997), p. 6.

4. Ibid., p. 7.

5. Personal communication. Chahine. Cairo: February 1997.

6. Muhammad Diyab, Interview with Youssef Chahine, *Al-Hayat*, 16 July 1999. Cinema section.

7. Ali Abu Shadi, *Waqa'i' al-sinema al-misriyya fi mi'at 'am 1896-1995*, (Cairo: al-Majlis al-ala lil-thaqafa, 1997), p. 203.

8. Nassri, *Muhawarat*, p. 12.

9. Muhammad Rida, 'Al-Bayt al-Zahri', *Al-Hayat*, 5 November 1999. Cinema section, p. 18.

10. Diyab, Interview with Youssef Chahine.

11. Ibid.

12. Ibid.

13. Ibid.

14. Nassri, *Muhawarat*, p. 16.

15. Felipe Fernandez-Armesto, *Sadat and His Statecraft*, (London: Kensal Press, 1982), p. 108.

16. Ibid., p. 111.

17. Personal communication with Marianne Khoury. Cairo: January 1997.

18. Personal communication with Khaled Youssef. Cairo: February 1997.

19. Muhammad Diyab, Interview with Chahine. *Al-Hayat*, 29 October 1999. Cinema section.

20. Humbert Balsan, 'Produire Chahine', *Cahiers du cinéma*, October 1996, p. 36.

21. Abbas Yari, 'Tawfik Saleh Talks to Film International: Out of History', *Film International*, Summer 1993, p. 53.

22. Personal communication with Youssef Chahine. Cairo: February 1997.

23. Ibid.

24. Personal communication with Samir Farid. Cairo: February 1997.

25. Diyab, Interview with Chahine.

3. Social Dramas and Melodramas

1. Personal communication. Interview with Hind Rustum. Cairo: February 1997.

2. Geoffrey Nowell-Smith, Lecture at Oxford University: January 1997.

3. Ibid.

4. Ronald Bergan, and Robyn Karvey, *The Faber Companion to Foreign Films* (Winchester, MA: Faber & Faber, 1992), pp. 105–6.

5. Roy Armes, *Third World Film Making and the West* (Berkeley: University of California Press, 1987), p. 246.

6. Erika Richter, 'Realistic Film in Egypt', Berlin, 1974. Included in an article by

Von Rolf Richter, p. 47. (No more information available.)

7. Anwar Sadat, *In Search of Identity*. Quoted by Muhammad al-Sawi, p. 188.

8. Samir Farid, 'Uridu an atahadath an hayati wa zamani' *al-Hilal*, November 1976, p. 95.

9. Ibid.

10. Ibrahim al-Aris, *Rihlah fi al-sinema al-Arabiyyah* (Beirut: Dar al-Farabi, 1979), p. 78.

11. David Kehr, 'The Waters of Alexandria: The Films of Youssef Chahine' *Film Comment*, Vol. 32, November – December 1996, pp. 25–6.

12. Pauline Kael, Quoted in Louis Giannetti's *Understanding Movies* (5th edn), (Englewood Cliffs, NJ: Prentice-Hall, 1988), p. 366.

13. Armes, *Third World*, p. 248.

14. Kehr, 'Waters of Alexandria', p. 27.

15. Jean-Louis Bory, 'The Arab Georgics' *Cahiers du Cinéma*, October 1996, p. 42.

4. Wartime and Postwar Films

1. Hassan S. Haddad and Basheer K. Nijm, eds, *The Arab World: A Handbook* (Wilmette, IL: Medina Press, 1978), p. 41.

2. David Kehr, 'The Waters of Alexandria: The Films of Youssef Chahine', *Film Comment*, Vol. 32, November – December 1996, p. 25.

3. Ibid.

4. Six-page document prepared by Magda's office, and the author's interview with her. Cairo: February 1997.

5. Muhammad al-Sawi, *Sinema Youssef Chahine: rihlah idyulojiyyah* (Alexandria: Dar al matbu'at al-jadidah, 1990), p. 147.

6. Document prepared by Magda's office, p. 3.

7. Labib Fumil, 'Youssef Chahine yaqul banaitu al-najah', *al-Kawakib*, October 13, 1959.

8. al-Sawi, *Sinema Youssef Chahine*, p. 147.

9. Robyn Karney, *Chronicle of the Cinema* (London: Dorling Kindersley, 1997), p. 602. See also Roy Armes, *Third World Film Making and the West* (Berkeley: University of California Press, 1987), pp. 248–9.

10. Kamal Ramzi, in Abd al-Mun'im Talima, ed., *Al-howiyyah al-qowmiyyah fi al-sinema al-Arabiyyah (National Identity in Arab Cinema)* (Beirut: United Nations Centre for Arab Union Studies, 1986), p. 71.

11. Abd al-Mun'im Talima, in *National Identity in Arab Cinema*, p. 73.

12. Samir Farid, 'Al-sinema wa al-dowla fi-l-alam al-Arabi', in *National Identity in Arab Cinema*, p. 109.

13. Ibid.

14. Karney, *Chronicle of the Cinema*, p. 639.

15. Personal communication. Cairo: January 1997.

16. Samir Farid, 'Uridu an atahadath 'an hayati wa zamani', *al-Hilal*, November 1976, p. 101.

17. Ali Abu Shadi, *Klasikiyyat al-sinema al-Arabiyyah* (Cairo: Al-hai'at al-ammah liqusour al-thaqafah, 1994), p. 303.

18. Derek Hopwood, *Egypt: Politics and Society 1945-90* (London: Routledge, 1991), pp. 72–3.

19. Abu Shadi, *Klasikiyyat*, p. 303.

20. Samir Farid, 'Uridu an atahadath 'an hayati wa zamani', p.101. Chahine reveals that the inspiration for this scene came from observing the French students revolt in 1968.

5. Autobiographical Trilogy

1. Malcom Cowley, ed., *The Faulkner-Cowley File: Letters and Memories, 1944–1962* (New York: no publisher given, 1966), p. 14.

2. Joseph Massad, 'Art and Politics in the Cinema of Youssef Chahine', *Journal of Palestine Studies*, XXXIII, No. 2, Winter 1999, p. 91.

3. Ali Abu Shadi, *Klasikiyyat al-sinema al-Arabiyyah* (Cairo: Al-hai' at al -ammah liqusour al-thaqafah, 1994), p. 392.

4. Ibrahim al-Aris, *Rihlah fi al-sinema al-Arabiyyah* (Beirut: Dar al-Farabi, 1979), p. 206.

5. Ella Shohat, *Israeli Cinema: East / West and the Politics of Representation* (Austin: University of Texas Press, 1989), p. 279.

6. al-Aris, *Rihlah*, pp. 201-2.

7. Shohat, *Israeli Cinema*, p. 280.

8. al-Aris, *Rihlah*, p. 206.

9. Massad, 'Art and Politics', p. 91.

10. William Shakespeare, *Hamlet*, Act II, Scene II, Lines 558–9.

11. Samir Farid, *Adwa' ala sinema Youssef Chahine*, (Cairo: al-maktabahal-thaqafiyya, 1992), p. 96.

12. Ibid., p. 99.

13. Ibid., p. 97.

14. Edwar Al-Kharrat, 'Random Variations on an Autobiographical Theme', in Robin Ostle *et al.*, eds, *Writing the Self* (London: Saqi Books, 1998), p. 9.

6. Historical Films

1. William Faulkner, *Requiem for a Nun* (New York: Random House, 1975), p. 80.

2. Afaf Lutfi al-Sayyid Marsot, *A Short History of Modern Egypt* (Cambridge: Cambridge University Press, 1985), p. 25.

3. Talima, *Al-howiyyah-al-qowmiyyah fi al-sinema al-Arabiyyah* (Beirut: United Nations Centre for Arab Union Studies, 1986), p. 27.

4. Ali Abu Shadi, *Klasikiyyat al-sinema al-Arabiyyah* (Cairo: Al-hai' at al-ammah liqusour al-thaqafah, 1994), pp. 23–36.

5. For further information on the Crusades, see: Amin Maalouf, *The Crusades Through Arab Eyes*, (New York: Schocken Books, 1987).

6. Sa'd Iddin Tawfiq, 'A Step Beyond Ballroom Films', *al-Kawakib*, (data not available).

7. Personal communication. Yousry Nasrallah. Oxford: June 1997.

8. Erika Richter, 'Realistic Film in Egypt', *Naher Osten*, Berlin, 1974, p. 48.

9. Personal communication. Oxford: May 1998.

10. Joseph Massad, 'Art and Politics in the Cinema of Youssef Chahine', *Journal of Palestine Studies*, XXXIII, No. 2, Winter 1999, p. 81.

11. 'Venice Wins Chahine Feature, Egyptian Offended by Cannes', unsigned, *Variety*, 19 May 1982, p. 30.

12. Personal communication. Ali Abu Shadi. Cairo: March,1997.

13. Edward Said, *Orientalism* (New York: Vintage Books, 1979), pp. 42-3.

14. Ibid., p. 82.

15. Abd al-Rahman al-Jabarti, *Al-Jabarti's Chronicles of the French Occupation*, (Princeton and New York: Markus Wieneer Publishing, 1993), p. 112.

16. Ibid., p.152.

17. Ibid., p. 113.

18. al-Jabarti, *Chronicles*, p. 93.
19. Samir Farid, *Adwa' ala sinema Youssef Chahine* (Cairo: al-maktabah al-thaqafiyya, 1992), p. 77.
20. Ibid., p. 71.
21. Jean Coutances, 'L'émigré', From *Télérama*, No. 2356, 8 March 1995, pp. 37–8.
22. Ibid.
23. Muhammad al-Quddusi, 'The Adventurous Immigrant Succeeds in Making the Impotent Egyptians Accept Normalization', *Al-Risalah*, 18 October 1994, p. 9.
24. Galal Amin, 'Harabu al-irhab bi-l-ghuna', *Dustur*, 3 September 1997, p. 16.
25. Ibid. See Salah Hashim 'Fight extremism with singing', *Al-Jadida*, 4 June 1997, p. 42.
26. Galal Amin, 'An al-fann, al-hub wa-d-din', *al-Hilal*, October 1997, p. 120.
27. Ibid.
28. Personal communication. London: SOAS, 23 October 1997.
29. Massad, 'Art and Politics', p. 82.
30. Stephen Holden, 'Philosophy as Red-Hot Adventure in 12th-Century Spain and France', *New York Times*, 4 October 1997 (n.p.g.).
31. Majdi Hasanayn, 'The Creator Must Have Political Opinions', *Al-Quds al-Arabi*, No. 25, 15 September 1997.

Conclusion

1. Nadir Adli, 'Far'oun al sinema al-misriyyah', *Nisf al-Dunia*, No. 242, 2 October 1994, p. 60.
2. Mahmud Sa'd, 'Masiruhu wa masiruna', *al-Kawakib*, No. 204, 26 August 1997, p. 9.
3. Serge Daney, 'Chahine, champagne d'Egypte', *Libération*, 17 May 1985. Reprinted in *Cahiers du cinéma*. October 1996, p. 43.
4. Samir Nassri, *Muhawarat Youssef Chahine ma' Samir Nassri*, (Cairo: Samir Farid, 1997), p. 34.
5. Ibid.
6. Christian Bosséno, 'Un humaniste fou de cinéma', *Revue du cinéma*, December 1984, pp. 106–9.
7. David Kehr, 'The Waters of Alexandria: The Films of Youssef Chahine', *Film Comment*, Vol. 32, November - December 1996, p. 26.
8. Bérénice Reynaud, 'Everywhere Desire', *Sight and Sound*, August 1997, p. 22.

9. Kehr, 'The Waters of Alexandria', p. 25.

10. Ibid.

11. Khaled Osman, 'Le style Chahine', *La revue du cinéma*, December 1984, pp. 114–5.

12. Ibid.

13. At the press conference following the premiere of *Destiny* at the Cannes Film Festival in May 1997.

14. Joseph Massad, 'Art and Politics in the Cinema of Youssef Chahine', *Journal of Palestine Studies*, XXXIII, No. 2, Winter 1999, p. 91.

15. Roy Armes, *Third World Film Making and the West*, (Berkeley: University of California Press, 1987), p 252.

16. Ibid., p. 353.

17. Teshome H. Gabriel, *Third Cinema in the Third World* (Ann Arbor, MI: UMI Research Press, 1982), p. 2.

18. Teshome H. Gabriel, 'Third Cinema as Guardian of Popular Memory: Towards a Third Aesthetic', in Jim Pines and Paul Willemen, eds. *Questions of Third Cinema* (London: BFI Publishing, 1989), p. 61.

19. Miriam Rosen, in John Wakeman (ed.), *World Film Directors* Vol. 1, p. 1003.

20. Ibid., pp. 1004–5.

21. Massad, 'Art and Politics', p. 90.

22. Ferid Boughedir, From his documentary *Camera Afrique*. Tunis, 1983.

23. Massad, 'Art and Politics', p. 89.

24. Jack G. Shaheen, *Reel Bad Arabs: How Hollywood Vilifies a People* (Brooklyn, NY: Interlink, 2001).

25. Personal communication. Interview with Chahine. Cairo: January 1997.

26. Humbert Balsan, 'Produire Chahine', *Cahiers du cinéma*, September 1996, p. 36.

27. Michel Fargeon, 'Youssef Chahine: An Interview', *The Unesco Courier*, September 1997, p. 49.

28. Ibid., p. 27.

29. Personal communication. Cairo: 5 February 1999.

30. Personal communication. Cairo: 5 February 1997.

31. Rosen, *World Film Directors* Vol. 1, p. 202.

32. Ibid.

33. Ibid.

34. Ibid.

35. Virginia Danielson, *The Voice of Egypt Umm Kulthum, Arabic Song and Egyptian Society in the Twentieth Century* (Chicago and London: University of Chicago Press, 1997), p. 145.

36. Ibid., p. 172.

37. Ibid., p. 182.

38. Ibid., p. 176.

39. Personal communication. Cairo: February 1997.

40 Hashim al-Nahhas, *Salah Abu Seif: Hiwar ma'Hashim al-Nahhas* (Cairo: al-hay'a al-amma li-l-kitab, 1995).

41. Abdel-Latif Khatir, 'Istifta' fi alam al-fann', *Al-Quds al-Arabi*, 7 March 2000. p.12

42. Ibid., p. 77.

43. Ibid., p.193.

44. Ibid., p. 226.

45. Ibid. See 'Toward a Theory of Film History', in Andrew Sarris, *The American Cinema: Directors and Directions 1929–1968* (New York: E. P. Dutton, I968), pp. 19–37.

46. Ibid.

47. Gabriel, Teshome H. 'Third Cinema as Guardian of Popular Memory', p. 60.

SELECT BIBLIOGRAPHY

Abu Shadi, Ali. *Klasikiyyat al-sinema al-Arabiyyah* (*Classics of Arab Cinema*) (Cairo: Al-hai'at al-ammah liqusour al-thaqafah, 1994).

Abu Shousheh, Muhammad al-Sayyed. *Dirasah wa al-sinario al-kamil lil al-Azima* (*A Study and the Complete Screenplay of al-Azima*) (Cairo: al-hay'a al-misiyya al-amma lil-kitab, 1975).

Adli, Nadir. 'Far'oun al sinema al-misriyyah' ('Pharaoh of the Egyptian Cinema'), *Nisf al-Dunia*, No. 242, 2 October 1994.

Arasoughly, Alia (ed.). *Critical Film Writing from the Arab World* (Quebec: World Heritage Press, 1996).

al-Aris, Ibrahim. *Rihlah fi al-sinema al-Arabiyyah* (*A Journey in Arab Cinema*) (Beirut: Dar al-Farabi, 1979).

Armes, Roy. *Third World Film Making and the West* (Berkeley: University of California Press, 1987).

Badawi, M. M. *Modern Arabic Drama in Egypt* (Cambridge: Cambridge University Press, 1987). *Early Arabic Drama* (Cambridge: Cambridge University Press, 1988).

al-Bandari, Mona, *et al. Mawsu'at al-aflam al-Arabiyya* (*Encylcopedia of Arabic Films*) (Cairo: Bayt al-ma'rifa, 1994).

Bosséno, Christian (ed.). *Youssef Chahine l'Alexandrin* (Paris, CinémaAction. 33rd and Édition du Cerf., 1985).

——. Khaled Osman and Mona de Pronocal. 'Youssef Chahine', *La Revue du Cinéma*, December 1984.

Book World. *On Centennial Cinema: Last Warning*, Issue 52, November /December 1996.

Cahiers du cinéma. Special edition on Youssef Chahine. August / September 1996.

El-Charkawi, Galal. 'Representing the Prophet of Islam on the Screen', in *History of the Arab Cinema 1896-1962*, in George Sadoul (ed.) *Cinéma et arabe culture*, 3 vols. (Beirut: Arab Film, 1964).

Cluny, Claudia Michel. *Dictionaire des nouveaux cinémas arabes* (Paris: Sinbad, 1978).

Danielson, Virginia. *The Voice of Egypt: Umm Kulthum, Arabic Song, and Egyptian Society in the Twentieth Century* (Chicago and London: University of Chicago Press, 1997).

Darwish, Mustafa. *Dream Makers on the Nile: A Portrait of Egyptian Cinema* (Cairo: American University of Cairo Press, 1998).

Dawood, Abdulghany. *al-Rahilun fi mi'at sana': al-juz' al-awwal, fil ikhraj (Ancestory of Egyptian Cinema, Part I: The Directors)* (Cairo: Ministry of Culture / Egyptian Film Centre, 1997).

Farid, Samir (ed.). *Tarikh al-sinema al-natiqa (History of Arab Sound Cinema, Research Part III)*. Al-Ittihad al-Amm lil-fannanin al-Arab in Collaboration with Cairo Cinema Festival, 1993.

—. *Adwa' ala sinema Youssef Chahine (Lights on the Cinema of Youssef Chahine)* (Cairo: al-maktabah al-thaqafiyya, 1992).

—. 'Uridu an atahadath an hayati wa zamani', *al-Hilal*, November 1976, pp. 90–101.

Fumil, Labib. 'Youssef Chahine yaqul banaitu al-najah', *al-Kawakib*, 13 October 1959.

Gabriel, Teshome H. *Third Cinema and the Third World: The Aesthetics of Liberation* (London: Halwals, 1987).

al-Hadari, Ahmad. *Tarikh al-sinema al-misriyya: al-juz' al-awwal min bidayat 1896 ila nihayat 1930 (History of Egyptian Cinema, Part One, from the beginning of 1896 to the end of 1930)* (Cairo: Cinema Club Press, 1989).

Haddad, Hassan S. and Basheer K. Nijm (eds). *The Arab World: A Handbook* (Wilmette, IL: Medina Press, 1978).

Ibrahim, Munir Muhammad. *Dirasat fi al-sinema al-misriyya: Ruwwad wa aflam (Studies in Egyptian Cinema: Pioneers and Films)* (Cairo: al-mak-tabah al-thaqafiyyah, 1985).

Kassan, Jan. *Al-sinema fi-l-watan al-Arabi (Cinema in the Arab World)* (Kuwait: alam al-ma'arifa, 1982).

Kehr, David. 'The Waters of Alexandria: The Films of Youssef Chahine', *Film Comment*, Vol. 32, No. 6, November/December 1996.

Khan, Mohamed. *An Introduction to Egyptian Cinema* (London: Informatics, 1969).

Malkmus, Lizbeth and Roy Armes. *Arab and African Film Making* (London: Zed Books, 1991).

Mandour, Muhammad. *Al-masrah (The Theatre)* (Cairo: Dar al-ma'arif bi-misr, 1959).

Marei, Farida (ed.). *Cinema Press in Egypt: The First Half of the 20th Century* (Cairo: Ministry of Culture, Egyptian Film Centre, n.d.g.)

Marsot, Afaf Lutfi al-Sayyid. *A Short History of Modern Egypt* (Cambridge: Cambridge University Press, 1985).

al-Nahhas, Hashim. *Salah Abu Seif: Hiwar ma' Hashim al-Nahhas* (Cairo: al-Hay'a al-Misriyya. al-amma lil-kitab, 1996).

Nassri, Samir. *Muhawarat Youssef Chahine ma'* Samir Nassri *(Conversations with Youssef Chahine)* (Cairo: Samir Farid, 1997).

Nassar, Zain. *Al-Musiqa al-Misriyya al-mutatawira (The Evolving Egyptian Music)* (Cairo: al-Maktabah al-Thaqafiyyah, 1990).

Ostle, Robin, *et al.* (eds). *Writing the Self* (London: Saqi Books, 1998).

Pines, Jim and Paul Willemen (eds). *Questions of Third Cinema* (London: BFI Publishing, 1989).

Qalyubi, Muhammad Kamel. *Al-Ra'id al-awwal fi al-sinema al-Misriyya* (Cairo: Arts Academy, 1994).

Raquda Publishing. *Hikayat Film al-Masir (The Story of the film, al-Masir)* (editor not credited), (Cairo: Raquda Publishing, 1998).

Rushdi, Fatma. *Kifahi fi-l-masrah wa al-sinema* (Cairo: Dar al-Maarif bi-Misr, 1971).

Sadoul, George. *The Cinema in the Arab Countries* (Beirut: Interarab Centre of Cinema and Television, 1966).

al-Sawi, Muhammad. *Sinema Youssef Chahine: Rihlah idyuljiyya (Cinema of Youssef Chahine: An Ideological Journey)* (Alexandria: Dar al-matbuat al-jadida, 1990).

Shafik, Viola. *Arab Cinema: History and Cultural Identity* (Cairo: American University of Cairo Press, 1998).

Shaheen, Jack G. *Reel Bad Arabs: How Hollywood Vilifies a People* (Brooklyn, NY: Interlink, 2001).

Talima, Abd al-Mun'im (ed.). *Al-howiyyah al-qowmiyyah fi al-sinema al-Arabiyyah (National Identity in Arab Cinema)* (Beirut: United Nations Centre for Arab Union Studies, 1986). (Not to be confused with a book by the same title by Hisham al-Nahhas)

Throval, Yves. *Regards sur le cinéma égyptien* (Beirut: Dar al-Mashreq, n.d.g.)

ARTICLES (English, French, German, Italian)

Télérama, Vol. Canne, No. 2574, 12 May 1999, pp. 86–8. Illustrated.

Film Français, No. 27771, 30 April 1999, p. 15. Illustrated. Interview.

Film International, Vol. 6, No. 4. Spring 1999, pp. 64–7. Illustrated.

Avant-Scène du cinéma, No. 474, July 1998, p.91. Interview.

Télérama, No. 2522, 13 May 1998, p. 70. Illustrated. Interview.

Première, No. 248, November 1997, pp. 92–3. Illustrated. Interview.

Alif, Journal of Comparative Poetics, No. 15, 1995, American University of Cairo.
Arab Cinematics: Toward the New and the Alternative.*Télérama*, No. 2356, 8
Mar 1995, pp. 34–6, 38. Credits and review for *al-Muhajir*: interview with
director Youssef Chahine and article about the film's reception in Egypt.

Film Français, No. 2540, 6 Jan 1995, p.41. Illustrated. Youssef Chahine's *al-Muhajir*
has had an adverse reception in Egypt and been banned – a victim of Islamic
fundamentalism – as was also Onat Kutlar who was seriously injured in a bomb
attack by a radical Islamic group in Istanbul on 30 December 1994.

Écrans d'Afrique, No. 9/10, 1994, pp. 14–23. Illustrated. (In French and English.)
Interviews with several African film-makers on the importance of the
centenary celebrations for Africa, pp. 15–16. Youssef Chahine.*La Revue du
Cinéma / Image et Son*, No. 475, October 1991, p. 8–9. Illustrated.

Film und Fernsehen, No. 6/7. June/July 1991, p. 46–51 Illustrated. Article on the
director, with biographical details and an examination of his work and films.

Première, No. 160, July 1990, pp. 30–31 Illustrated. Article on the director's career.

Cinématographe, No. 125, December 1986, pp. 62–5. Interview with Youssef
Chahine about his film *le Sixième Jour*.

Cahiers du Cinéma, No. 386, July/August 1986, p. 57 'Le journal', insert No. 64,
p. iv. Discussion of film-making in Egypt, with comments from Chahine on his
latest film in production, *le Sixième Jour*.

Cinématographe, No. 112, July/August 1985, pp. 28–30. Interview with Chahine
about his film *Adieu Bonaparte*.

Jeune Cinéma, No. 168, July/August 1985, pp. 6–8. Interview with Youssef Chahine
about his films.

Jeune Cinéma, No. 168, July/August 1985, pp. 6–8. Interview with Chahine about
his film *Adieu Bonaparte*.

Cinéma, No. 318, June 1985, pp. 19–20. Details of the homage to Chahine arranged within the festival for Arab films held in Paris in April.

Avante-Scène du Cinéma, No. 373, June 1985, pp. 65–7. Interview with Youssef Chahine about his film *Adieu Bonaparte*.

Avante-Scène du Cinéma, No. 341, June 1985, pp. 12–13. Notes on Chahine's films.

Avante-Scène du Cinéma, No. 341, June 1985, pp. 89–90. Notes on Chahine's career and film *al-Iskandariyya ... leh?*

Avante-Scène du Cinéma, No. 341, June 1985, pp. 91–4. Bio-filmography.

Télérama, No. 1844, 15 May 1985, pp. 11–13. Chahine talks about his film *Adieu Bonaparte*.

La Revue du Cinéma / Image et Son, No. 400, December 1984, pp.105–18. Article about Chahine's career and films. Authors: Christian Bosséno, Khaled Osman et Mona de Ponocal.

La Revue du Cinéma / Image et Son, No. 400, December 1984, p. 109. Filmography.

La Revue du Cinéma / Image et Son, No. 400, December 1984, pp.110–13. Production report on Chahine's new film *Adieu Bonaparte*.

La Revue du Cinéma / Image et Son, No. 400, December 1984, pp. 114–16. Article on Chahine's style.

La Revue du Cinéma / Image et Son, No. 400, December 1984, pp. 116–18. Article on the major themes in Chahine's work.

Télérama, No. 1814, 17 October 1984, pp. 3–33. Article on the making of Chahine's film *Adieu Bonaparte* and its poor reception in Egypt.

Télérama, No. 1814, 17 October 1984, p. 33. Short bio-filmography.

Cahiers du Cinéma, No. 358, April 1984, 'Le journal' insert No. 42, p. XVI. Note that Chahine has been sentenced to one year in prison in Egypt, for distributing a film showing the profession of lawyer in an unfavourable light.

La Revue du Cinéma / Image et Son, No. 385, July/August 1983, pp. 44–5. Interview with Chahine on *Hadduta Misriyya*.

Cinéma Nuovo, Vol. 32, No. 283, June 1983, pp. 37–44. Analysis of Chahine's work.

Cinéma Nuovo, Vol. 32, No. 283, June 1983, p. 44. Filmography.

Jeune Cinéma, No. 150, April 1983, pp. 1–5. Interview with Chahine about his film *Hadduta Misriyya*.

Deux Écrans, No. 52, December 1982, pp. 31–3. Interview with Chahine about his work, particularly *Hadduta Misriyya*.

Cahiers du Cinéma, No. 333, March 1982, 'Le journal', insert No. 22, 1982, p. VII–VIII. Interview with Chahine on Egyptian cinema and his own work.

Index on Censorship, Vol. 10, No. 4, August 1981, pp. 39–44. Profile of the director, and his experiences of film censorship.

Framework, No. 14, Spring 1981, p. 11. Interview with Chahine, on his film *al-Iskandariyya ... Leh?*

Framework, No. 14, Spring 1981, pp. 12–15. Articles on Chahine and Egyptian cinema.

Framework, No. 14, Spring 1981, p. 15.

National Film Theatre Programmes, January 1981, pp. 8–9. Season of films.

Adhoua, No. 3, January/March 1981, pp. 9–15. Articles about Chahine's work.

Adhoua, No. 3, January/March 1981, p. 15. Filmography.

Cinéma, No. 256, April 1980, pp. 48–55. Interview with Chahine on his film career, particularly *al-Iskandariyya ... Leh?*

Cahiers du Cinéma, No. 310, April 1980, pp. 21–5. Interview with Chahine, on his film *al-Iskandariyya ... Leh?*

Jeune Cinéma, No. 119, June 1979, pp. 28–30. Interview with Chahine on his latest film *al-Iskandariyya ... Leh?*

Image et Son, No. 291, December 1974, pp. 61–6. Interview with Chahine about the making of *al-Usfur*.

Jeune Cinéma, No. 83, December/January 1974/75, pp.15–17. Interview with Chahine on film-making in Egypt, and his film *al-Ard*.

Cinéma, No. 159, September/October 1971, pp. 127–31 Interview with director Chahine on his film, *al-Ard*.

Cinéma 3, No. 3, September 1970, pp.31–52. In depth interview with the director and detailed filmography.

Image et Son, No. 238, April 1970, pp. 56–64. Interview with Chahine on his career, his films and the Egyptian cinema today.

Cahiers du Cinéma, No. 22, pp. VII–VIII. Interview with Chahine on Egyptian cinema and his own work.

Première, No. 98, pp. 227–8. Bio-filmography.

Framework, No. 14, Spring 1981, pp. 12–15. Articles on Chahine and Egyptian cinema.

Film Comment, No. 32, Vol. 6, November/December 1996. 'The Waters of
   Alexandria: The Films of Youssef Chahine' by David Kehr.

Cahiers du Cinéma, Supplement No. 506, October 1996, No. 2, Special Edition:
   Youssef Chahine. Filmography

Sight and Sound, August 1997. Article on Youssef Chahine: 'Everywhere Desire' by
   Bérénice Reynaud.

Journal of Palestine Studies, XXXIII, No. 2 (Winter 1999), pp. 77–93 'Art and Politics
   in the Cinema of Youssef Chahine' by Joseph Massad.

FILMOGRAPHY

Baba Amin (*Daddy Amin*, 1950)
Screenplay: Hussein Hilmi al
  Muhandes, based on an idea by
  Youssef Chahine. Dialogue: Ali al-
  Zorkani. Photography: Massimo
  Dellamano. Editing: Kamal Abu al-
  Ala. Music: Mahamoud al-Sharif
  and Ahmad Sabri.
Cast: Hussein Riyad, Faten Hamama,
  Kamal al-Shinnawi, Marie Munib,
  Hind Rustum.
Production: Mabazin and Zayed Films.
  Distribution: Al-Qahira li-l Alam.
  Running time: 110 minutes. Black
  and White.

Ibn al-Nil (*Nile Boy*, 1951)
Screenplay, dialogue: Neirouz Abd al-
  Malik, based on the novel *Nature
  Boy*, by Grant Marshall.
  Photography: Alvise Orfanelli.
  Sound: Nivio Orfanelli. Music:
  Ibrahim Haggag, Youssef Saleh, Abd
  al-Halim Noweira, Ahmad Sedqi.
  Editing: Kamal Abu al-Ala.
Cast: Faten Hamama, Yehia Chahine,
  Shukri Sarhane, Mahmoud el-
  Milligi, Samiha Tawfik, Nader Galal.
Production: Mary Queeny Films.
  Distribution: Behna Films.

Running time: 120 minutes. Black
  and White.

al-Muharrij al-Kabir (*The Great
Clown*, 1952)
Screenplay: Youssef Chahine, based on
  an idea by Mahmoud Ismail.
  Dialogue: Mahmoud Ismail.
  Photography: Abd al-Halim Nasr.
  Music: Ibrahim Haggag, Hussein
  Gueneid and Ibrahim Hussein.
  Editing: Kamal al-Shaykh.
Cast: Youssef Wahbi, Faten Hamama,
  Nabi al-Alfi, Fardous Muhammad,
  Wedad Hamdi, Hassan Fayek.
Production: Abd al-Halim Nasr.
  Distribution: Behna Films.
  Running time: 110 minutes. Black
  and White.

Sayyidat al-Qitar (*Lady on a
Train*, 1952)
Screenplay, dialogue: Neirouz Abd al-
  Malik. Editing: Kamal Abu al-Ala.
  Photography: Mahmoud Nasr.
  Music: Mahmoud al-Sharif,
  Hossein Gueneid, Ibrahim Hegazi.
Cast: Laila Muurad, Imad Hamdy, Sirag
  Mounir.
Production: Abd al-Halim Nasr.

Running time: 100 minutes. Black
and White.

Nisa' bila Rigal (Only Women, 1953)
Screenplay: Youssef Chahine, based on
an original story by Ihsan Abd al-
Koddous and Neirouz Abd al-Malik.
Photography: Alvise Orfanelli.
Cast: Mary Queeny, Imad Hamdy, Huda
Sultan, Elouia Gamil, Said Abu
Bakr, Kamal al-Shinnawi.
Production: Mary Queeny Films.
Distribution: Behna Films.
Running time: 115 minutes. Black
and White.

Sira' fi-l -Wadi (The Blazing Sun,
1954)
Screenplay: Ali el-Zorkani, Helmi
Halim. Photography: Ahmad
Khorsheed. Music: Fouad el-Zaheri.
Editing: Kamal Abu al-Ala.
Cast: Faten Hamama, Omar Sharif, Zaki
Rostom, Farid Shawqi, Abd al-
Warres Asser.
Production: Gabriel Talhami Films.
Distiribution: Misr International
Films. Running time: 106 minutes.
Black and White.

Shaitan fil Sahra (Devil in the
Desert, 1954)
Screenplay: Hussein Hilmy al-
Mohandes. Photography: Alvise

Orfanelli and Bruno Salvi. Editing:
Sayed Bassiouni.
Cast: Omar Sharif, Mariam Fakhr al-
Din, Ghany Kamar, Loula Sidqi,
Tawfiq al-Dekn.
Production: al-Intisar Films. Running
time: 110 minutes. Colour. (Black
and White).

Sira' fil Mina (Dark Waters, 1956)
Screenplay: Youssef Chahine,
Muhammad Refaat and Liette
Fayad. Photography: Ahmad
Khorsheed. Music: Fouad el-
Saheri. Editing:
Kamal Abu al-Ala.
Cast: Faten Hamama, Omar Sharif,
Ahmad Ramzi, Hussein Riyad,
Fardous Muhammad, Tawfiq al-
Dekn.
Production: Gabriel Talhami Films.
Distribution: Misr International
Films. Running time: 120 minutes.
Black and White.

Wadda'tu Hubbak (Farewell, My
Love, 1957)
Screenplay: al-Sayid Bedir.
Photography: Ahmad Khorsheed.
Music: Farid al-Atrash. Editing:
Said al-Shaykh and Hussain Afifi.
Cast: Farid al-Atrash, Shadia, Ahmad
Ramzi, Abdel Salam Nabulsi,
Tawfiq al-Dekn.

Production and distribution: Farid al-
Atrash Films. Running time: 100
minutes. Black and White.

Inta Habibi (My One and Only Love,
1957)
Screenplay and dialogue: Abu el-Seoul
el-Ibiari. Photography: Ahmad
Khorsheed. Music: Farid al-Atrash.
Costumes: Fouzia Higazi. Editing:
Said al-Shaykh, Hussain Afifi.
Cast: Farid al-Atrash, Shadia, Hind
Rustum, Abdel Salam Nabulsi,
Sirag Mounir, Mimi Chakib.
Production and distribution: Farid al-
Atrash Films. Running time: 120
minutes. Black and White.

Bab al-Hadid (Cairo Station, 1958)
Screenplay: Abdel Hay Adib.
Photography: Alvise Orfanelli.
Music: Fouad al-Zahery.
Cast: Youssef Chahine, Hind Rustum,
Farid Shawqi, Hassan al-Baroudi.
Production: Gabriel Talhami Films.
Distribution: Misr International
Films. Running time: 90 minutes.
Black and White.

Jamila al-Jaza'iriyya (Jamila, the
Algerian,1958)
Screenplay and dialogue: Naguib
Mahfouz, Aderrahman Sherkaoui,
Ali el-Zorkani, Waguih Naguib.

Original idea: Youssef el-Sebai.
Photography: Abdel Aziz Fahmi.
Editing: Muhammad Abbas.
Cast: Magda, Ahmad Mazhar, Zahrat al-
Ula, Salah Zulfiqar, Hussein Riad,
Rushdi Abaza.
Production and distriubtion: Magda
Films. Running time: 120 minutes.
Black and White.

Hub ila al-Abad (Forever Yours,
1959)
Screenplay: Waguih Naguib. Dialogue:
Muhammad Abu Youssef.
Photography: Muhammad Nasr.
Editing: Ateya Abdo.
Cast: Ahmad Ramzi, Nadia Lutfi,
Mahmoud el-Milligi, Fekri Ramzi,
Zaki Ibrahim.
Production: Ramses Naguib Films.
Distribution: Orient Films.
Running time: 95 minutes. Black
and White.

Bayn Idayk (Only You, 1960)
Screenplay and dialogue: Waguih Naguib.
Photography: Ahmad Khorsheed.
Editing: Rashida Abdel Salam.
Cast: Magda, Choukri Sarhan, Zenat
Sidqi, Kismat Shereen, Ibrahim
Negm, Alweyya Gamil.
Production: Chahine and Naguib
Films. Running time: 95 minutes.
Black and White.

Nida' al-Ushaq (Lovers'
Complaint, 1961)
Screenplay: Abdel Hay Adib and
    Waguih Naguib (supervision by
    Abderrahman Sherkaoui).
    Photography: Alvise Orfanelli.
    Sound: Nasri Abdel Nour. Music:
    Fouad el-Zahiri. Decor: Antoine
    Polizois. Editing:
    Rashida Abdel-Salam. Assistant
    directors: Ali Reda and Samir Nasri.
Cast: Berlanti Abd al-Hamid, Shoukri
    Sarhan, Farid Shawqi, Abd al-
    Ghany Kamar, Tawfiq al-Dekn,
    Aziza Helmy, Souraya Fakhry.
Production and distribution not
    credited. Running time: 110
    minutes. Black and White

Ragul fi Hayati (A Man in My Life,
1961)
Screenplay and dialogue: Abderrahman
    Sherkaoui and Waguih Naguib.
    Photography: Alvise Orfanelli.
    Editing: Rashida Abdel Salam.
Cast: Samira Ahmad, Shukri Sarhan,
    Sami Nagib, Tawfiq al-Dekn,
    Ibrahim Nigm, Samir Khalil.
Production: Samira Ahmad Films.
    Running time: 105 minutes. Black
    and White.

al-Nasir Salah al-Din (Saladin, 1963)
Screenplay: Abdel Rahman al
    Shariqawi, Naguib Mahfouz,
    Izzedine Zulfiqar, based on a
    suggestion by Youssef el-Sebai.
    Dialogue: Youssef el-Sebai,
    Abderrahman Sherkaoui.
    Photography: Walid Serry. Music:
    Francesco Lavagnino, Ahmad
    Saadedin. Editing: Rashida Abdel
    Salam.
Cast: Ahmad Mazhar, Nadia Lutfi,
    Salah Zulfiqar, Laila Fawzi, Salah
    Nazmi, Noman Wasfi.
Production: Assia Films and General
    Organisation of Egyptian Cinema.
    Distribution: Misr International
    Films. Running time: 145 minutes.
    Colour.

Fajr Yawm Jadid (Dawn of a New
Day, 1964)
Screenplay: Samir Nasri. Dialogue:
    Abderrahman Sherkaoui.
    Photography: Abdel Aziz Fahmi.
    Music: Angelo Lavgnino. Editing:
    Rashida Abdel Salam.
Cast: Sana Jamil, Seifeddn, Youssef
    Chahine, Hamdi Gheisse, Madiha
    Salem.
Production: Mary Queeny Films.
    Distribution: Movies and Film
    Distributing Co. Running time: 125
    minutes. Colour.

Bayya' al-Khawatim (*The Ring Seller*, Lebanon, 1965)
Screenplay: Brothers Rahabani, based on the operetta of Sabry Cherif. Photography: Andre Domage. Music: Brothers Rahabani. Artistic director: Sabry Cherif. Editing: Sabah Haddad. Costumes: Salha and Joseph Rabbat.
Cast: Fairuz, Youssef Azar, Nasri Shams al-Din, Youssef Nassif, Salwa Haddad, Elia Shoueri, Philmon Wahbeh, William Haswani, Hubba and Lebanese Folkloric Troupe.
Production: Nader al-Attasy, Tannous Frangie for Phoenicia Films (Studio Asry Beyrouth [*sic*]) Distribution: Oriental Society for Film Distribution. Running time: 95 minutes. Colour.

Rimal min Dhahab (*Golden Sands*, 1966)
Screenplay: Youssef Chahine, Ihasan Abdel Kuddous. Dialogue: Ihsan Abdel Kuddous. Photography: Claude Robin. Music: Ali Ismail.
Cast: Faten Hamama, Paul Barje, David Laham, Abdel Wahhab el-Doukkali, Elina Maria, Téjeiro, Carlos Munoz, Ruben Rojo, Nohad Kalii, Afwalla Ahmad Batoul, Muhammad Afifi, Lisette Enokian.
Production: Ibrahim al-Moudalal.

Distribution: Cinematic Association for Production and Distribution. Running time: 110 minutes. Colour.

Eid al-Mairoun (*Sacred Oil*, 1967)
Screenplay: Youssef Chahine, Choukri Raffael. Editing: Rashida Abdel Salam. Photography: Abdel Aziz Fahmi.
Cast: Muhammad Tawfic, Hussein Asr. Running time: 13 minutes. Black and White.

al-Nass wa al-Nil (*People and the Nile*, Egypt-USSR, 1968)
Screenplay: Nicolai Vikroski and Hassan Fouad. Photography: Abdel Aziz Fahmi, Chlinkov, Watchen and Peter Tisko. Music: Khatechadourian.
Editing: Rashida Abdel Salam.
Cast: Salah Zulfiqar, Izzat al-Alayli, Mahmoud el-Milligi, Seifeddin.
Production: General Organisation of Egyptian Cinema, Theatre and Music. Running time: 105 minutes. Colour.

al-Ard (*The Earth* aka *The Land*, 1969)
Screenplay: Hassan Fouad, based on the novel by Abderrahman Sherkaoui. Photography: Abdel

Halim Nasr. Sound: Hassan el-
Touni. Music: Ali
Ismail. Decor: Salah Gaber,
supervised by Gabriel Karraz and
Muhammad Tanun al-Naggar.
Editing: Rashida Abdel Salam.
Cast: Mahmoud el-Milligi, Nagwa
Ibrahim, Izzat al-Alayli, Yehia
Chahine, Tawfiq al-Dekn, Ali al-
Sharif, Abdel Rahman el-Khamisi.
Production: General Egyptian
Organization for Cinema.
Distribution: Misr International
Films. Running time: 130 minutes.
Colour.

al-Ikhtiyar (*The Choice*, 1970)
Screenplay: Youssef Chahine and
Naguib Mahfouz. Photography:
Ahmad Khorsheed. Music: Ali
Ismail. Editing: Rashida Abdel
Salam.
Cast: Suad Husni, Izzat al-Alayli,
Seifeddin, Youssef Wahbi.
Production: General Organisation of
Egyptian Cinema. Running time: 110
minutes. Colour.

Salwa (*The Girl Who Talked to
Cows*, 1970)
Screenplay: Youssef Chahine.
Photography: Abdel Aziz Fahmi.
Editing: Rashida Abdel Salam.
Music: Ali Ismail.

Cast: Seifeddin, Galal Issa, Hamdi
Ahmad, Nadia and Hanan.
Running time: 20 minutes. Colour.

al-Usfur (*The Sparrow*, 1973)
Screenplay and dialogue: Youssef
Chahine and Lotfi al-Khouli.
Photography: Moustapha Imam.
Music: Ali Ismail. Editing: Rashida
Abdel Salam.
Cast: Mahmoud el-Milligi, Muhsina
Tawfiq, Seifeddin, Salah Kabil, Ali
al-Sherif.
Production: Misr International Films
(Cairo), National Office for Cinema
Industry (Algeria). Running time:
100 minutes. Colour.

al-Intilaq (*Forward We Go*, 1973)
Photography: Aly Badrakhan, Waguih
iad. Editing: Rashida Abdel Salam.
Production: Egyptian Army. Running
time: 10 minutes. Colour.

Awdat al-Ibn al-Dal (*Return of the
Prodigal Son*, Egypt-Algeria 1976)
Screenplay and dialogue: Youssef
Chahine, Salah Jahin, Farouk
Beloufa. Music: Salah Jahine.
Photography: Abdel Aziz Fahmi.
Editing: Rashida Abdel Salam.
Cast: Mahmoud el-Milligi, Magda el-
Roumy, Suheir al-Murshidi, Ragga
Hussein, Huda Sultan, Sid Ali

Khouiret, Ahmad Mehrez, Hisham
Selim, Shukri Sarhan.
Production: Misr International Films
(Cairo), ONCLC (Algeria).
Distribution: Misr International
Films. Running time: 120 minutes.
Colour.

al-Iskandariyya ... Leh?
(Alexandria ... Why?, 1978)
Screenplay and dialogue: Youssef
Chahine, Mohsen Zayed. Editing:
Rashida Abdel Salam. Photography:
Mohsen Nasr. Music: Fouad al-
Zahiry.
Cast: Mohsen Mohieddin, Nagla Fathi,
Izzat al-Alayli, Mahmoud el-Milligi,
Mohsena Tawfiq, Ahmad Mihrez,
Gerry Sandquist, Youssef Wahbi,
Yahia Chahine, Laila Fawzi, Akila
Rateb, Zeinab Sidqi.
Production: Misr International Films
and Algerian Television. Production
director: Abd el-Hamid Daoud.
Distribution: Misr International
Films. Running time: 120 minutes.
Colour.

Hadduta Misriyya (An Egyptian
Story, 1982)
Cincematic conception: Youssef
Chahine. Photography: Mohsen
Nasr. Sound mixer: Hassan el-
Touny. Music: Gamal Salama.

Editing: Rashida
Abdel Salam.
Cast: Nour el-Cherif, Mohsen
Mohieddin, Oussama Nadir, Yousra,
Magd al-Khatib, Laila Hamada,
Hanan, Ragga Hussein, Ahmad
Mihrez, Muhammad Munir,
Seifeddin, Suheir al-Bably,
Mahmoud el-Milligi,
Tawfiq al-Dekn.
Production director: Fouad Salah al-
Din. Production and distribution:
Misr International Films. Running
time: 120 minutes. Colour.

al-Wada' ya Bonaparte (Adieu
Bonaparte, 1985)
Screenplay and dialogue:Youssef
Chahine, assisted by Yousry
Nasrallah, Mohsen Mohieddin,
Jean-Michel Comet. Photography:
Mohsen Nasr. Music: Gabriel Yared.
Editing: Luc Barnier.
Cast: Michel Piccoli, Mohsen
Mohieddin, Patrice Chéreau,
Mohsena Tawfiq, Ahmad Abd al-
Aziz, Dalia Younes, Muhammad Atef,
Abla Kamel, Huda Sultan, Gamil
Rateb, Salah Zulfiqar, Tahia Carioca,
Tawfiq al-Dekn, Seifeddin, Hassan
Hussein, Christian Patey, Claude
Gernay, Hassan al Adl, Muhammd
Dardiri, Alexandra Katzaflis, Farid
Mahmoud, Jean-Pierre Michaud.

Production: Misr International Films, Ministry of Culture (Cairo), Lyric International, Ministry of Culture (France). Producer's delegate: Marianne Khoury, Humbert Balsan, Jean-Pierre Mahut. Distribution: Misr International Films. Running time: 114 minutes. Colour.

al-Yawm al-Sadis (*The Sixth Day*, 1986)

Screenplay: Youssef Chahine, an adaptation of the novel by Andrée Chedid. Dialogue: Naguib Iskandar. Photography: Mohsen Nasr. Music: Omar Khairat. Costumes: Yvonne Sassinot and Nahed Nasrallah. Choreography: Ingy Essolh. Editing: Luc Barnier.

Cast: Dalida, Mohsen Mohieddin, Maher Ibrahim, Chewikar, Hamdy Ahmad, Muhammad Mounir, Youssef Chahine.

Production: Misr International Films and Lyric International. Running time: 105 minutes. Colour.

al-Iskandariyya ... Kaman wa Kaman (*Alexandria Again and Forever*, Egypt-France, 1989)

Screenplay: Youssef Chahine. Director assistant: Yousry Nasrallah. Photography: Ramses Marzouk. Choreography: Ingy Essolh. Editing:

Rashida Abdel Salam.

Cast: Yousra, Youssef Chahine, Hussein Fahmi, Amro Abdel Guelil.

Production: Misr International Films, Paris Classics Production. Running time: 105 minutes. Colour.

al-Qahira munawwara bi ahliha (*Cairo ... as Told by Chahine*, 1992)

Cinematic conception: Youssef Chahine. Photography: Tariq al-Telmisani, Samir Bahzan. Editing: Rashida Abdel Salam.

Production: Misr International Films (Cairo), Mirroirs (Paris) with the participation of the National Cinema Centre (Paris). Running time: 22 minutes. Colour.

al-Muhajir (*The Emigrant*, Egypt-France, 1994)

Screenplay: Youssef Chahine. Photography: Ramses Marzouk. Music: Muhammad Nouh. Editing: Rashida Abdel Salam. Costumes: Nahed Nasrallah. Choreography: Walid Aouni.

Cast: Yousra, Khaled Nabaoui, Mahmoud Hemida.

Production: Misr International Films, Ognon Pictures. Running time: 129 minutes. Colour.

al-Masir (*Destiny*, 1997)

Screenplay and dialogue: Youssef
    Chahine, Khaled Youssef.
    Photography: Mohsen Nasr. Editing:
    Rashida Abdel Salam. Music:
    Muhammad Nouh and Kamal el-
    Tawil. Costumes: Nahed Nasrallah.
Cast: Nour el-Cherif, Laila Elouie,
    Mahmoud Hamideh, Muhammad
    Mounir, Hani Salama.
Production: Misr International Films.
    Distribution: Misr International
    Films and Pyramid. Producers:
    Humbert Balsan and Gabriel
    Khoury. Running time: 135 minutes.
    Colour.

Kullouha Khatwa (*It's Only One
Step*, 1998)

Director of Photography: Mohsen Nasr.
    Editing: Rabab Abdel Latif. Sound:
    Gasser Khorcheed. Lyrics: El Rayes
    Bira. Music: Mohammed Asfour.
Cast: Mohammed Ragab, Hani Salama,
    Regina, Ahmed Fouad Selim.
Production: Misr International Films.
    Running time: 270 minutes. Colour.

al-Akhar (*The Other*, 1999)

Screenplay: Youssef Chahine, Khaled
    Youssef. Photography: Mohsen Nasr.
    Editing: Rashida Abdel Salam.
    Music: Yehia El Mougy. Costume

Designer: Nahed Nasrallah.
Cast: Nabila Ebeid, Mahmoud Hemeda,
    Hanan Tork, Hani Salama, Lableba,
    Edward W. Said (cameo).
Production: Ognon Pictures, Misr
    International Films. Executive
    Producers: Humbert Balsan,
    Marianne Khoury, Gabriel Khoury.
    Running time: 105 minutes. Colour.

Skout ... Hansawar (*Silence ...We
are Shooting*, 2001)

Screenplay: Youssef Chahine. Director:
    Youssef Chahine. Director of
    Photography: Pierre Dupouey.
    Executive Producers: Humbert
    Balsan, Marianne Khoury, Gabriel
    Khoury. Song Writer: Gamal Bekhit
    and Kawssar Mostafa. Composer:
    Omar Khairat. Choreographer:
    Karim Tonsy. Editing: Rachida
    Abdel Salam. Assistant Director:
    Khaled Youssef. Production
    Manager: Hisham Soliman. Art
    Director: Hamed Hemdane.
    Costumes: Nahed Nasralla.
Cast: Latif, Ahmed Wafik, Ahmed
    Bedeir, Magda El Khatib, Mustapha
    Chaaban, Hanan Tork, Zaki Abdel
    Wahhab.
Production: Misr International Films
and Ognen Pictures.
    Running time: 100 minutes. Colour.

INDEX

Bold type denotes detailed analysis of a film; Italics denote illustrations (only where there is no textual reference on the same page)